In Praise of *No War for Oil*

"*No War for Oil* is a tour de force of history, myth-busting, and sturdy policy analysis. It is at once an excellent overview of the development and quirks of the world oil market, a slaying of eleven monstrous but widely believed falsehoods, and a description of how and why our wars for "energy independence" have had quite the opposite effect. At a time when ill-conceived, unwinnable foreign wars are driving runaway deficits, we need more than a mild course correction. We need the facts, the truth, and the analysis to question the foundational assumptions that have driven American foreign policy for the past 60 years. This book could not be more valuable or more timely."

> —**Michael C. Munger**, Professor of Political Science, Public Policy and Economics, Duke University

"Here at long last is a book that explodes all of the myths underlying the use of military force to protect the global flow of oil. *No War for Oil* not only provides an invaluable account of the misguided policies that have led to ever-increasing U.S. military involvement in the Middle East, but also shows how the de-militarization of U.S. energy policy would better serve the nation's long-term interests."

> —**Michael T. Klare**, Professor of Peace and World Security Studies, Hampshire College

"In *No War for Oil*, Ivan Eland shows that U.S. dependence on oil is no big deal; that thinking otherwise has led to huge costs, including at least one war; that we are not running out of oil; that a free market in oil is the best energy policy; and that oil is incredibly cheap compared to the alternatives. Eland beautifully weaves history and economics to tell a compelling and, more important, true story. He has hit a home run."

> —**David R. Henderson**, Research Fellow with the Hoover Institution, Associate Professor of Economics at the Naval Postgraduate School, and former Senior Economist for Energy Policy with the President's Council of Economic Advisers

"In *No War for Oil*, Eland provides a catalog of sharply argued rebuttals of the many myths that pervade Americans' understanding of oil and national security. His comprehensive, methodical presentation will be very useful for reorienting the policy debate to firm, analytical ground. Not everyone will agree with every point Eland raises, but he is setting the right ground for crucial foreign policy debates. And the clear preponderance of evidence and analysis in the book convincingly presents the case for substantial changes in American foreign policy."

> —**Eugene Gholz**, Professor, Lyndon B. Johnson School of Public Affairs, University of Texas

"Ivan Eland provides a clear and powerful analysis of a major driver of U.S. foreign policy and military strategy. He offers a fascinating history of oil and its beguiling allure. For anyone with a serious interest in American defense and foreign policies, the Middle East, or the perilous pursuit of 'strategic goods,' the splendid book *No War for Oil* is a *must* read."

> —**Donald L. Losman**, Professor of Economics, Industrial College of the Armed Forces, National Defense University

"Ivan Eland has produced a devastating indictment of the 'oil rationale' for the intrusive, counterproductive U.S. military presence in the Middle East. *No War for Oil* should help debunk the most prominent justification for that misguided policy. Eland shows that on this issue, as on so many others, allowing the free market to operate is both less expensive and less disruptive. Abandoning the attempt to police the Muslim world in the name of preserving Western access to oil will end the terrible price that the American people have paid in blood as well as treasure."

> —**Ted Galen Carpenter**, Senior Fellow, Cato Institute; author, *Smart Power: Toward a Prudent Foreign Policy for America*

NO WAR FOR OIL

NO WAR FOR OIL

U.S. DEPENDENCY AND THE MIDDLE EAST

Ivan Eland

The INDEPENDENT INSTITUTE

Oakland, California

No War for Oil
Copyright © 2011 by The Independent Institute

The Independent Institute
100 Swan Way, Oakland, CA 94621-1428
Telephone: 510-632-1366
Fax: 510-568-6040
Email: info@independent.org
Website: www.independent.org

Cover Design: Roland de Beque
Cover Image: © Matthias Kulka/Corbis
Interior Design and Composition by Leigh McLellan Design

Library of Congress Cataloging-in-Publication Data

Eland, Ivan.
  No war for oil : U.S. dependency and the Middle East / Ivan Eland.
      p. cm.
  Includes bibliographical references and index.
  ISBN 978-1-59813-054-6 (hardcover) -- ISBN 978-1-59813-046-1 (pbk.)
  1. Energy policy--United States. 2. National security--United States. 3. Petroleum industry and trade--United States. 4. Petroleum products--Prices. 5. Middle East--History, Military 6. Persian Gulf Region--Strategic aspects. I. Title.

HD9502.U5E48 2012

338.2'72820973--dc23

2011023157

Contents

1

Trading Blood for Oil

OIL HAS A BLOODY HISTORY. The ghost of petroleum hovers in the background even of wars that have liberty and democracy among their rationales. But occasionally statesmen are blunt about trading blood for oil. George W. Bush's invasion and occupation of Iraq was wrapped in an idealistic blanket, but George H. W. Bush, the younger Bush's father and a realist, showed more candor, baldly stating that securing petroleum supplies for the United States was the major reason he prosecuted the first Persian Gulf War. Blatant or veiled, the grab for oil resources has been a major factor behind many conflicts and military deployments.

Ever since the British Navy changed the propulsion of its ships from coal to oil in 1911, oil has been deemed a "strategic" commodity. National governments focused on securing enough oil to power their militaries—armies, navies, air forces, marines, and coastal protection forces—and eventually on seeking oil for their economies. The word "strategic" as it relates to oil has come to mean a product so vital to the military or economy that the government must step in, even to the point of war, to ensure adequate supplies or low prices. However, oil is not strategic, and war for oil is not necessary to ensure the flow of petroleum or to create security.

Besides, other key products that *are* as vital to the military or economy cause the government, media, and public much less concern than petroleum. Such products include rubber (there was a rubber shortage during World War II), semiconductors, and the platinum group metals, which are more rare and expensive than petroleum and are required to crack oil into gasoline, diesel fuel, and other products. If governments manage or use the military to secure oil, there are many other products that they should also be worried about. In that case, the government might as well be skittish about and manage every product in the economy, but that sort of government over-management is often disastrous—at its extreme it is called "communism."

Instead, governments should just allow the market to deliver oil. Oil is a valuable commodity, and therefore people, companies, and countries have a huge incentive to explore for, extract, and export it to consumers. Even in the Persian Gulf, where petroleum is cheaper to extract, oil-producing countries that are major sellers to the United States have oil exports that represent 32 to 44 percent of GDP. Furthermore, since the 1973 oil "crisis," the United States has reduced its oil imports from 6 to 3 percent of gross domestic product (GDP). Thus, it would seem that oil-producing nations have even more incentive to sell oil than the United States has to buy it. Because oil is valuable, it has flowed despite economic embargoes and around, and even through, wars.

That is not to say that the market for oil is perfect. In the short term, the price of oil can be irrational as world events or new discoveries cause either anxiety or exhilaration. The relatively wealthy American public—which doesn't even have to get out of its vehicles to know what gasoline is selling for and which puts pressure on its politicians when it considers the price to be too high—knows deep down that oil and its products are fairly cheap.

Governments, often under pressure from either their publics or oil companies, should take a longer-term view and rely on markets to buy and sell oil, but sometimes they don't. For example, even though governments do not have to go to war to secure oil that the market will provide more efficiently, they sometimes do so to surreptitiously subsidize oil companies' vested interests.[1] Sometimes countries nationalize their oil production, although doing so is grossly inefficient and actually restricts worldwide oil production more than the famed producing cartels of companies (the Seven Sisters and Texas Railroad Commission of yore) or countries (Organization of Petroleum Exporting Countries—OPEC). None of these cartels has been very successful in holding the long-term price much above what oil would bring with an unfettered market. Furthermore, the 1973 oil embargo was disastrous for the OPEC cartel's Arab members and will likely not be tried again, even if the now more efficient oil markets would allow it, which they probably will not. Governments also irrationally distort the market by holding unneeded strategic petroleum reserves.

The U.S. government also worries about whether key oil transportation routes, for example, the Straits of Hormuz, will be blocked or that "rogue states," or terrorists will use oil profits for nefarious ends. Of course, the country that could block the Straits of Hormuz—Iran—has little incentive to do so because its oil exports, the main source of its foreign exchange earnings, must be shipped through that narrow passage too. Terrorists rely on kidnapping and drug dealing more than on oil to raise money for their diabolical deeds. Rogue states may or may not earn money from oil, so it is unfair to focus blame on oil per se. And even if the United States became independent of foreign oil, which is unlikely to happen anytime soon, rogue states would just sell their valuable oil to countries that care less about meddling into other nations' business than does the United States (for example, China and India).

Most politicians (regardless of party affiliation), the media, and the public all believe that oil independence, or at least reducing U.S. dependence on foreign oil, is a good idea. They are all wrong. Barring some unlikely breakthrough in nonpetroleum energy technologies, most of which are very expensive or otherwise infeasible, it would cost Americans significantly to reduce their dependence on foreign oil. Oil produced in the United States tends to be costly compared to petroleum produced in other places—for example, the Persian Gulf. That's a major reason why the United States imports a significant portion of the oil it uses. There is nothing wrong with that, and oil prices would go up if such imports were curtailed or stopped. Thus, despite politicians' promises, oil independence is unachievable and even undesirable.

Popular Myths about Oil

So what do most people actually believe about oil and its availability? If we look closely at the myths and beliefs that surround oil, we find that in almost every case the truth differs from the popular myths that swirl throughout American culture. For an extended discussion about each of these myths, please see Chapters 12 through 22; for now, here is a quick review of what most of us believe in spite of the evidence to the contrary.

The first popular myth is that no viable market exists for oil. Some allege that a free market for oil does not exist because of government subsidization, protection, and politicization. But it is now clear that embargoes are illusory and the market just reorders itself like it did during the 1973 oil "crisis." Additionally with the advent of the spot and futures markets today, countries have no real control over who buys their oil, so oil is bought and sold through a global networking system that assures us that where there is demand there is supply.

A second myth is that big oil and OPEC collude in order to stick consumers with high prices for oil and gas. The oil industry has one of the poorest public images of any industry. When the price of oil is high—for example, when record real price levels occurred in 2008—the oil companies are usually pilloried in the media, which often imply that oil companies and/or foreign oil-producing countries collude to price-gouge innocent consumers. Yet repeated government studies—including one in 2006 by the Federal Trade Commission (FTC), the government's antitrust watchdog—have found no collusion among the oil companies to artificially raise prices.[2]

A third myth says that oil reserves have peaked, and we are running out of oil. Erroneous predictions of peak oil have been made before, however. In fact, such peak oil predictions usually occur when the market is tight and prices are high, and evaporate when prices go back down. The peak oil craze coinciding with the high prices during 2007 and 2008 was the fifth time predictions have been made that the world was running out of oil—they started in the 1880s, and the penultimate episode was during the tight oil markets of the 1970s.[3] In between, World War I and World War II sucked up much oil and caused the U.S. government each time to predict that global oil supplies would soon peak. All four previous times, the peak oil predictions proved unfounded. Similarly, recent predictions of peak oil lack sufficient evidence to back them up. In fact, statistics show that the world's oil reserves are increasing in size.

A fourth myth is that oil is a "special product" and even strategic, and so it must be secured by the government. Yet, there are many critical products that the market is allowed to supply amply at efficient prices. Oil should be no different. If governments avoid enacting counterproductive policies, industrial economies are fairly resilient even to significant oil-price hikes. Furthermore, enough oil is produced domestically, many times over, to meet the needs of the U.S. military in time of war, and this supply can be augmented with petroleum from nearby friendly countries—for example, Canada and Mexico. Thus, oil is not strategic.

A fifth myth is that we need a strategic petroleum reserve (SPR) in case of emergency. Prior to the 1973 oil crisis there was no SPR; its subsequent history reveals that it was a product of the Cold War mindset. Although it contained oil, it was as much about demonstrating the U.S. government's will to protect its economy from oil supply disruptions in order to deter foreign countries from shutting off supplies. The ninety-day supply was supposed to give the United States that long to negotiate a resumption of the oil flow or to use force to get the supplies moving again. But as Donald Losman of the National Defense University has cogently argued, if the U.S. government goes into hysterics over oil by declaring it as a strategic commodity, when it is best allocated by the market, it will only tempt any potential U.S. adversary to strike at the perceived U.S. Achilles Heel.[4] Sarah Emerson, an analyst at Energy Security Analysis, Inc., noted, "In a way, the SPR is an anachronism." Government policies, the result of slow processes, often come along too late to make a difference. Oil could still be released from the SPR to attempt to reduce the world oil price, but there is no clear policy to do that.[5]

In our sixth myth, a bipartisan consensus exists among politicians and the public about the desirability of American independence from oil and foreign oil. Can so many people be wrong? Yes.

Somehow the implication is that if the United States were independent of foreign oil, U.S. military personnel would not have to die in the Middle East, and the United States would not have to meddle in or be allied with nasty, corrupt Middle Eastern countries. The good news is that if we rely on market forces to bring us the oil we need, we will not need independence from foreign sources of petroleum to achieve these laudable objectives.

Even if the consensus view on the desirability of being independent of foreign oil is right, independence has been difficult to achieve. Although every president since Richard Nixon has endorsed independence from foreign oil, the percentage of America's oil consumption that is imported has risen from 34 percent in 1973 to more than 70 percent now.

Before the early 1970s, the United States had market power in petroleum as a producer, but now its market power is based on it being the world's largest oil consumer. Because the United States has the biggest and wealthiest economy in the world, it accounts for only 5 percent of the world's population but consumes about a quarter of the world's oil. Because the United States is such a large market, it is closely watched for trends, and even anti-U.S. oil producers, such as Libya and Venezuela, court U.S. sales. Saudi Arabia even discounts oil to maintain its share of the American market. As business and environmental journalist for *Harper's Magazine*, Paul Roberts, has noted, ". . . . the sheer extent of American demand, coupled with the country's own booming production (the United States is still the number-three producer), gives Uncle Sam a degree of influence over world oil markets and world oil politics that goes well beyond anything the U.S. might achieve militarily."[6]

The seventh myth says that price hikes in oil and gas cause economic disasters. This myth can usually be traced to the stagflation that followed the 1973 Arab oil embargo and production cutback. Yet, inflation—increases in the general price level in the economy—is not caused by increases in the price of one item, such as oil or gasoline. Increases in the price of one item mean that people have less to spend on all other items, thus lowering prices for those other items and putting offsetting downward pressure on the overall price level. Only when the government increases the money supply in the economy can people spend more money on oil or gasoline and on other items too.[7] Thus, only increases in the money supply can cause general price inflation. Burgeoning U.S. money supplies were primarily responsible for the stagflation of the 1970s.

Myth eight is the belief that the United States wants to control oil supplies in order to keep the price of oil low. But in fact, the United States does not want the price of oil to go too low. From 1959 to 1971, the U.S. government imposed controls on imported oil to raise the price of oil for domestic producers—which was a huge subsidy. Even before that, the Texas Railroad Commission and other state regulatory commissions formed a cartel that restricted and allocated production to try to keep the domestic price of oil higher than the international market price. The federal government attempted to aid and abet this cartel. In the early 1970s, when the Nixon administration imposed price controls on the U.S. economy—including the price of oil—the U.S. domestic oil price went from being artificially high to artificially low.[8] So there is some minor manipulation in the market, but it is not universally about low prices for oil.

Myth nine says that possession of oil vastly increases a country's economic and political power. Current history refutes this notion easily. Post–World War II Japan and Europe (especially Germany) and the Asian Tigers (Singapore, Hong Kong, Taiwan, and South Korea) have all experienced economic miracles though they possess little or no oil. The U.S. position as a supplier in the oil market has been in relative decline since the late 1800s, when it had a virtual monopoly, but during that same period it grew into a world power and then a superpower. And countries with the most oil, like the Middle Eastern countries or Venezuela, have not grown into superpowers.

Myth ten says that the United States must coddle autocratic and terrorist-supporting Saudi Arabia because of its huge oil reserves and supply. The story behind this myth is a bit more complicated than it appears, and it is explained in more detail in Chapter 21, but it is to some degree based on the notion that we get a majority of our oil from Saudi Arabia; in fact, we obtain only about 18 percent from the Saudis.

And finally, myth eleven is that the dependence of Europe on Russian energy is a threat to U.S. security. Although Russia has the largest natural gas reserves in the world (27 to 28 percent of the global total), the United States also has large natural gas reserves and produces 84 percent of the gas it consumes. It adds to this domestic supply with imports, via pipeline, from Canada—another 15 percent of U.S. consumption.[9] So it is unlikely that the United States will ever be as directly dependent on Russia for energy as are the Europeans.

Thus, there is little threat to U.S. security from European dependence on Russian energy, and the U.S. has little direct dependence on Russian energy. However, U.S. hand-wringing continues to this day—as is evidenced by the uneconomic U.S. governmental jockeying to compete with Russia in its sphere of influence over oil and gas pipeline routes to Europe through the Caucuses and Central Asia.[10]

Conclusion

With all of the irrationality of government (the nationalization of oil resources, producer cartels, price controls, economic embargoes, the use of force to "defend" oil, strategic petroleum reserves, government subsidies for alternative fuels, and so on), the media, and the public, isn't oil "strategic" just because everyone thinks it is? The market, although somewhat distorted by these government measures and consumer irrationality, is still the best vehicle to deliver oil most efficiently from the producer to the consumer. If there is money to be made, commerce will go around and through these obstacles. The price might be slightly higher than a completely free market would deliver, but even in this imperfect world, the market remains the best alternative. And if governments and the public become better informed, perhaps the oil market would become freer.

This discussion is intended to make governments, the media, and citizens think more rationally about oil and the use of military power to secure it. The history of oil and the debunking of myths about petroleum, including the recurring fears about peak oil, takes us right up against the unnecessary U.S. use of military presence and power—a form of imperialism and mercantilism—to secure oil. In fact, because the military lacks enough post–Cold War conventional missions to justify all of its expensive weapons systems, it is becoming an oil-protection force. Yet buying oil on the market is actually cheaper than commandeering it at gunpoint.

The use of U.S. military power to secure oil is not only unneeded and costly in lives and money, but also counterproductive to U.S. security. Osama bin Laden, the late head of al Qaeda, said the main reasons he attacked the United States were its ("infidel") support for autocratic governments in and its military presence on Muslim Middle Eastern lands. Instead of using U.S. military power to invade and meddle in Muslim oil producing nations (such as Iraq and Yemen, respectively)—which fuels Islamist terrorist attacks on American targets—the United States, contrary to conventional wisdom, could reduce such attacks by eliminating, or at least reducing, the motivating factor: unnecessary U.S. intervention in the oil-rich Persian Gulf.

Realizing that the alleged need to secure oil with military power is a canard, withdrawing all U.S. forces from the Persian Gulf, and eliminating that mission for the U.S. military—or at least carrying it out with over-the-horizon forces that don't wave a red flag in front of the Islamist terrorist bull—would enhance U.S. security. Hopefully, this discussion will work toward taking some of the irrationality out of U.S. energy and national security policies.

PART I

A History of Oil and the Use of Military Power to Control Supplies

2

American Dominance in Oil

FOR CENTURIES, oil has seeped out of the ground, and people have made use of it. But the first attempt to go after the underground reservoirs by drilling (as was done to bring up salt water) was near Titusville, Pennsylvania—where the world's first oil well hit pay dirt in 1859. The first oil boomtown was created there, ultimately dying out as supplies eventually dwindled. From that day forward until the early 1970s, the United States was dominant in the world market for oil production, refining, and marketing.

John D. Rockefeller, a seller of grocery supplies in Cleveland, Ohio, got into the business of refining the oil into kerosene for lamps. The gasoline-powered car had not been invented yet. Rockefeller was originally leery of getting into producing oil at the wellhead because of its unpredictability.

Rockefeller was not the first to develop the technology to drill for oil, pump it out of the earth, refine it into kerosene or gasoline, or transport it through pipelines. Furthermore, he did not start the first oil company, develop the corporate trust or invent horizontal or vertical corporate integration.[1] But he did eventually create the Standard Oil Company (1870), which gained dominance of the U.S. oil refining, pipeline, and transportation markets by the late 1870s; became the first industrial monopoly in America and the model for others to come; became one of the first transnational corporations ever; and made Rockefeller the richest man in the world and the single most important figure in the history of oil.

By the early 1880s, Standard controlled 90 percent of U.S. oil refineries and pipelines, 80 percent of the oil marketing business, the overwhelming majority of tank cars used to move petroleum by rail and road, and the largest seagoing tanker fleet to transport oil worldwide. Furthermore, Standard had finally entered the oil-drilling business and was producing about 25 percent of U.S. crude oil—thus creating the first vertically integrated petroleum company. Rockefeller's position was made even more dominant by the fact that the United States produced and refined 85 percent of the world's oil.[2]

Curiously, however, despite his dominance of the U.S. refining market, Rockefeller's problem was that the price of his product was dropping—and it was partly because his cost cutting philosophy and economies of scale from a larger, more efficient organization reduced the price of kerosene from 45 cents per gallon in 1863 to six cents by the mid-1890s.

The Dominance Erodes

Also, by the early to mid-1880s, a few short years after his virtual monopoly was established, Rockefeller encountered his first international competitors—the Nobels of Sweden and the rich banking family of French Rothschilds. They both got their oil from Baku, which was then in Russia (it was later in the Soviet Union and now is in Azerbaijan). Another competitor was what would eventually become Royal Dutch Shell—a combination of a Dutch and a British firm—which began producing oil in the Dutch East Indies (now Indonesia) in 1885 and other places across the globe.

So toward the end of the nineteenth century, Standard's competitive position had eroded. By 1892, foreign competition had broken Rockefeller's hold on the global kerosene trade. Even more important, in the United States, oil fields were discovered in Texas, Oklahoma, Kansas, and California during the first decade of the twentieth century, shifting the epicenter of oil production from the eastern United States to the Southwest. Emerging companies—such as Union Oil of California (1893), Texaco (1902), and Gulf Oil (1907)—eroded Standard's dominance in the domestic market. Standard's control over U.S. oil refining facilities had declined from 90 percent in 1880 to 60 to 65 percent by 1911.[3]

Despite the dropping prices and increasing competition in the oil industry, both foreign and domestic, the progressive movement was aflame in the United States, "big was bad," and busting big business trusts was the rage. Rockefeller was quintessentially portrayed as the ruthless capitalist competitor that progressives loved to hate.

In 1906, long past Standard's peak dominance in the industry, the administration of Theodore Roosevelt brought an antitrust suit against the company.

Eventually, in 1911, the U.S. Supreme Court broke up the trust into thirty-four companies, with the biggest parts becoming Standard Oil of New Jersey (nearly 50 percent of the original company, which later became Exxon), Standard Oil of New York (9 percent of the company, which became Mobil Oil), Standard Oil of California (which became Chevron), Standard Oil of Ohio (which became Sohio and then the U.S. arm of British Petroleum), Standard Oil of Indiana (which became Amoco), Continental Oil (which became Conoco), and Atlantic (which became part of ARCO and then Sun Oil).

The fact that foreign and domestic competition had eroded Rockefeller's monopoly position long before the antitrust suit was brought indicates that the market pressures—through such competition, new technology, or fresh ways of doing business—are a better way of naturally reducing a company's market power than are belated and arbitrary government antitrust legislation and litigation.

The breakup of the trust was designed by Standard Oil itself. For a time, former Standard companies still cooperated with each other (in part because the government waved antitrust considerations for the war effort during World War I) instead of competing, thus rendering the outcome of the antitrust proceeding largely negligible. The government didn't enforce the breakup too ardently. Over time, however, the breakup did affect the business, and the former Standard companies became genuine competitors in the 1920s. According to a Federal Trade Commission (FTC) study completed in 1927, the market share of former Standard Oil companies for U.S. refined petroleum products had been reduced to only 45 percent.[4]

By 1914, the start of World War I, the United States produced about two-thirds of the world's oil. With the cutoff of Russia's oil from the global market because of war and revolution, the United States supplied 80 percent of the allies' oil during the world conflict.[5]

3

Iran, Iraq, World War I, and the Interwar Years

OIL IN THE MIDDLE EAST was first discovered in 1908 in Iran by the Anglo-Persian Oil Company (eventually becoming British Petroleum). In 1911, during the naval race between Germany and Britain, Winston Churchill, then First Lord of the British Admiralty decided—on the advice of oil-advocate retired Admiral Jacky Fisher—to switch the most powerful fleet in the world from coal-powered vessels to oil-powered ships. Oil gave British ships more range, speed and efficient use of personnel than the largely coal-burning German fleet. The British Navy would switch its propulsion from coal, produced at home in Wales, to oil, which was produced overseas in Iran.[1]

This development was significant, because governments came to believe, from this day forward, that oil was a strategic commodity—that is, a product requiring heavy state intervention in the market. In addition to patrolling and protecting the rest of the expansive global British Empire, the fleet would now be concerned with where it got the oil to power its own ships. The British now had to keep a fleet in the Mediterranean, designed to protect oil coming from the Persian Gulf through the Suez Canal.[2] The imperial army, including some troops from British colonies, would be needed to ensure that the British Navy had adequate supplies of bunker oil for its ships.

Churchill, perceived nowadays as a conservative, believed that the world's oil corporations had too much power and decided that the British government had to get into the oil business. Thus, in June of 1914, Churchill obtained his goal of majority government ownership of a private company, Anglo-Persian— an act that meets the textbook definition of socialism.[3]

Even before Britain began hostilities against Germany in Europe on August 4, 1914, the British began operations to seize the oil in Abadan (in Iran) and the important port of Basra (in what is now Iraq), from which Abadan oil was shipped. Iraq was then part of the Ottoman Empire, which, along with Germany and the Austro-Hungarian Empire, was on the opposite side from Britain in the war. The British and others knew well the potential Iraq had for producing oil. After three years, the Brits eventually captured Baghdad; but at the end of the war, the Ottoman Turks still controlled the potentially oil-rich province of Mosul, which had few connections with what is now the rest of Iraq.

Under an agreement to end hostilities with the Turks, the British were not supposed to move into potentially oil-rich Mosul and, under another agreement, the British had agreed to give Mosul to France. The British had also duplicitously agreed to give France—or to keep—other lands that were supposed to make up a great independent Arab nation (including Palestine). These same lands were falsely promised to the Arabs in exchange for their revolt against the Turks during the war; the British caused that rebellion by awakening Arab nationalism. Alarmed by the shortages of oil during the war, the British violated all the agreements, demanded that the Turks withdraw from Mosul and occupy it.

Military possession was nine-tenths of the law, and the French eventually agreed to British possession in exchange for 25 percent of the oil and a British recognition of their claim to Syria. The artificial country of Iraq was born because of oil. Britain created Iraq by combining the largely unrelated provinces of Mosul, Baghdad, and Bara into one country, so that it could control the oil in Mosul too. Britain's cobbling together of such disparate provinces—which had no common political or cultural history—into Iraq, and installing a king who had been deposed from a neighboring country, has haunted the world up until the present and figures mightily in the world of "oil security."

During World War I, the Germans had superior rail transportation, but the allies dominated new means of transportation—cars, trucks, and tanks—powered by internal combustion engines. Such engines were also used in aircraft and submarines during the conflict. During the war, the rise of those engines over propulsion by horses and coal-fired train power plants led to a new market for oil (just in time, because the incandescent light bulb was replacing kerosene lamps) and the view that oil was a strategic commodity—meaning that it had to be managed by governments rather than by free markets.[4] In other words, the politics of governments would often clash with, modify, or override the economic decisions of private companies. World War I had been the first war to use oil on a large scale, and this sent governments scurrying to get oil from where it came out of the ground, especially the Middle East. Governments focused on oil being crucial to any future war effort (ignoring other important minerals and raw materials, such as rubber). Britain sought to expand its oil reserves from Iran to Iraq and Kuwait, France to Iraq, the U.S. to the Persian Gulf, and Japan to the Dutch East Indies (Indonesia).[5]

Interwar Years

Following shortages of oil during World War I—caused by high demand and price controls—excessive fears of U.S. and world oil depletion continued into the early 1920s. The rapid increase in the number of motor vehicles paralleled the rise in petroleum consumption of 50 percent from 1914 to 1918. Toward the end of the war, the output of Russia, one of the largest producers in the world, plunged because of war damage, the Bolshevik Revolution, and Lenin's decision to nationalize the Russian oil industry.[6]

During the same period, the U.S. government pessimistically and erroneously forecast a rapid decline in American oil production and the exhaustion of U.S. petroleum reserves (U.S. oil production did not actually peak until 1970). New discoveries of petroleum deposits had been scarce from 1917 to 1920, and prominent geologists felt discouraged about the future of U.S. production. The director of the U.S. Bureau of Mines warned that "within the next two to five years the oil fields of this country will reach their maximum production, and from that time on we will face an ever-increasing decline." In the winter of 1919 to 1920, predictions were that the United States would soon be a large importer of oil. George Otis Smith, the director of the U.S. Geological Survey, estimated that known U.S. oil reserves would be completely depleted in precisely 9 years and 3 months and predicted a gasoline famine. Such fears led U.S. oil companies to go overseas to look for new supplies. Because the British had no oil at home, they had beaten the United States into the Middle East and staked a claim to Iranian oil in 1908.

After World War I, one of the places desperate U.S. oil companies went abroad to find oil was Iraq. In the 1928 Red Line Agreement, American oil producers got 23.75 percent of Iraqi oil, with equal shares to Anglo-Persian (future British Petroleum), Royal Dutch Shell, and a French company. Calouste

Gulbenkian, a private Armenian investor, got the other 5 percent. The Iraqi people got zero percent. The signatories to the agreement also agreed that they would not undertake oil projects in most of the Middle East region (Kuwait, Iran, and Egypt were excepted) without the consent of the others.

Because gasoline prices began to affect so many people in America, rising prices in the early 1920s led to the first of many government investigations, much posturing by politicians, and intense media coverage—a cycle that has repeated itself throughout U.S. history every time oil markets are tight. In 1923 and 1924, Senator Robert La Follette's congressional investigation—which uncovered bribes given to Albert B. Fall, Warren Harding's secretary of the interior, for the corrupt leasing of U.S. naval oil reserves to private oil companies—was one of the few such oil investigations in U.S. history that produced legitimate results rather than mere political demagoguery. The Harding administration's Tea Pot Dome scandal, when combined with John Rockefeller's ruthless competitive tactics and secrecy, led to a public skepticism about the honesty and competitiveness of the oil industry that unfortunately endures until this day.

As would be the case in the future, fears in the early 1920s of reduced supplies were vastly overblown. As in previous and later tight markets, rising prices predictably led to increased exploration, and new oil technology made such efforts more successful in finding "black gold." Oil production increased during the late 1920s and scarcity turned to abundance until the late 1930s, when another world war threatened. In 1925, J. Howard Pew of Sun Oil noted, "My father was one of the pioneers in the oil industry. Periodically ever since I was a small boy, there has been an agitation predicting an oil shortage, and always in the succeeding years the production has been greater than ever before."[7] This would not be the last time false doomsday predictions of peak oil production would be followed by an oil glut.

Cheap oil during the later 1920s led to the proliferation of automobiles in the United States. Oil supplies in the United States also skyrocketed, however, with the 1930 discovery of the Black Giant oil field in East Texas, the largest oil find to date in the country. Oil prices plummeted, and the U.S. oil industry eventually sought welfare from the government, as many conservative business interests often do when economic times are bad. The new "liberal" administration of Franklin Delano Roosevelt (FDR) was more than willing to help.

For some strange reason, the administration believed that raising the prices of raw materials (really the price of everything) would help economic recovery along. Initially, the plight of the oil industry was covered under the National Industrial Recovery Act (NIRA), the heart of FDR's New Deal. NIRA allowed the oil industry to cartelize, reduce competition, set mandatory production quotas by state, and thus increase prices. A tariff on oil imports also helped keep domestic oil prices higher than world market levels. With its excessively high prices, any cartel provides incentives to cheat on the production quotas. The advantage to a government-sponsored cartel is that it can prosecute "hot oil"—that is, oil sold above the quotas.

Even when the Supreme Court ruled the NIRA unconstitutional in 1935, states were willing to enforce "voluntary" production quotas established by the federal government.[8] An artificially high price for oil (and everything else) was the last thing that the impoverished public needed during the Great Depression.

Attempts were also made to cartelize the international oil market, beginning with the "As-Is" Agreement among the major oil companies in 1928. The first cartel attempt was called the "Seven Sisters" and lasted until the early 1970s. It consisted of the three largest Standard companies after the 1911 breakup—Standard Oil of New Jersey (Exxon), Standard Oil of New York (Mobil), and Standard Oil of California (Chevron)—Gulf Oil, Texaco, and the British companies Shell and British Petroleum.[9] (Total, a French company, was really the eighth sister.) By the early 1930s, the Seven Sisters had control of Middle Eastern oil. Like the later OPEC, the Seven Sisters tried to divide up markets, agree on production quotas, and set a uniform world price. The discovery of the giant field in Texas put a crimp on this attempt and oil prices sank during the 1930s. So as with the later Texas Railroad Commission and OPEC oil cartels, price collusion usually fails when there are too many sources of production outside the cartel's jurisdiction. Also, as the price rises, even members of the cartel have huge incentives to cheat and produce more of the product.

As World War II became imminent, the FDR administration once again liked a large and integrated oil industry, which was more efficient for production during wartime. For the war, under government orchestration and order, the large integrated oil firms, the independent producers, and the refiners and marketers all acted as if they were in one organization. The government allowed an antitrust exemption that allowed them to coordinate their efforts and pool their supplies of oil.[10]

Mexico

Oil was discovered in Mexico in 1910. In 1938, General Lázaro Cárdenas, the radical leftist president of Mexico, nationalized the Mexican oil industry and expropriated the assets of foreign oil companies. Fearing a bad socialist precedent that would adversely affect their global operations, the companies tried to organize embargoes on Mexican oil worldwide, arguing that such exports were stolen goods. The British government led the effort to impose sanctions on Mexican oil because the company most affected by the nationalization, Mexican Eagle, had mainly British stockholders.

Yet, with war on the horizon, Britain was heavily dependent on secure oil supplies from Mexico and Venezuela. The perverse effect of trying to close off Mexico's oil export markets to much of the world via sanctions led that country to redirect its exports and become the leading supplier of petroleum to the Axis powers. In addition, the United States only provided lukewarm support for Britain's efforts—mainly because, given the downward spiral toward war internationally, FDR did not want to allow the Axis powers to make inroads into the Western Hemisphere as a result of Western powers angering any Latin American country. Also, given his "liberal" ideology, FDR believed in a nation's right to expropriate foreign assets as long as just compensation was given to the companies.[11]

Thus, Mexican nationalization stood and became a very bad precedent down to the present. The artificially high oil prices paid today by the world's consumers aren't a result of the greed, intrigue, and corruption of large transnational oil companies (the conventional wisdom), but rather occur because most of the world's oil is now controlled by inefficient nationalized state-owned companies.

Saudi Arabia

While the British were preoccupied with Iranian oil, Royal Dutch Shell was worrying about Indonesia, and the French, British, Dutch, and later the Americans were colluding to keep others out of the oil in the old Ottoman Empire (including Iraq), the richest oil prize of all was sitting undiscovered.

The Anglo-Persian Oil Company, virtually all of the world's geologists, and even the king of Saudi Arabia were skeptical about finding oil in the kingdom. In 1938, a well hit pay dirt in the kingdom—a poor, sparsely populated desert wasteland in the center of the Middle East. American companies SoCal and Texaco—cut out of the Red Line Agreement among international oil companies that had divided up the oil of the former Ottoman Empire—had formed a joint venture called the Arab-American Oil Company (Aramco) and were thus in the lucky position of being able to exploit what turned out to be very rich oil deposits in eastern Saudi Arabia.

Oil was discovered only shortly after King Abdul Aziz Al-Saud finished his 30-plus year conquest of the Arabian Peninsula, united its disparate tribes, and founded the nation of Saudi Arabia in 1932. Not trusting the British, King Abdul Aziz allowed U.S. companies to develop the kingdom's oil.

The United States saw demand for its oil greatly increase during World War II (the United States supplied six out of every seven barrels of oil used by the allied countries[12]), and the discovery of new U.S. oil fields had decreased because the low prices during the Great Depression of the 1930s discouraged the long-term development of new technology and oil fields. As World War II ended, one of the many gloom-and-doom forecasts in the oil industry's history estimated that the United States would have only enough oil to last two years in any war with the Soviet Union.[13]

Even before World War II ended, the U.S. government saw it this way: eventually, the United States would be a net oil importer and would need a foreign source for such imports. In the 1940s, fears of future oil shortages led to the "conservation theory," whereby the United States would buy scarce oil from foreign sources and save its own petroleum to ensure American security (interestingly, the opposite is thought today by the U.S. government, public, and media—that the United States should become independent of foreign sources of oil and drill for more oil in the United States).[14]

The U.S. government realized during the war that the vast reserves of oil in the Persian Gulf would transfer the global epicenter of oil production from the U.S. Gulf Coast to another gulf halfway across the world. Going where the British did not have the oil locked up, the United States focused on Saudi Arabia, which had recently found the world's biggest oil deposits. In February 1944, FDR told Lord Halifax, the British ambassador to the United States, that the British had Persian oil, that the United States and Britain shared Iraqi and Kuwaiti oil, and that the Americans had the oil in Saudi Arabia.[15]

But taking his cue from the British and believing that World War II showed that oil was a strategic commodity, during the war, in 1945, FDR held a summit meeting with King Abdul Aziz that implicitly traded Saudi oil for U.S. protection. At the summit, FDR made an agreement with Abdul Aziz that U.S. companies could drill for oil in the kingdom. Saudi Arabia had already become one of only three Arab countries during the war to receive U.S. lend-lease assistance, and in 1943, FDR had declared that the security of the desert kingdom was "vital to the defense of the United States."[16] In a 1945 memo, the State Department concluded, "The oil resources of Saudi Arabia [are] among the greatest in the world" and they "must remain under American control for the dual purpose of supplementing and replacing our dwindling reserves, and of preventing this power potential from falling into unfriendly hands."[17] (Decades later, President Ronald Reagan was even more blunt in 1981: "There is no way" that the United States would allow Saudi Arabia to be "taken over by anyone that would shut off that oil."[18])

Saudi Arabia had only small military forces, so the U.S. agreed to put the kingdom under its security umbrella. FDR got the king to agree to the construction of an U.S. air base in Dhahran, Saudi Arabia. Due to concerns about internal unrest arising from any large U.S. military presence, however, the United States chose indirect means of providing the kingdom's security—for example, deputizing regional powers and augmenting the Saudi military.[19] (Unfortunately, the United States forgot this largely "offshore" strategy after the Cold War and first Gulf War ended, stationed troops in the kingdom, and had to endure blowback from terrorists on 9/11 who didn't like that U.S. military presence.) In 1950, FDR's successor, Harry S. Truman, more clearly and publicly defined the security-for-oil agreement that FDR and Abdul Aziz had reached.

Yet from 1949, in apparent contravention of the agreement, the United States, not knowing how to defend Saudi oil fields on the other side of the world from a much closer Soviet Union, had a secret plan to destroy those oil fields, rather than defend them, in the event that the Soviet Union ever invaded them. Even as early as 1945, the United States had U.S. oil executives in the kingdom store explosives under their beds to be used in that event.[20]

At any rate, as oil analyst Lisa Margonelli has concluded, American independence from foreign energy died as early as the Roosevelt-Abdul Aziz summit in 1945.[21]

4

World War II

NO DOUBT EXISTS that oil is required to run the aircraft, ships, and vehicles—armored and otherwise—during a war, and that during a world war, normal trade patterns are sometimes disrupted. This reality makes petroleum "strategic" in a narrow sense. Of course, even then, there are many "strategic" items needed to conduct a war, of which oil is only one. For example, during World War II, the United States experienced a severe rubber shortage because Japan's conquest of Malaya and the Dutch East Indies had shut off 90 percent of the natural rubber coming to U.S. ports and because of price controls on rubber in the United States during the war.

Similarly, oil is used as a raw material in a nation's economy and for producing items used during war. The disrupted trade patterns during a catastrophic world war make countries worried about having enough oil for economies and war production. Yet again, other raw materials are also critically needed for economies and war production. Because of oil's role in operating military equipment during World War I and its uses in industry, all countries in World War II made acquiring oil supplies a top war goal. They may, however, have overemphasized acquiring oil in their war objectives and underemphasized other critical raw materials needed for war.

Europe and the Middle East

Oil played a significant part in the largest war in world history. Nazi Germany had little oil within its borders and had to either manufacture it synthetically (46 percent of its total supply in 1940) or get it from abroad. Like the

Imperial Japanese (and in contravention of the advice of the classical economists of the eighteenth and nineteenth centuries), Adolf Hitler wanted to conquer oil and bring it within the boundaries of the empire rather than taking the more cost-effective route of simply buying it abroad. Hitler wanted and got Romania's Plotesti oil fields (producing 58 percent of Germany's imports in 1940) by an alliance, invaded Russia in part to grab Soviet petroleum in Baku (now in Azerbaijan) and other oil fields in the Caucuses, and fought in the Middle East in part for oil (for example, his bid to get Iraqi oil).

The allies bombed Plotesti refineries so that the Nazis would not get the oil. The Soviets were able to stop Hitler before he captured the oil at Baku—ironically because the Germans ran out of fuel (including at the critical battle of Stalingrad)—and the British ejected the Germans from Iraq. Hitler, however, did capture the Grozny oil fields in Chechnya. The allied strategic bombing campaign was ineffectual—German industrial production increased in spite of the pounding from the air—until it started targeting the German synthetic fuels industry.

From Pearl Harbor to the dropping of the atomic bombs, the United States provided six-sevenths of the oil for the allied war effort, and half the total tonnage of items shipped from the United States was oil. Because Britain was an island, early in the war, German U-boats began targeting shipments of oil and other war materiel coming from the United States, which was helping Britain even before formal U.S. entry into the war. The U.S. Navy was even patrolling the Atlantic and helping the Brits find German U-boats in mid-1941—long before Germany declared war on the United States just after the Japanese bombed Pearl Harbor in December of that year. German U-boats were very lethal and came close to shutting down the sea connection between Britain and the United States during the spring of 1943. Britain's oil supply was at its lowest ebb. Then the allies broke the new U-boat codes, further improved their radar, fielded a new long-range aircraft to patrol distant areas, and added a counterattack capability to their convoys. This turned the tide, and allied convoys carrying oil and other vital supplies could cross the Atlantic.

After the Nazis invaded the Soviet Union and made rapid gains there and in North Africa, the allies feared that the two German armies would link up in Iran. In mid-1941, the British and Russians occupied Iran to protect the large petroleum refinery in Abadan and the oil supply route from the Persian Gulf to Russia. They deposed Reza Shah, who had exhibited Nazi sympathies, and replaced him with his son, Mohammed Reza Pahlavi.[1] Erwin Rommel, Germany's commander in North Africa, had his tactical brilliance negated by shortages of oil-based fuel, one of the many critical items required by the military in wartime.

Asia

At the time of World War II, the United States was the world's leading producer of oil and Japan's principal supplier—80 percent of its petroleum imports were from the United States. Japan had modernized, wanted an empire just like the British, French, and U.S. possessed, and was prepared to use brutal force to get it.

FDR did not like Japan's expansion, especially its incursion into Manchuria in 1931 and its invasion of China in 1937. In 1940 he slapped on a limited and ineffective ban on aviation gasoline to Japan. FDR eventually embargoed U.S. metal and oil exports to the island nation and froze Japanese financial assets in the United States, which were primarily used to buy oil. As Japan was preparing to invade southern Indochina in late July of 1941, FDR froze the Japanese assets in the United States, thus effectively cutting off oil shipments to Japan. Britain followed the U.S. lead with an asset freeze and also imposed an oil embargo, which cut off Japan from supplies in Borneo in the British East Indies. The Dutch East Indies also enacted a freeze and oil embargo. The Japanese had known that taking all of Indochina might precipitate a U.S. oil embargo, but they felt they needed control of all Indochina to invade the oil-rich Dutch East Indies farther south.[2]

Since Japan had no oil of its own, it had become desperate for petroleum supplies. Japan would have to give up its expansionist aims if it could not obtain fuel for its military and industry. The Dutch East Indies (now Indonesia) had rich oil deposits, and the effective U.S. cutoff of supplies sealed the Japanese plan to invade these islands. The de facto U.S. oil embargo caused the Japanese Navy to realize that an absence of petroleum would render its ships worthless; it began to take a harder line toward invading the Dutch East Indies. But in any such invasion, Japanese supply lines would run near the U.S. colony of the Philippines. This scenario would mean certain war with the Americans.

With support from the Japanese Navy, however, Japan's Prime Minister Prince Konoye tried to get a last ditch personal meeting with FDR to avoid war and was even willing to give up Japan's alliance with the Axis powers to avoid war with the potentially much stronger America. In early October 1941, FDR rebuffed Konoye's peacemaking effort. Thus, because Konoye could offer no other option besides war, the hawkish Hideki Tojo replaced him. The debate in Japan over whether to go to war centered on the longer-term availability of oil for the Japanese military, which the United States was trying to cut off.[3]

In a desperate move, the Japanese decided to attack the not-so-sleeping giant of the United States, which had an economy larger than Imperial Japan and Nazi Germany combined. They devised a simultaneous attack on the American fleet headquarters at Pearl Harbor, Hawaii, and the Philippines. The Japanese hoped that a surprise attack would cripple the U.S. fleet that threatened its supply lines and either cause "isolationist" U.S. public opinion to accept Japanese expansion or at least provide time for Japan to fortify rings of island defenses to withstand a U.S. counterattack. Even the commander of the Japanese Navy, Admiral Isoroku Yamamoto, who had spent four years in the United States, was skeptical that the United States would not fight. He believed Japan's cause probably would be doomed by the United States' industrial might, but he dutifully launched the surprise attack anyway.

Had FDR not embargoed metals and oil and frozen Japan's assets in the United States, there might have been no war with Japan. FDR knew that an oil embargo against Japan might very well spur the Japanese to invade the Dutch East Indies, meaning war with the United States, because Joseph Grew, then-U.S. ambassador to Japan, warned of him of this possibility. The United States chose to risk war and knew by the end of November 1941, through earlier breaking of the Japanese code, that an attack was imminent. But U.S. officials thought any Japanese attack would come in the Philippines, along the invasion route to the Dutch East Indies, not at Pearl Harbor. Ambassador Grew had warned Washington of rumors that Japan would attack Pearl Harbor, but U.S. officials believed such a long-range attack was impossible for the Japanese. Nevertheless, the Japanese realized that the American fleet at Pearl Harbor could launch a flanking assault on their invasion of the East Indies and Singapore. Thus, they plotted to attack Pearl Harbor and U.S. positions in the Philippines simultaneously.[4]

Perhaps, however, the Japanese could have tried to buy oil from non-U.S., non-British, or non-Dutch sources or on the black market rather than invade the Dutch East Indies and attack the United States. At that time oil made up only 7 percent of Japan's energy needs—although most of the oil was consumed by the Japanese military and shipping. Prior to World War II, eight countries accounted for 94 percent of world oil production—the United States, the Soviet Union, the Dutch East Indies, Iraq, Iran, Venezuela, Mexico, and Romania.[5] In 1942, when the United States entered World War II, it accounted for only about half the world's oil reserves.

Could Japan have purchased oil from non-embargoing nations or on the black market? Daniel Yergin, an oil expert, pooh-poohs this idea, saying that no other significant sources of petroleum were available to the Japanese.[6] Although oil supplies were tight in a world already at war, embargoes are notoriously leaky for those willing to pay above the market price on the black market. Such premiums make producers willing to cheat on formal embargoes. It still would have been much cheaper for Japan to try this alternative rather than to start a desperate and probably futile war against the American colossus.

But as with so many other countries in world history, Japan was mesmerized by having an empire and didn't heed the work of the classical economists of the eighteenth and nineteenth centuries. These economists said that it was cheaper to conduct free trade with foreign countries and merely buy their wares than to incur the large costs of building a big military, invading and administering such nations, or coercing them to sell—or blatantly stealing—their products at gunpoint. (Because shockingly, U.S. post-World War II oil security policy looks a lot like what our wartime adversaries were trying to achieve, this book is intended to make the same point to the U.S. government, media, and public about the immorality and inefficiency of using military force, or the threat thereof, to secure oil supplies.)

The U.S. attempt to strangle Japan prior to World War II by cutting off its oil is rarely mentioned in U.S. history books—as if the Japanese bombed Pearl Harbor out of the blue for no reason. In the end, during the war, U.S. submarines did strangle Japan's island nation, cutting it off from oil from the East Indies, other raw materials, and war materiel. U.S. submarines and other naval vessels were so effective that 95 percent of Japanese merchant shipping was either sunk or put out of action by U.S. torpedoes.[7] By the end of the war, the Japanese air force was completely out of fuel.

In fact, continuing this almost total naval strangulation of the vulnerable Japanese home islands—essentially maintaining the naval quarantine and allowing only medicine and the minimum requirements for food to pass through it—would have been morally preferable to dropping A-bombs and firebombs on the civilian population of that island nation in an attempt to compel surrender.

5

The Cold War

THE HEAVY USAGE of U.S. petroleum during World War II and feared shortages led to increased popularity for the "conservation theory." The theory had originated in similar circumstances in the 1920s after the feared oil shortages during the First World War.

The administration of Franklin Delano Roosevelt (FDR) conducted the first analysis of the security ramifications of declining U.S. petroleum reserves. In November 1941, before the United States got into World War II, the State Department advocated conserving U.S. oil reserves and becoming more dependent on foreign oil, especially that from the Middle East.[1] Later, Navy Secretary James Forrestal believed that Persian Gulf oil was going to be crucial in preparing to counter the Soviet Union during the Cold War. During peacetime, he wanted to use that oil and conserve U.S. oil so that the United States would have its reserves to fall back on during any subsequent world war. Eugene Rostow and the National Security Resources Board believed the same thing. When it passed the Marshall Plan aid to Europe, Congress recommended that Europe get its energy outside the United States.[2]

The first tension of the Cold War appeared over U.S. fears that the Soviet Union was trying to grab oil fields in the Persian Gulf. At the beginning of World War II, the British and Soviets had occupied Iran—then the Gulf's largest oil producer—to keep it from falling into German hands. They had both agreed to withdraw their forces six months after the war ended. The Soviets showed no signs of leaving northern Iran by March 2, 1946, as promised. Truman gave the U.S. Navy orders to augment its presence in the eastern Mediterranean. Stalin withdrew Soviet forces in May 1946. Although the United States believed the Soviets wanted the oil-rich Persian Gulf and warm-water ports on the Mediterranean, the latter is more likely because the Soviet Union already had much oil. But even after the Soviet withdrawal, the U.S. Joint Chiefs of Staff believed oil was critical in any future U.S.-Soviet conflict and wanted to keep the Soviet Union far away from Gulf oil.

According to Michael Klare, even Truman's provision of military assistance to Greece, Turkey, and Iran under the Truman doctrine of 1947 was to bolster a northern tier of countries to prevent the Soviets from penetrating south to the other oil producing nations of the Persian Gulf, thus threatening U.S. access to Gulf petroleum. This was an extreme case of what later would be called the "domino theory," because Greece has no border with and is not that close to the Gulf oil-producing states. At this time, the U.S. also established a permanent naval presence near the Persian Gulf.[3]

Forrestal supported the original attempt to create an international government cartel in oil—the Anglo-American Petroleum Agreement—a direct descendent of the "As-Is" agreement and the Texas Railroad Commission. In order to deal with excessive supply, the Anglo-American Petroleum Agreement set production quotas for countries based on reserves and economic factors. When the agreement was introduced in mid-1944, the entire oil industry opposed it, and FDR withdrew it from Senate consideration. Putting a ceiling on American production and relying more on imported oil would ruin the U.S. domestic oil business. This was the beginning of the canard—now endorsed by every politician, the domestic oil industry, and many duped citizens—that the U.S. must eradicate "dependence on foreign oil" (everyone else in the world liked the cheap foreign oil).

Even with Forrestal's support, the Truman administration was finally forced to give up on this proposed cartel in 1947. Nevertheless, to conserve U.S. oil, Forrestal and the U.S. government continued their quest to increase Persian Gulf production.

Throughout the Cold War, the U.S. fear of Soviet penetration of the Middle East, and U.S. politicians' self-serving political interest in dubbing Israel the only bastion of anticommunism and democracy in the region, sometimes led to conflict with the oil companies' championing of the Arab cause.[4] Sometimes, domestic considerations trumped the U.S. government desire to control Middle Eastern oil. In 1948, all of Truman's foreign policy advisors—including Forrestal, Secretary of State George Marshall, the military chiefs of staff, the CIA, and

George Kennan, head of the State Department's Policy Planning Staff—argued that America's only vital interest in the Middle East was to have a good relationship with Saudi Arabia and other Arab oil producers, thus necessitating opposition to a new Jewish state in British-controlled Palestine. But Truman was in desperate straits for the 1948 election. One of his few advisors who favored a Jewish state, domestic advisor Clark Clifford, told him that very few presidential candidates had won elections without winning New York and that the Jewish vote was crucial there. Truman, a good politician, didn't hesitate for a minute, overruled his entire foreign policy team, and endorsed a policy that was favorable to the United Nations partition of Palestine in November 1947 and the rapid recognition of the new state of Israel in 1948.[5] Previously, Truman famously once told a group of American diplomats posted in the Middle East, who were urging Truman not to give in to Zionist desires, "I'm sorry, gentlemen, but I have to answer to hundreds of thousands who are anxious for the success of Zionism: I do not have hundreds of thousands of Arabs among my constituents."[6]

The return of resources to the private sector after World War II made the demand for oil skyrocket sixfold during the Golden Age of Oil from 1948 to 1973.[7] Increases in the number of cars, roads, and suburbs increased oil consumption dramatically. In 1947 and 1948, oil shortages arose and prices spiked quickly, leading to the usual cries of "energy crisis" and congressional investigations into oil company conspiracies to increase the price. Yet despite the high demand, pessimistic predictions about the U.S. running out of oil were upended when new regions began production in the United States and Canada. This new production caused U.S. oil reserves to be 21 percent higher in 1950 than in 1946.

Huge oil fields were also discovered in the Middle East during the late 1940s (for example, Ghawar, Saudi Arabia, the world's largest oil field[8]), 1950s, and 1960s. Although U.S. production was increasing, the Middle East finds made world production rise even faster—leading to a decline of U.S. dominance in the world market, as its share of production declined from 64 percent in 1948 to 22 percent in 1972. In all, global production rose faster than even the rapid spike in world consumption, thus driving prices down. New technology, such as the ability to drill deeper and drill off shore, increased oil supplies.

A similar phenomenon happened in proved oil reserves: U.S. reserves increased, but world reserves rose more rapidly. In 1950, estimates were that the world had enough proved oil reserves for 19 years; by 1972, despite the rapid increase in consumption, the estimated proved reserves were 35 years. Thus, the U.S. share of the world's reserves declined from 34 percent in 1948 to 7 percent in 1972.

The post–World War II production surge from Venezuela and the Middle East made oil and natural gas supplant coal as the dominant fuel by the mid–twentieth century. It was the fastest replacement of a dominant fuel in history—with coal still predominant in providing the world's energy needs in 1950 and oil replacing its preeminence by the mid-1960s. Petroleum was easier to move, environmentally cleaner, and less costly than coal.

In 1948, for the first time, U.S. imports of crude oil and oil products exceeded exports—that is, the United States became a net importer of oil. The influx of petroleum from overseas eventually caused President Dwight D. Eisenhower in 1959 to reluctantly impose import quotas on foreign oil, which was the most significant energy policy in the postwar era and lasted until the 1973 oil "crisis." The major U.S. oil companies, with much petroleum production overseas, opposed the quotas, but domestic independent producers were politically more powerful and won the day. Clarence Randall, then chairman of the Council on Foreign Economic Policy, complained to then–Secretary of State John Foster Dulles that those who were claiming "national security" to curtail imports had it backwards. He argued that "our policy should be to conserve that which we have rather than to take measures which would cause our supplies to be exhausted more rapidly." In other words, he wanted to encourage—not restrict—imports to conserve domestic supplies.[9]

As foreign imports of oil increased, securing those overseas supplies of oil became a primary goal of the West during the Cold War—even rivaling the maintenance of Western Europe's independence from communism. U.S. policy-makers felt that the Persian Gulf's oil fields, especially the rich prize of Saudi Arabia, had to be kept free from Soviet influence or control to guarantee the economic survival of the West. However, U.S. military planners didn't know how such fields could actually be defended in a long war and spent as much time figuring out how to scuttle them as defend them.[10] Nevertheless, to carry out Truman's explicit "oil for security" trade with Saudi Arabia, he created a U.S. program to train the Saudi military and established an American airfield at

Dhahran near the oil fields in the eastern part of the country. This airfield guarded these deposits and contributed to the strategic ring of air bases to contain the Soviet Union.[11]

Eisenhower also regarded the protection of the Persian Gulf as vital to U.S. security and promulgated the Eisenhower doctrine, which Congress approved to authorize U.S. forces to defend friendly nations against Soviet-sponsored actors in the Middle East and to increase aid to anticommunist governments in the region. John F. Kennedy sent U.S. aircraft to the Gulf area in 1963 when Gamal Abdel Nasser's Egypt backed Yemeni forces in their attack on Saudi Arabia.[12]

Because of U.S. overstretch during the Vietnam War, Nixon was forced to modify the Eisenhower doctrine, substituting a flood of U.S. arms, advisors, and technicians to the Middle East for U.S. troops and for the British, who had dominated the Middle East after World War I but were pulling out because of their own imperial overextension. The reality of heavy and direct U.S. military involvement in a small, backwater country in Southeast Asia at the expense of U.S. forces to safeguard Gulf oil throws suspicion on the whether that petroleum was as strategic as U.S. policymakers claimed.

Moreover, although the threat to oil after the Cold War is much less than during it, even the threat of Soviet control over the Persian Gulf oil fields was overstated. The Soviets, always desperate for hard-currency foreign exchange, would have had an incentive to sell this valuable commodity, albeit at a higher price than prior to any conquest of Gulf oil.

Developing Countries Wanted a Bigger Piece of the Pie

Venezuela and Saudi Arabia

Before World War II, in the 1930s, Mexico had nationalized its oil industry. The left had taken power in Venezuela, and American oil companies and the U.S. government feared a similar nationalization of some of the most important oil reserves in the world. During any world war, however, Venezuela's oil, like Mexico's, was also fairly secure. In 1943, a landmark "50–50" agreement was reached that equalized the oil companies' profits from Venezuelan oil and the Venezuelan government's take on taxes and royalties. This agreement would set a precedent for others to come, as nationalism became dominant in the postwar years, and developing countries wanted a bigger chunk of oil profits. A similar "50–50" agreement with Saudi Arabia and other Middle Eastern producers followed in 1950. [13]

Iran

In the case of Iran, 50–50 was not enough for its new government. In 1951, as Mexico had done in 1938, the elected anticommunist prime minister of Iran, Mohammed Mossadegh, nationalized Iranian oil fields out of British hands. The Anglo-Iranian Oil Company—with a majority ownership by the British government—believed that Iran's royalty plus 20 percent of the company's worldwide profits was a good deal and had been the best arrangement in the world for an oil-producing nation, with the exception of the Saudis' recent 50–50 deal. Mossadegh didn't see it that way, even when Anglo-Iranian also offered Iran a 50–50 agreement.

In 1953, the CIA, colluding with the British, facilitated the overthrow of democratically elected and Western-oriented Mossadegh, restored the autocratic Shah, and grabbed part of the oil loot for U.S. companies. Although Soviet troops had withdrawn from Iran after World War II in 1946, the United States ostensibly feared that the Soviets would get Iranian oil by subversion and was also afraid of falling dominoes in the Middle East region, which held 60 percent of the world's oil reserves. But economic mercantilism by the U.S. government was likely the real reason for the U.S.-facilitated coup.

Surprisingly, however, at the time, U.S. oil companies were not thrilled about getting into Iran, because they had lucrative production in Saudi Arabia and elsewhere in the Middle East that would face competition from Iranian oil. Also, the oil companies initially resisted U.S. government pressure to join a consortium in Iran because, as it had at other times, the U.S. government was pushing the companies to cooperate with each other at the same time it was gearing up to prosecute them for being an "international petroleum cartel." The Truman administration eventually reduced the criminal prosecution to civil litigation and gave the oil companies an antitrust waiver to participate in the Iranian consortium.

The consortium was eventually established and was precedent setting. Previously, foreign oil companies would own rights to oil in developing countries.

After the deal, although the restored and grateful Shah allowed U.S. and British oil companies to stay in Iran, the national Iranian oil company—and thereafter other national oil companies—would own the oil and the foreign oil companies would manage the local industry and buy the output. The consortium also made the United States the major player in Middle Eastern oil.[14]

But one thing was certain. As usual, such foreign meddling by the U.S. government produced future unintended consequences for "oil security" far greater than the immediate benefits. When the British pulled out of the Middle East in 1971, the United States then began to rely even more heavily on the Shah to secure Middle Eastern oil supplies and be a bulwark against the Soviet Union and its surrogates in the Persian Gulf region (for example, Iraq). This policy was part of the post-Vietnam Nixon doctrine of letting regional actors take up more of the security burden rather than always relying on U.S. military might. Unfortunately, this improvement in U.S. policy was short-lived. The oppressive Shah ran afoul of his own people by buying too many weapons from the United States and other Western nations at the expense of economic development. A revolution overthrowing him in early 1979 led to the rise of a radical anti-Western fundamentalist Muslim regime under the equally authoritarian Ayatollah Ruhollah Khomeini.

Suez Crisis—1956

Oil played a triple role in the Suez crisis. Gamal Abdel Nasser, Egypt's pan-Arab nationalist ruler, was annoyed that the United States cut promised aid to build the Aswan High Dam on the Nile River. He nationalized the Suez Canal, which was on Egyptian territory, hoping to use the added revenues to complete the dam project.

The British and French previously owned the canal and conspired with Israel to use military force to get it back. The canal was Europe's major route for importing oil from the Persian Gulf, and Nasser's nationalization threatened this lifeline, at least in the minds of the British and French. Without the canal, oil tankers going from the Persian Gulf to Europe had to go around the Horn of Africa, a much more long and costly route. The Israelis invaded Egypt, and the British and French told the world that they would occupy the Canal Zone to "save" the internationally used canal from the war. Before they could do so, Nasser blockaded the canal with rubble, making it impassable.

President Eisenhower refused to support his European allies and instead sided with Nasser—currying favor with developing nations during the Cold War, especially the oil-producing ones. In support of Egypt, the first of three Arab oil embargoes was imposed (the later two happened during the 1967 and 1973 Arab-Israeli wars)—this time on oil exports to Britain and France.[15] (Oil pipelines from Iraq and Saudi Arabia to the Mediterranean Sea were also closed.) Britain and France assumed that if Nasser closed the canal, their U.S. ally would provide emergency petroleum supplies. Europe faced oil shortages during the impending winter. Not only did Eisenhower decline to provide Europe with oil, but he said that he would do so only when the British and French began withdrawing from the Suez. True to his word, he did when they took that action.

During the crisis, the Soviets threatened military intervention and maybe even nuclear attacks on Britain and France. Eisenhower made clear that if the latter happened, he would launch nuclear weapons against the Soviet Union. In the end, as has been the case in many wars in the Middle East, the Israelis—and in this case, their British and French conspirators—achieved a tactical victory, but suffered a strategic defeat. Nasser had won.

In cutting off oil supplies to Europe, the U.S. government, fearing petroleum shortfalls, had asked major oil companies to take certain actions that the Justice Department later prosecuted them for under the Sherman Antitrust Act. This double-crossing of the oil companies by the government had happened previously in U.S. history. During the 1930s, the Justice Department successfully prosecuted oil companies for cooperating with the Interior Department's "market stabilization" regime (read: cartel).[16]

The other development stemming from the war was an increase in the size of oil tankers; the supertanker was born. The insecurity of the Suez Canal required bigger tankers that could make the long journey around the Horn of Africa. Again, the resilient oil market adapted to political blockages of oil and even war. Furthermore, as during other times in oil history, fears of a long-term oil shortage gave way to surplus. In this slack market, U.S. oil import quotas and domestic production restrictions and allocations tried to hold the U.S. price artificially high.

One of the reasons that Eisenhower imposed quotas on imported oil in 1959 was to reduce U.S. dependency on such imports, thus obviating the need to send troops to the Middle East to safeguard them.[17] The former general was usually and laudably reluctant to send U.S. conventional forces into war, but he had just done so for what would be the only time in his eight-year presidency the year before with an intervention in the Middle East, the U.S. invasion of Lebanon in 1958. Although Lebanon had little oil, the president was demonstrating the Eisenhower doctrine, which claimed American resolve to support friendly countries against communism—especially oil producers in the Middle East. Of course, Eisenhower would have been better off to import the cheaper oil and simply realize that he could rely on the market to deliver it, instead of adopting the mercantilist policy of using force or covert action to ensure such incoming supplies. The oil import quotas to the world's largest oil consuming economy made the U.S. oil price artificially high and the world price artificially low, thus contributing to the formation of the OPEC cartel to attempt to push the world price back up.[18] So the United States helped create its future nemesis.

1967 Middle East War

Those much larger supertankers came in handy during the 1967 war, when the Suez Canal and pipelines from Iraq and Saudi Arabia were again closed and oil going from the Persian Gulf to Europe again had to go the long route around the Cape of Good Hope in southern Africa. This time, the oil disruption was potentially more severe, because not only were petroleum transportation routes through the Middle East closed, but also 60 percent of Arab, Middle Eastern, and North African oil production was shut down by strikes, riots, and sabotage to protest the war—that is, operations in Saudi Arabia, Libya, and the big refinery in Abadan, Iran. Three-quarters of Europe's oil supply came from Arab, Middle Eastern, and North African producers, thus threatening shortages there. At the same time, a civil war in Nigeria, caused by a fight over oil revenues and ethnic and religious issues, resulted in a Nigerian government embargo on oil exports from the oil-rich Biafra region, which was attempting to secede.

Also, Arab oil producers embargoed oil exports to friends of Israel—that is, the United States, Britain, Germany, Japan, and so on. U.S. producers in Aramco were ordered by the Saudis to embargo their own country; fearing nationalization, they complied. Yet, cleverly knowing that the amount of oil on the world market was more important to those consuming countries than which nations sold it to them, Kuwait and Saudi Arabia sold oil into the market as long as they got guarantees that it wouldn't go to the embargoed nations. Thus, Kuwait and Saudi Arabia got the symbolic benefit of embargoing friends of Israel without actually hurting those consuming nations or eroding their own oil profits.

As in any embargo of a product with a worldwide market, supplies simply reordered. Arab oil found new markets outside the embargoed countries. The embargoed countries bought from non-Arab producers. The temporary shortage from Arab countries, which eventually got their production back on line, was made up for by increased production in other countries—the United States, Iran, Indonesia, and Venezuela. (This spare U.S. capacity would not be there in the 1973 oil embargo.) Even while they imposed the targeted embargo, the Arab countries had an incentive to increase production by 8 percent to maintain market share!

As long as producers sell oil into the worldwide market, the embargo of any selected countries will be ineffectual. Because of market reordering, the targeted 1967 Arab oil embargo was a flop, and the Arab embargoing countries were the biggest losers. (The same was actually true in the more famous 1973 Arab oil embargo, which was perceived as being much more effective.) In fact, international oil companies managed to handle the market reordering without Western government help.

As in the aftermath of the 1956 war, fears of shortages gave way to accelerated production after the 1967 war ended. For a long time, supply would exceed demand.[19] And producing countries continued to demand a bigger share of the pie. In 1970, Libya's successful negotiations with the major international oil companies for a greater portion of oil revenues tipped the balance in favor of the producing states.

6

Three Cartels

The Seven Sisters, the Texas Railroad Commission, and OPEC

THE ORGANIZATION OF Petroleum Exporting Countries (OPEC) was formed in 1960 but didn't have much impact until 1973. In the late 1950s, to reestablish their market share, the Soviet communist government engaged in some free-market competitive slashing of the oil price. The Seven Sisters Western oil cartel, grousing about the new competition, followed suit without consulting the oil-producing nations. As a result of such price cuts, OPEC was born from the efforts of the Iraqi government of Abdul Karim Kassem and the Saudi and Venezuelan oil ministers. OPEC was a "cartel to confront the cartel"—that is, for oil-producing nations to cooperate in an attempt to receive a better deal for their oil (on production, prices, and taxation) from the Western cartel.[1] At its founding, OPEC's five members accounted for 80 percent of the world's oil exports.

In the 1960s, international oil companies still owned, by concession, the oil in the ground in most producing countries, and the global market was glutted with oil—thus, rendering OPEC weak. And in the 1950s and 1960s, the number of international oil companies proliferated.[2]

Like all natural resource cartels, OPEC has had trouble dictating the long-term price of its commodity. As Sheikh Ahmed Zaki Yamani, the famous Saudi oil minister, said in the late 1970s, "Political decisions cannot permanently negate the divine laws of supply and demand."[3] OPEC had some effect on the short-term price of oil in the 1970s, but only because the market was already tight (demand was increasing relative to supply). In the 1960s and again in the 1980s and 1990s, OPEC lost influence over the price as the market slackened.

OPEC learned everything it knows about trying to keep prices high from two American-led oil cartels and was a push back to them. First, "the Seven

Sisters"—seven private transnational oil companies, five of which were U.S. companies and two of which were British firms—dominated the world oil market from 1928 until 1971. For the most part, the American government looked the other way when it came to prosecuting the companies under U.S. antitrust laws.

In 1949, the seven companies controlled 82 percent of the world's oil reserves, 80 percent of its production, and 76 percent of its refining capacity, excluding the United States and the communist bloc. However, the main problem throughout most of the period of dominance by the Seven Sisters (except during World War II) was that the price of oil was too low; the companies tried to keep it propped up by establishing production quotas for each country. This indicates that the cartel, like its successor OPEC, was not very successful in trying collusion to keep prices artificially high, because of production outside the cartel (for example, the Soviet Union) and cheating by cartel members. Even right up to the oil price shock in 1973, real prices were much lower than before World War I or during the oil boom of the 1920s. For the producing nations, Western oil companies' extensive oil concessions (ownership within their territories) left them no say in oil-related decisions.[4]

OPEC replaced the Seven Sisters as the dominant cartel, as many oil producing countries, in a fit of anti-colonialism, nationalized their oil resources and their governments joined OPEC. This wave of nationalizations from 1970 to the mid-1980s was the most important development in the nature of the world oil market since the formation of Standard Oil. In 1972, the Seven Sisters still produced 77 percent of the world's oil outside the United States, Eastern Europe, and China and 90 percent of the oil from the Middle East. But from 1977 to 1984, the companies' oil reserves dropped by two-thirds, their profits plummeted, and they desperately tried to find new sources of petroleum.[5]

These large transnational companies still exist today and are still very profitable, but so much state involvement exists in oil production around the world that they are harder pressed to find and develop new oil fields than in the past. At the time of the 1973 oil crisis, the Seven Sisters earned two-thirds of their profits overseas. By the mid-1980s, however, OPEC governments had fully nationalized their oil, and the U.S. giants, needing oil reserves, then turned homeward; they had previously ceded the U.S. domestic market to smaller independent and midsized oil companies. With scarce oil reserves available, the majors also increased their involvement in oil refining and marketing and now account for about 60 percent of those U.S. businesses. Then from the 1990s until 2004, the giants began buying each other, including the ironic combination of the two largest pieces of the old Standard Oil Trust—Exxon (formerly Standard Oil of New Jersey) and Mobil (formerly Standard Oil of New York). Such combinations were needed to acquire scarce oil reserves and to pool resources to afford exploration and development of harder-to-get-at deposits using more expensive techniques.[6]

The second cartel was the Texas Railroad Commission, which attempted to prop up the price of domestic oil production, much of which—until oil was found on the north shore of Alaska and began being piped during the 1970s—was produced in Texas. Until 1971, the commission (and other state commissions, which were swayed by Texas's leadership in production) restrained production below capacity in order to artificially elevate the U.S. domestic oil price. Ironically, OPEC, now hated in the United States, modeled its production quotas on the commission's efforts to limit and allocate production. Also, OPEC believed that its "oil weapon" could not be used effectively until the United States no longer had the world's spare capacity of petroleum to bring onto the market to offset any OPEC production cuts. In 1971, Saudi Arabia began to have the spare capacity, not the United States. U.S. producers could no longer keep up with domestic consumption, and this lack of U.S. surplus made the 1973 oil crisis more painful than the 1956 and 1967 oil embargoes.

The Texas Railroad Commission was helped in its efforts to keep prices artificially high for smaller domestic independent producers by quotas on imported foreign oil imposed by President Eisenhower beginning in 1959 and lasting until 1971. Such quotas had the effect of more rapidly depleting U.S. fields instead of relying on greater imports of cheaper Middle Eastern oil from the major international oil companies. Although the international oil companies were huge, they lost on the quota issue because the smaller independent oil companies were more politically powerful in the United States. The independents employed local people, affected the domestic economy more greatly, and gave heavily to political campaigns.[7]

The U.S. import quotas helped lead to the formation of OPEC in the first place by artificially lessening demand for non-U.S. oil, thus lowering its price. OPEC was created to help defend that price.[8] When U.S. import quotas were eventually lifted—because U.S. oil production peaked in 1970 (discovery of oil in Prudhoe Bay, Alaska, would only slow the growth of U.S. imports) and

U.S. demand was increasing—imports soared from 19 percent of total U.S. consumption in 1967 to 36 percent in 1973.[9]

With rapidly rising demand for oil as countries around the world industrialized during the late 1960s, such quotas and cartels were no longer needed to try to artificially prop up the price. In fact, for the United States the problem then became that the price of oil was too high. The old saying about banks—that they only want to lend money to people who don't need it—is similar to the problem with cartels: they are set up to artificially hike prices but have their maximum political influence when they are already high, not when they are low and the cartel is trying to raise them.

OPEC's heyday lasted a shorter time than that of the Seven Sisters cartel, and it had even less control over the oil price (although the sisters didn't do a very good job either). This occurred because OPEC had even less market share than the sisters (OPEC maintained more than 50 percent during the 1970s and has less than 40 percent today), exhibited less discipline, and did not have integrated production, refining and distribution operations (the sisters helped distribute OPEC's oil).[10]

OPEC's political influence peaked in 1973, under the then-tightest post–World War II market conditions, and in 1979 and 1980, when Iran's revolution dramatically lessened that country's oil production. In the former case, huge demand increases in the late 1960s and early 1970s contributed to the doubling of the price of oil between 1970 and 1973. The price spike was caused by rapid post–World War II global industrialization, by fewer oil wells being drilled in the U.S. from the mid-1950s to the early 1970s because of new environmental laws, and by the environmental movement's push for cleaner air and water, which compelled a fast change over from coal to fuel oil. But even those two episodes of OPEC's influence were overblown and were exacerbated by mistakes made by some oil consuming nations, especially the United States.

7

Another Middle East War and Embargo, Shortages, and Price Rises

IN 1973, Israel and the Arabs again went to war. Because the United States supported and resupplied Israel with military items, Arab OPEC producers and other Arab countries, in solidarity with the warring Arab nations, embargoed oil to the United States and the Netherlands. The cartel also cut production quotas for individual members in an attempt to make the United States and the West pay more for petroleum. The production cutback was only 8 or 9 percent of the free world's oil (7 percent of U.S. supplies) and was made possible only because of the tight petroleum market and because the revenues from rising prices more than offset those forfeited from lost volume. (The Arabs actually had to increase production during the 1967 embargo on the United States, Britain, and Germany, because the market was much more slack—and the oil price lower—than during the 1973 embargo.) As in the 1967 war, again fearing nationalization, U.S. oil companies helped implement the embargo and production cutbacks against their own country.

The 1973 Oil Crisis Shows the Problems with Cartels

The conventional wisdom has been that the cartel unleashed a powerful weapon that showed that it could bring the West's oil consuming nations, including the United States, to their knees. In reality, the 1973 Arab oil embargo and production cutbacks were a colossal failure that made oil producers' third embargo their last.

OPEC, like all cartels, has had some hidden problems in controlling the long-term price of oil or banning sales to specific countries. First, a worldwide market exists for oil. If some producing countries refuse to sell to some consuming nations—as during the Arab embargo—those buying nations will find other non-embargoing sellers. And the embargoing countries then will have to export to the customers of the non-embargoing sellers or lose revenues. As noted earlier, this same "market reordering" happened during both the 1956 and 1967 Middle Eastern war and oil crises. The embargoed countries will assume some extra costs in switching suppliers, but they shouldn't ever be that severe. Even Sheikh Yamani, then Saudi Arabia's oil minister and the architect of the 1973 embargo, admitted that it was merely an illusion. He said that the embargo "did not imply that we could reduce oil imports to the United States. . . . The world is really just one market. So the embargo was more symbolic than anything else." In addition, rampant cheating occurred, as tankers from Arab countries bound for non-embargoed countries mysteriously changed course on the high seas and headed for the United States.[1]

However, the cartel's illusion did make Japanese and European foreign policies tilt more toward the Arabs rather than Israel—but that was merely because the Europeans foolishly believed that any embargo could really be effective. In addition, many in the United States were at least partially hoodwinked by this chimera. If senior U.S. policymakers in the Nixon administration had been more knowledgeable about how both embargoes and the oil market worked, their economic responses to the cartel's action might have been less counterproductive than they turned out to be. But there is some indication that administration officials knew that prior embargoes in 1956 and 1967 had been ineffective because the Arabs had to sell their oil to someone, if not the United States or other embargoed countries.[2] Yet U.S. policymakers often feel pressure to "do something" to satisfy domestic audiences, even if it makes the situation worse. Retaining price controls from before the embargo and initiating consequent government rationing in its wake were disasters. Politically, however, and in contrast to European appeasement, the threat of an Arab embargo did not deter the United States from saving Israel by resupplying it with weapons. In fact, a nationalist reaction in the United States to the Arab actions actually increased support for Israel.

Despite the panic induced by the oil embargo, the cartel's production cutbacks caused more of a problem in oil consuming nations—but only in the short term. In a global market, anytime any supplier cuts production, the world price will go up for all consumers (likewise, if any supplier increases production, the price will go down for all consumers). For example, although once the

Japanese and Europeans had tilted their foreign policies to be more pro-Arab and were exempted from further production cuts, the aforementioned world market—remaining affected by the production cutbacks to the United States and the Netherlands—still dealt Japan and Europe and all other consumers price increases. (After 1973, further integration of the world's oil market magnified the indiscriminate hurt of any production cutback anywhere in the world, which, when combined with the disaster for the cartel of this embargo, likely renders any such future uses of the "oil weapon" much less likely.)

When the suppliers of the cartel cut production (the cuts amounted to only about 8 or 9 percent of the free world's supply), the world oil price quadrupled.[3] According to Leonardo Maugeri, an executive in the Italian energy company Eni, the international crisis was caused less by the actual shortage of oil than by a collective psychology fearing shortfalls—a psychology that led to irrational actions.[4]

Even when the oil price is high, however, the power of cartels has been exaggerated. Because the demand for oil is inelastic (a fancy economic term for demand responding slowly to price changes), cartel nations can increase revenues even when they cut production. But the problem with cartels is that promising to abide by the quota and then cheating by hiking production is even more profitable. Countries want to cash in on the high prices caused by promised production cutbacks, and to do that they secretly pump even more oil than their production quotas. Of course, all of this cheating under the table eventually increases the supply of oil on the world market and drops the price. As the 1973 Arab oil embargo and announced production cutbacks endured, oil came out of the woodwork and back onto the market. Just as when the international oil companies controlled oil in the producing nations and got pressure from these countries to increase production to generate more producer royalties, the same incentive for more revenues encouraged increased production by the new nationalized oil industries of the cartel.

Although U.S. Secretary of State Henry Kissinger obliquely threatened U.S. military action to seize oil fields if the 1973 oil embargo was not relaxed (a secret U.S. plan was created to seize Persian Gulf oil fields), and the Saudis countered that any such action would bring a fouling of oil wells, Saudi Arabia, during both the 1967 and 1973 embargoes, secretly violated its own embargo by allowing oil to flow under the table to a U.S. military that was trying to contain the Soviet Union worldwide. After all, oil tankers can mysteriously change course once at sea.[5] (Of course, the U.S. produced enough oil domestically to fuel its military many times over.) The threat of Soviet intervention in the Gulf, with the accompanying threat of escalation to nuclear war, also might have given the U.S. significant pause before using force to grab the oil fields.

In September 1974, after the 1973–1974 oil crisis was over, President Gerald Ford, attempting to deter future cartel oil shocks, obliquely threatened, "Throughout history, nations have gone to war over natural advantages, such as water or food."[6] In January 1975, Henry Kissinger again made a threat to use force to grab oil. He declared that force should not be used "in the case of a dispute over price" but should be an option "where there is some actual strangulation of the industrialized world." Of course, this statement shows that Kissinger was either disingenuous or ignorant of how the oil market worked and of how unlikely it would be for the cartel to be able to "strangle" the West using oil as a weapon. In May of 1975, then–Secretary of Defense James Schlesinger echoed Kissinger's threat: "We might not remain entirely passive to the imposition of [another oil] embargo. I'm not going to indicate any prospective reaction, other than to point out that there are economic, political, and conceivably military measures in response."[7]

In the mid-1970s, U.S. threats aside, most oil-producing nations won control over their oil resources from the international oil companies, and 1974 to 1978 is referred to as "OPEC's Golden Age." Even during that limited time span, however, OPEC had bitter internal battles when trying to set an oil price.[8] Moreover, the cartel has always had problems with a lack of discipline—that is, cheating members.

One other problem with cartels exists. Countries with large oil reserves in the ground—Saudi Arabia—don't want to drive up the price too high, because this rise can lead to a long-term or even permanent reduction in the demand for oil. The cuts in demand from high prices can result from conservation by consumers or from making alternative fuels more economical. For example, because of the oil crises in the 1970s, the electric power generation industry and other industrial users, in the 1980s, moved almost completely away from oil as a fuel source and toward coal, natural gas, and nuclear power. In areas other than transportation, these fuels eroded oil's share of the world energy market because they were cheaper and more efficient.

The 1973 oil crisis brought the double horror of price increases and gas lines. The lines were caused by government price controls that actually held price hikes below what they should have been and thus required government petroleum rationing when demand exceeded supply. Although the world oil price went up by more than 200 percent, price controls held the U.S. price to only a 56 percent increase.[9]

Nevertheless, higher prices spurred greater conservation and a move to alternative fuels, which caused a significant decrease in long-term demand for oil in the 1980s and even into the 1990s. The United States was 25 percent more energy-efficient and 32 percent more oil-efficient in 1985 than in 1973.[10] Refined oil products as a proportion of the world's primary energy supply declined from their peak of 44 percent during the 1970s to 37 percent in 1990 (in 2005 their share was 36 percent because of greater use of natural gas, coal's expansion in Asia, and less oil being used in residences and electricity generation).[11] In total U.S. energy consumption, fossil fuels—oil, coal, and natural gas—declined from 93 percent in 1973 to 86 percent in 2004.[12] From 1975 to 2000, the amount of energy needed to produce one dollar of U.S. GDP fell 40 percent.[13]

The United States imported 34 percent of oil consumed in 1973 and imports more than 60 percent today, yet, because of advances in auto fuel efficiency, less use of oil by electric utilities, and a post-industrial (services-based) economy that requires less fuel, the ratio of oil consumption to GDP (about three percent) is now half of what it was 1970 (roughly six percent).[14] Although the economic effects of oil price spikes have always been exaggerated (see below), this last statistic shows that the U.S. economy has become even more resilient to them in recent years.

Although the oil crises of the 1970s produced the usual gloom-and-doom forecasts about running out of oil, the higher prices spurred production from non-OPEC sources—Mexico, Alaska, Norway, Great Britain, and the Soviet Union. (The Soviet Union always declined to enter OPEC because the Russians could take advantage of higher prices when OPEC nations cut production, yet foist the costs on the cartel.) Because of reduced demand for OPEC oil and increased non-OPEC production, OPEC's share of the world market declined from greater than 50 percent to 29 percent.[15] Higher prices also motivated the use of new technology to extract oil previously unavailable—for example, deep drilling offshore in the North Sea by Britain and Norway.

Saudi Arabia, the largest oil producer in and leader of OPEC, does not want to go through the trauma of another backlash to the 1973 oil embargo and price hikes. Having learned their lessons from the oil shocks of the 1970s, the Saudis have aimed to keep the oil price below a level that would spur long-term reductions in demand. Subsequently, the Saudis, by hiking their production, would often sabotage OPEC's efforts to increase world prices. And ironically, the U.S. and other Western governments did not want the oil price to go too low—because it might destabilize the Shah's Iran, Saudi Arabia, and other oil producers and because it might render uneconomical higher cost oil investments, such as those in the North Sea. Instead, Western governments merely wanted price stability.[16]

Finally, OPEC is also not immune from the exaggerated fear that high oil prices can damage petroleum-consuming economies. This fear has given OPEC countries an incentive not to drive up oil prices too high, because they fear that their own investments, from the recycling of petro-dollars back in to consuming nations, will be harmed.

Consuming Governments Caused the Ill Effects of the 1973 Oil Crisis, Not OPEC

Unfortunately, the fuel shortages and gas lines in the 1973 oil crisis seared the importance of "oil security" into the American consciousness. First, although oil had first become a political commodity during World War I, the 1973 oil crisis made it even more so. Second, the queues at U.S. gas stations could have been avoided by lifting oil price controls and letting higher prices naturally allocate gasoline to the users who needed it most—rather than using incomprehensible federal oil allocation rules and having U.S. state governments ration fuel by, for example, requiring motorists to buy gas only on even and odd days. Britain and Italy adopted similar ill-fated petroleum rationing systems. At the same time, Japan and Switzerland experienced oil price hikes and yet experienced no disruptions because they let the price rise all the way to market levels.

Richard Nixon didn't want to do that in 1971. As part of his anti-inflation program, he had imposed—by Executive Order—economy-wide price controls, which included restraints on oil prices. In time of oil surplus, the U.S. price had been kept artificially high from 1959 to the early 1970s because the Texas Railroad Commission and other state commissions restrained domestic production and because the U.S. government had imposed quotas on less expensive competing foreign imports. Now abruptly in a tight oil market, the government did an about-face, ended import quotas on cheaper foreign imports, and even made the oil price artificially low with price controls. Also, because oil is such a political commodity, Congress went further and legislated oil price controls, which Nixon signed. Thus, even when price controls on the rest of the economy were lifted in 1974, they foolishly remained on oil.

Nixon had wanted to get re-elected in 1972. To do so, in 1971, he urged Federal Reserve Chief Arthur Burns to pump up the money supply to give the economy an artificial stimulus. Such expansionary monetary (and fiscal) policy was also designed to counter the perceived dragging effects on the economy of higher oil prices. Hiking the money supply almost always causes inflation sooner or later. Nixon wanted it to be after the election, especially because fighting the Vietnam War without raising taxes had already caused some inflation. So this former opponent of wage and price controls, as president, cynically imposed them. Paul Volcker, then Nixon's under secretary of the Treasury, later admitted that the twin policies were designed to give Nixon the best electoral situation possible—surging production and restrained prices.

The oil price controls induced artificially low prices, which reduced production and increased demand, thus creating oil shortages even before the Arabs imposed their oil embargo and production cutbacks in late 1973 and early 1974. In April 1973, to try to relieve the shortages, Nixon was forced to remove import quotas on foreign oil.[17] The reasons that the Arab oil embargo and production cutbacks during the 1973 Middle East war presented more hardship to consuming nations than similar measures during the 1956 and 1967 wars was because the oil market was much tighter and the world's spare production capacity had moved from the United States to Saudi Arabia.

Even though the economy had been pumped up by a loose money supply, price controls restrained the general price level for a while—through the 1973 oil crisis—but resulted in stagflation (slow economic growth and rampant inflation) in the mid- and late 1970s when the controls were eased and pent-up inflation surged.

Dramatically increasing the money supply also usually creates an artificial bubble in the economy. When it pops, a recession ensues when excess investments are liquidated. Conveniently for Nixon, the ill effects of the inflated money supply didn't cause a recession until the 1973–1975 period—long after he had been reelected. This recession had less to do with the 1973 oil embargo and price increases than it did with the expansion of the money supply for Nixon's re-election.

Thus, stagflation has been blamed on the 1973 oil embargo and high petroleum prices. In reality, the Vietnam War, increases in the money supply, and wage and price controls were the culprits. (For example, price controls induce economic drag by misallocating oil and wasting peoples' time lining up for gasoline.) Economist Doug Bohi has estimated that economic growth suffered only .35 percent from oil crises of the 1970s.[18]

Furthermore, Western policymakers worried that high oil prices would suck billions of dollars out of the industrial oil-consuming countries, but those dollars were "recycled" as cash-flush oil producers consumed more from and invested more in those same industrial nations. For example, in the case of Saudi Arabia, recycled petro-dollars into the United States—for example, revenues from U.S. exports to the desert kingdom, Saudi investments in the United States, and U.S. oil company profits and dividends from activities in the kingdom—dwarfed U.S. payments for Saudi oil annually by a factor of two to five, even during the days of high oil prices in the mid- to late-1970s.[19] One important factor involved was the attractiveness of the United States as an investment haven.

It is also a fallacy to believe that a rise in oil prices can cause significant inflation—the general upward movement of prices in the economy. If the price of one good goes up, people normally have less money to spend on other things. This tends to reduce the demand for the other products and thus their prices, leaving the overall price level fairly unchanged. For example, between the oil embargo of 1973 and the later oil "crisis" at the end of the decade during the Iranian revolution, OPEC made only two small price increases, but general inflation ran amok. Only increases in money supply can cause a rampant hike in the general price level in the economy. Such inflation does not come mainly from the oil market but is a government-induced phenomenon. For example, during the 1973 oil price hikes, Germany, Switzerland, and other countries following the German-led tight monetary policy had little inflation, and Japanese disinflation (prices increasing at a decreasing rate) also resulted from a restrictive monetary policy.

Also, the 1973 oil crisis caused the U.S. political leadership to begin touting U.S. independence from foreign energy to enhance U.S. security—directly the opposite of the approach taken in the early Cold War years, during which the government wanted to use more Middle Eastern petroleum and "conserve" U.S. oil for future national security purposes (for example, any war against the Soviets). In late 1973, President Nixon introduced the protectionist Project Independence by saying, "Let us set as our national goal, in the spirit of Apollo, with the determination of the Manhattan Project, that by the end of this decade we will have developed the potential to meet our own energy needs without depending on any foreign energy source." His staff had told him that this goal by 1980 was impossible and that he was foolish to announce it.[20] Fortunately, his staff was correct. But although the success of John F. Kennedy's public goal of putting men on the moon is often touted, the failure to reach Nixon's aim has been swept under the rug, and politicians of both parties are still endorsing this undesirable objective. As this book will show, the discipline of microeconomics should tell us autarkic and protectionist energy policies are no more economically efficient than such policies for other products.

In sum, the Arab oil embargo appeared to be more effective than it was. However, Israel won the 1973 war on the battlefield, and the Arab oil embargo and production cutbacks were eventually rescinded without achieving any of their political objectives. When combined with the second oil shock in 1979 and 1980, however, the shortages and gas lines became seared into the American consciousness and have adversely affected American energy policy ever since.

The Iranian Revolution and Oil "Crisis"

Then record-high oil prices in 1979 and 1980 were caused by panic in the world market when the Iranian revolution in 1978 and 1979 cut off the production and exports of the world's second largest oil exporter. Although Saudi Arabia and other OPEC producers increased output so that the oil global supply dropped only 4 to 5 percent (the world supply dropped eight or nine percent during the 1973 cartel production cuts), the panic boosted the world price more than 100 percent.[21] The price more than doubled from $44 a barrel to a then-record

$104 a barrel.[22] (These values are in 2008 dollars, still below the now record level of $147 a barrel in 2008.)

Although oil imported into the United States actually increased by 8 percent, oil companies engaged in panic buying and hoarded the stocks, predicting even greater price increases. As in the 1973 crisis, and caused by the continued fear of shortages carrying over from that crisis, the apprehension exceeded the actual supply reduction.

The reduced world supply also resulted in some supply disruptions in the United States because U.S. oil price controls were still around. By the end of the 1970s, the U.S. oil price was still only 60 percent of the world price.[23] Although President Ford had had the chance to remove the controls in 1975, he had declined to do so. Carter had only started the ball rolling in June of 1979 on a gradual decontrol of oil prices.[24] Had the price been allowed to rapidly rise to world levels, shortages and rationing through gas lines would have disappeared.

As in the oil crisis of 1973, slashed production, this time due to the Iranian revolution, had a greater effect than any oil embargo. After U.S. hostages were taken in Iran, Jimmy Carter unilaterally banned imports of Iranian oil, and the Iranians initially retaliated by banning their oil exports to any American firm. (Later, however, American companies actually began selling Iranian oil, but not in the United States because of U.S. sanctions.) Although these largely symbolic acts roiled the spot market price for a time, the market merely reordered as it had in 1973.

U.S. intervention had contributed to Iran's revolution. After the British abandoned much of the Middle East in 1971, succeeding U.S. administrations pursued a "twin pillars" strategy in the Middle East—relying on Iran and Saudi Arabia to ensure stability. Yet U.S. political hugging of and huge American arms sales to the bigger pillar—Iran—actually ended up destabilizing the country and leading to the revolution.

Oil prices would have been—and should have been—even higher had the Republican-instituted price controls not existed. Presciently recognizing the problem, Democrat Jimmy Carter began decontrolling oil prices toward the end of his term, and Ronald Reagan, his Republican successor, finished the task by 1981. The gasoline price is a political problem for any administration—Democratic or Republican—because the price is much more visible to the public than the prices of other goods. People see the gasoline price plastered on roadside signs that they can view without ever having to leave their car and go into a store. That's why Carter's decision was courageous as the 1980 election approached. Reagan's follow-up was a little less so, because oil companies usually give many of their political contributions to the Republican Party. The decontrol of oil prices eventually brought greater supplies at cheaper prices, thus validating that an unfettered market is the best means of efficiently getting oil to the consumer.

The oil "crisis" in 1979 and 1980 arising from the Iranian revolution was irrational—that is, based on only small actual oil shortages of four to five percent of global supply due to strikes by Iran's oil workers, nationalization of its oil industry, and reduced exports. The panic was induced by memories of the previously irrational chaos in 1973, which had also caused buyers to build up inventories and inadvertently aggravate the shortages. During the 1979–1980 crisis, the panic buying to build up inventories increased the shortage to about 10 percent of world supply, worse than the shortage in the 1973 oil crisis.

The erroneous lessons that the world drew from the 1973 embargo and the 1979–1980 Iranian-induced price spike were that the future energy outlook was bleak and that any governmental act by an oil-producing nation or nations, or political instability in any one of them, could trigger an economic crisis in the West. As this book will show, neither of these conclusions was correct. In both crises, panic buying and governmental controls magnified the effects of the rather small actual world shortages. High prices from the crises eventually caused conservation (oil is price-sensitive in the long term) and more exploration and production, leading to a glut of oil in the 1980s and 1990s. Such a slack market ran counter to the CIA's grim prediction in 1977 of imminent peak oil production, rapidly depleting global oil reserves, and aggressive competition among nations for dwindling energy resources[25] (another example throughout the oil industry's history of the market falsifying gloom-and-doom predictions of long-term shortages and permanent high prices).

Because of this oil glut, when Israel invaded Lebanon in 1982, Arab oil producers quickly dropped the idea of another disastrous oil embargo against the United States. The ineffectiveness of even the famed 1973 oil embargo has been demonstrated, if nothing else, by the fact that the Arabs have never tried to impose another one, despite later wars and crises in the Middle East.

In fact, with more oil coming onto the market from non-OPEC sources and the world price and their revenues declining, OPEC members, to parry the competition, found themselves giving unofficial price discounts and exceeding production quotas, sometimes by bartering oil for industrial manufactures or armaments. During the oil glut of the 1980s, many of the seemingly invincible oil-producing countries got sucked into the world debt crisis by borrowing too much money on the assumption that the oil price would never go down—historically an abysmal bet.

Finally, the 1979–1980 crisis also caused the oil market to become more efficient by moving the oil business from long-term contracts to buying and selling on the short-term spot market. In addition, the oil futures contract would reduce even OPEC's ability to set short-term prices in the market. Originally, Standard Oil tried to set the oil price, then it moved to the Texas Railroad Commission domestically and the Seven Sisters international oil companies worldwide, then to OPEC, and now to the NYMEX (New York Mercantile Exchange), which runs a truly global oil market. These developments led to the large integrated oil companies disintegrating and becoming more competitive by buying oil anywhere and everywhere. In the late 1980s, reintegration—that is, tying oil reserves for production to markets for refined products—was the trend.[26]

The tight oil markets and high prices of the 1970s did, however, give oil-producing countries more power vis-à-vis the international oil companies. Since the breakup of the Standard Oil Trust in 1911, the wealth and power of the oil industry has not been in refining and marketing, but in control of resources in the ground. In the 1970s, as a result of oil now being more valuable, Iraq, Kuwait, Venezuela, and most other OPEC countries would complete nationalization of their oil industries (the Saudis waited until the mid-1980s to do so). These nations, however, continued to contract with the international companies for technology, services, personnel, and marketing systems to sell their oil. The oil companies drilled only in the United States, the North Sea, and a few other places, and owned refineries and gas stations throughout the world.

The days of the oil concession—in which the international oil companies actually owned oil beneath the ground in developing countries and set prices and production rates—were over, and the companies, at best, could contract for part of the production that they discovered within the particular country. Exploration by the companies was foreclosed in many nationalized countries and was discouraged by the threat of nationalization in other developing nations. The oil companies shifted their exploration to industrial countries. Yet even Britain formed a national oil company during the 1970s to get more control over North Sea oil and also added a tax on oil revenues (bucking the world-wide trend, Margaret Thatcher wisely later dissolved the national company in 1985 and even sold off British government shares of British Petroleum).

More and more state owned oil companies—such as Venezuela's Citgo— were even marketing their own oil directly into the market and avoiding altogether the international companies as middlemen. In 1973, OPEC countries directly marketed only eight percent of their oil production, whereas in 1979 the amount had skyrocketed to 42 percent.[27] Unfortunately, this inefficient nationalization of oil production and marketing has done more to permanently and artificially prop up the world oil price than anything the largely ineffective OPEC cartel or political instability in oil producing countries could ever muster. Some countries, however, are now realizing that state-owned oil industries lack the technology to adequately explore and produce reserves within their borders and are inviting back the major private international oil firms or oil service companies, such as Halliburton or Schlumberger, to act as contractors to help do so.

8

The Carter Doctrine

NOT ALL OF Carter's policies were as enlightened as his decontrol of various industries, including energy. Carter went down to defeat in the 1980 election because of the stagflation caused by the Vietnam War, and the poor economic policies of Nixon, Ford, and himself (until he nominated as head of the Federal Reserve Paul Volcker, who ran a tight monetary policy and drained high inflation out of the economy[1]). But before Carter left office, he left an indelible and unfortunate mark on U.S. policy in the Persian Gulf.

Until 1971, the United States had relied on Britain to stabilize its ex-colonial lands in the Persian Gulf and Middle East. After the British withdrew from more than one hundred years of protecting the Gulf, the United States, from 1971 until 1979, relied on the Shah's Iran, and to a lesser extent Saudi Arabia, to stabilize the Gulf and act as a counterweight to any Soviet penetration. Under the more modest post-Vietnam Nixon doctrine, the United States provided military assistance to regional proxies to battle attempted Soviet inroads in various regions—in this case, Soviet military aid to Iraq.

The year 1979 was a tumultuous year for the Near East/South Asia region. The Shi'i fundamentalist Islamist cleric, Ayatollah Khomeini, overthrew the Shah in Iran early in the year; late in the year, the Sunni fundamentalist Islamic militants took over the holiest site in Islam, the Grand Mosque in Mecca, Saudi Arabia; and the Soviets invaded Afghanistan, which borders Iran on the east. Carter, unduly panicked by these events, in January 1980 enunciated the so-called Carter doctrine, when he stated:

> The region which is now threatened by Soviet troops in Afghanistan is
> of great strategic importance: It contains more than two-thirds of the

world's exportable oil. The Soviet effort to dominate Afghanistan has brought Soviet military forces to within 300 miles of the Indian Ocean and close to the Straits of Hormuz, a waterway through which most of the world's oil must flow. The Soviet Union is now attempting to consolidate a strategic position, therefore, that poses a grave threat to the free movement of Middle East oil.

This situation demands careful thought, steady nerves, and resolute action, not only for this year but for many years to come. It demands collective efforts to meet this new threat to security in the Persian Gulf and in Southwest Asia. It demands the participation of all those who rely on oil from the Middle East and who are concerned with global peace and stability. And it demands consultation and close cooperation with countries in the area which might be threatened.

Meeting this challenge will take national will, diplomatic and political wisdom, economic sacrifice, and, of course, military capability. We must call on the best that is in us to preserve the security of this crucial region.

Let our position be absolutely clear: An attempt by any outside force to gain control of the Persian Gulf region will be regarded as an assault on the vital interests of the United States of America, and such an assault will be repelled by any means necessary, including military force.

The Carter doctrine was designed to be a sequel to the Truman and Eisenhower doctrines, each pushing U.S. interests farther east.[2] And it was a reversal of the Nixon doctrine, which depended on pro-American regional proxies to stanch Soviet influence around the world. The Nixon doctrine was now rendered meaningless in the Gulf by the demise of Iran, the strongest regional pillar, into revolution and hostility toward the U.S.

Ever since the Truman administration, the United States had been scared that the Soviets would try to take over the oil fields in the Persian Gulf and use them to increase their influence over the Europeans and Japanese, who relied more on Persian Gulf oil than did the United States.[3] So in the minds of U.S. policymakers, the threat appeared to be not to the United States per se but to its informal empire of one-sided alliances.

Problems with the Carter Doctrine

There were several problems with Carter's analysis and doctrine. The first was that although the Russians and Soviets had always wanted a warm water port further south, Afghanistan was landlocked. The reluctant Soviet invasion of that country came about because of Soviet fears that a militant Islamist rebellion in Afghanistan would spill over into their Islamic republics in the south.[4] (The Carter administration foolishly provided the Islamists with assistance in order to tweak the Soviets.) If the Soviets had wanted a warm water port on the Persian Gulf and control of the oil that went through the Straits of Hormuz, they could have just directly invaded Iran, which then bordered on the both the Soviet Union and the straits. The Soviets in Afghanistan were only 300 miles from the straits, but to get there they would again have to go through Iran. The Soviets didn't invade Iran either directly from the Soviet Union or from Afghanistan, because Iran is much larger than even Afghanistan in land area and population, is as mountainous in some places, and also would have had zealous Islamist fighters who would have resisted the communist atheists fanatically. Besides, the Soviets were having enough problems trying to suppress the Islamist resistance in Afghanistan. So Carter's argument that Soviet forces in Afghanistan posed a grave threat to Middle East oil was greatly exaggerated.

In addition, although Carter called on collective action by other nations, especially those that imported oil from the Middle East, the United States pledged unilaterally to protect the Persian Gulf. At the time, even though Carter designated a Rapid Deployment Task Force to protect the Gulf, it had to borrow U.S. forces from other regions of the world to do so.

The Carter doctrine, however, set a precedent for the United States blatantly acknowledging that it would use military power to secure oil supplies. Carter's pronouncement, however, was a more explicit version of FDR's and Truman's promises to Saudi Arabia of providing security to the Persian Gulf in exchange for Saudi oil. The embarrassing similarity of the Carter doctrine to Imperial Japan's policy prior to and during World War II went unnoticed. Imperial Japan had also used military power to guarantee resources for use by its economy and armed forces.

Of course, making the case that the Soviets would try to conquer the Persian Gulf's oil was plausible, but the Soviets themselves were a major oil producer. And to say that the Soviets would then not operate by market considerations did not comport well with their history in the oil market. Except for oil, the nonviable state-owned Soviet economy produced nothing that the world wanted. Exports of oil were about the only source of foreign exchange earnings the Soviets had, and thus they had not joined OPEC because they did not want to be restricted in the amount of oil they sold into the market. Even if the Soviets had physically conquered some of the Persian Gulf's oil—the worst possible case and a Soviet objective that seemed to be more of a U.S. fear rather than actually in the Soviet mind—the Soviets, like any other actor, would be motivated to sell a valuable commodity for badly needed cash.

Ironically, in 1975, shortly before Carter took office, Secretary of State Henry Kissinger, on behalf of President Ford, had been pursuing a deal that would have made the United States dependent on direct imports of oil from its major superpower adversary during the Cold War—the Soviet Union. Although the deal eventually fell through, Kissinger hoped to undermine OPEC's influence in the world oil market by exporting American wheat in exchange for imports of petroleum from the Soviet Union. (U.S. hypocrisy was on display later, during the early 1980s, as Ronald Reagan imposed economic sanctions against a European pipeline project that would have made Western Europe more dependent on Soviet natural gas.)

Kissinger's lack of understanding of the oil market is starkly evident because he overvalued OPEC's influence; Carter's was too because he did not understand that the Soviets had few products that could earn them desperately needed foreign exchange and that they could not afford to play politics with a commodity their rickety economy needed to survive. The weak oil price of the middle to late 1980s was one of the reasons the Soviet Union collapsed. These two examples illustrate the great American tradition of regularly making its adversaries ten feet tall.

Even if the Carter doctrine was justified at the time, like most such government policies, it remained after conditions had changed. Even as the Soviet Union weakened and dissolved, dedicated U.S. forces were assigned to secure Gulf oil; pre-positioned weapons were put in place in the Gulf to use when they got there; transport ships and planes were purchased to get them and their equipment there; bilateral security or base access agreements were signed with Oman, Jordan, Egypt, Kenya, Somalia, and Diego Garcia in the British Indian Ocean Territory; the United States built an important facility in Saudi Arabia to command and control U.S. forces; and the designation of the effort was upgraded from the Rapid Deployment Task Force to the Central Command.[5] So at the very time that the major alleged threat to the oil was declining, U.S. plans to assert military control over the Persian Gulf were deepening. This reality should cause suspicion that the Soviet threat to Gulf oil had been hyped to justify a U.S. military presence in the Gulf. Thus, the Carter doctrine had an important lasting effect because it enshrined the securing of Gulf oil as the top U.S. military priority—where it has remained—and eventually led to real, unilateral U.S. military hegemony over the Gulf.[6]

9

The 1980s

*European Dependence on Soviet Energy
and the Iran-Iraq War*

DURING THE REAGAN administration, the energy-poor Western Europeans began construction of pipelines to one of the closest sources of natural gas—the Soviet Union. The hawkish and anti-Soviet U.S. administration didn't want its European allies to become dependent on Soviet natural gas, so it imposed economic sanctions on U.S. technology being used for the pipelines. This U.S. action was hypocritical because the Europeans were merely trying to do the same thing the United States did after the 1973 Arab oil embargo—diversify to different fuels and sources of fuels. Like Henry Kissinger, who was trying to trade U.S. grain to the Soviet Union in return for the rival superpower's oil, the Germans were trying reduce their dependence on Persian Gulf oil by importing natural gas from the Soviet Union.[1]

Reagan's sanctions not only enraged the Western Europeans and the Soviets but hurt U.S. companies, which didn't have a monopoly on the pipeline technology. The pipelines were built anyway, and Soviet and Russian gas has been flowing to Western Europe ever since through a pipeline system that links Europe with natural gas supplies from Russia, Algeria, and the North Sea. Although the Soviets and Russians have occasionally reduced or cut off energy supplies for political reasons, mainly to weak countries in their sphere of influence, they have never done so to the more powerful Western European nations, even during Cold War confrontations. Even during the 1973 Arab oil embargo, the Soviets refused to participate and pumped more oil to take advantage of the high prices. From the Cold War to this day, the faraway United States has worried more about potential regional threats to its allies than the allies themselves did.

One major factor leading to disintegration of the Soviet Union was the collapse of oil prices in the mid- to late 1980s. The bottom fell out of the global oil market—with the world price being cut by about 50 percent in 1986 alone, the year after Mikhail Gorbachev took power—and did not begin recovering until the year 2000. Being the world's largest oil producing nation from the late 1970s to its demise in 1991, the Soviet Union relied on energy as the basis for its economy. Energy was also the country's chief export and an important earner of desperately needed hard currency required to pay for meat, grain, and technological imports. With only shoddy products being produced by the entirely state-owned communist economy, the Soviet Union had to depend on energy exports.

Yegor Gaidar, using Soviet Politburo archives opened after the Soviet Union fell, says that the Soviet leadership panicked about the drop in oil revenues because they had far fewer gold reserves to pay their bills than the West believed. Some international bankers realized the dire straits the Soviets were in and refused to give them credits, thus making the Soviet Unions's financial situation even worse. According to Gaidar, Soviet General Secretary Mikhail Gorbachev even called German Chancellor Helmut Kohl and begged for immediate financial assistance, saying that the situation was "catastrophic."[2]

The 1980s: The Iran-Iraq War

The tight petroleum market and the two oil crises of the 1970s, as well as the resultant gas lines and price increases, encouraged people and governments in oil-importing countries to reduce their demand for petroleum products through conservation and the use of alternative energy sources. The lower demand for oil helped keep further crises in the Persian Gulf in the 1980s and 1990s from turning into oil shocks, as did the fact that higher prices in the 1970s led to the introduction of new energy technology and compensatory production increases by some OPEC members, such as Saudi Arabia, and non-OPEC oil producers, such as Mexico, Britain, Norway, the United States (Alaska), Malaysia, China, and Angola. Once again, as had happened so many times in the history of oil, dire predictions of permanently declining supply and rising prices in 1980 would give way to an oil glut and a price slump throughout most of the two decades after that time.[3]

After the Iranian revolution at the end of the 1970s, Iran appeared weak and chaotic to Iraq's Saddam Hussein. In 1975, Iraq had been forced to give up some sovereignty over the Shatt-al-Arab waterway—a critical route to the Persian Gulf for the oil exports of both countries—to the then-stronger Iran. Also, about 90 percent of Iranian oil resources are in Khuzestan, a province in southwest Iran right on Iraq's border; the province has a significant Arab population. Lastly, the Ayatollah Ruhollah Khomeini's fundamentalist Islamic revolution in Iran threatened to destabilize Saddam's Iraq. So Saddam decided to invade Iran to end this threat, re-establish Iraqi sovereignty over the entire Shatt-al-Arab, and maybe even grab Khuzistan and its oil.

Lasting almost a decade (1980 to 1988), the Iran-Iraq War—featuring attacks by both countries on each other's oil installations, ports, and tankers—reduced Iran's oil exports and nearly cut off Iraqi oil exports, which together made up roughly 5.8 percent of the world's production. But a number of factors, including conservation induced by the oil crises of 1973 and 1979–1980 (the United States alone increased oil efficiency by almost a third from 1973 to 1985); a move to alternative fuel sources for the generation of electricity (increased use of coal, nuclear, and liquefied natural gas); flush world inventories from panic buying during the 1979–1980 oil crisis; production increases from non-OPEC oil producers, including new Mexican, Alaskan, and North Sea oil coming on line (lessening the 5.8 percent loss); and cheating on production quotas by OPEC producers actually led to a slack oil market and declining real oil prices during the 1980s. Throughout the twentieth century, oil had been taking up an ever-increasing percentage of total energy demand; this trend was reversed as industrial countries lowered their percentage oil consumption as a percentage of total energy demand from 53 percent in 1978 to 43 percent in 1985 due to high oil prices and government action.[4] The 15 percent reduction in oil demand from the major industrialized countries more than compensated for the oil exports lost from Iraq and Iran during the eight-year war.[5]

Furthermore, in the early 1980s, OPEC members were cheating on their quotas. For example, contrary to postulated threat scenarios, the Ayatollah Ruhollah Khomeini did not intend to use oil as a weapon. Instead, the radical Islamist Iranian leader tried to maximize production—exceeding Iran's OPEC quota threefold—to bring in revenues to shore up his weak revolutionary regime and fund his war with Iraq, while retaliating against Arab OPEC members for supporting Iraq in the conflict.[6]

In 1986, Saudi Arabia, traditionally OPEC's largest producer and leader, decided that it was tired of bearing the costs of restricting oil production—and therefore lowering its market share and revenues—in a vain attempt to shore up sagging oil prices. Despite supposed OPEC production cuts and production losses from the Iran-Iraq War, prices continued to fall. To teach OPEC cheaters a lesson, the Saudis decided to substantially increase production, thus causing the bottom to drop out of the oil market. This dramatic action was designed to put higher cost OPEC producers out of business. Since the 1973 Arab oil embargo, OPEC members had been trying to earn revenues through production restriction and consequent price increases; now they would have to earn them through fighting for market share with the lowest cost producer.[7] The Saudis were able to regain some of their lost market share.

The petroleum price went so low that, to aid the politically powerful U.S. domestic oil producers under the perennial rhetoric of national security, then–Vice President George H. W. Bush, swerving from the official Reagan administration free-market posture, traveled to Saudi Arabia to plea for the Saudis' propping up of the oil price. The plea failed; the Saudis continued increasing production.

So despite severe curtailment of exports because of a war involving two of the largest oil producers in the world, the tsunami of market forces emanating from the two previous oil crises in 1973 and 1979–1980 drowned out this effect, and the oil market remained awash in product throughout the 1980s. The breakdown of OPEC discipline because of the war also contributed to the overproduction.

Since oil was the main industry of both Iran and Iraq, each nation tried to strike oil facilities to reduce the ability of the other country to wage war. Iran was also attacking the tankers of Iraq's nearby allies—Kuwait and Saudi Arabia. Despite the glut of oil on the world market in 1987, but in keeping with the Carter doctrine, Reagan decided to put Kuwait's oil tankers under an American flag so that the U.S. Navy could protect them in the Persian Gulf.

The U.S. naval operation even resulted in a full-blown naval fight with the Iranian Navy. The U.S. sank half of Iran's fleet and, by destroying two Iranian oil platforms producing 150,000 barrels a day, actually reduced the amount of oil flowing into the world market. Despite Reagan's rhetoric that "we will not return to the days of gas lines, shortages, economic dislocation, and international humiliation," the United States seemed to be destroying the oil in order to protect it. Furthermore, in 2003, the International Court of Justice ruled that U.S. destruction of the Iranian oil platforms could not be justified as "self defense." [8]

Despite public opposition in the United States to the naval mission and congressional objections that the United States didn't import that much oil from the Persian Gulf, the seven U.S. surface ships assigned to protect the tankers were the largest U.S. military presence in the Persian Gulf up to that time. [9]

In the Iran-Iraq War, the United States was secretly helping Saddam Hussein with intelligence, military planning, and dual-use technology, which could be used for civilian or military purposes. Although the United States feigned neutrality in the war and had embargoed weapons to both nations, it looked the other way while its allies sold arms to Iraq. Additionally, Western companies provided the precursor materials to Saddam Hussein for making biological and chemical weapons. Eventually, Iraq won the war, but by a fifteen-round decision, not a knockout blow. Thus, the United States and its allies had helped Saddam become the power to be reckoned with in the Gulf, and because the United States had taken upon itself the mantle of protector of Gulf oil, it would be dealt the task of doing the reckoning.

From 1984 to 1990, world oil reserves had increased almost 50 percent, but most of that increase came from Persian Gulf producers and Venezuela. No non-OPEC production—such as that from Mexico, Alaska, or the North Sea during the 1970s—was coming on line. Thus, the world began to depend more on Persian Gulf suppliers—that is, two-thirds of the world's reserves resided there. [10]

10

The U.S.–Iraq Wars

The First Gulf War

AFTER IRAQ WON the Iran-Iraq War, the George H. W. Bush administration, instead of recalibrating its policy to balance against the stronger Iraq, or staying out of the politics of the Persian Gulf region, kept trying to curry favor with now more powerful Saddam Hussein, the original aggressor in that war. But after the war ended, Iraq, now the most powerful nation in the Gulf region, became unhappy with its small Kuwaiti neighbor for several reasons. First, the Kuwaitis were slant drilling to take oil from under Iraqi soil and thus destroying pressure in the oil field that straddled the border between the two nations. Second, Kuwait would not forgive Iraq's debt for what the Iraqis regarded as Iraq's shouldering of the war burden for the Arab world against a hostile Persian Iran. Third, Kuwait would not support reducing OPEC oil production quotas so that Iraq could make more money from its oil. In fact, Kuwait was one of the two leading cheaters, producing more than its quota allowed—an act of war to cash-strapped Iraq. Finally, Iraq had only limited access to the Gulf for its oil exports, and annexing Kuwait would give it an entire Gulf coastline.

The United States then made the same mistake that it did in Korea in 1950. The United States had declared to the world that South Korea was not within the U.S. defense perimeter. North Korea interpreted such talk to mean that the U.S. would not come to the aid of South Korea if attacked; the North then invaded the South. In the case of Iraq and Kuwait in 1990, as tensions heated up between the two countries, U.S. officials declared that the United States did not get involved in "inter-Arab territorial disputes." Margaret Tutwiler, an aide to then–Secretary of State James Baker, stated that the United States had no "special defense or security commitments to Kuwait."[1] Like the North Koreans in 1950, Saddam Hussein read that as a green light to invade Kuwait, which he did. After invading and occupying Kuwait, Saddam controlled 19 percent of the world's oil.[2] Iraq and Kuwait, next to Saudi Arabia, had the second and third-largest oil reserves in the world.[3] Together, Iraq, Kuwait, Saudi Arabia, and the United Arab Emirates accounted for more than 50 percent of the world's oil reserves.[4]

In both 1950 and 1990, U.S. policy brought about the worst of all worlds. If the U.S. superpower thought that both South Korea and Kuwait were strategic (highly suspect in both cases), it should have made that clear to the potential aggressors to dissuade them from invading in the first place. If the United States didn't think either nation was strategic—the seeming implicit conclusion derived by examining U.S. actions before the invasions—then it shouldn't have done anything about the attacks rather than becoming hysterical after they happened. Doing nothing was the best choice in both cases to save blood and treasure.

In 1950, South Korea, then a poor country with little technology, had already been written off by the Joint Chiefs of Staff as likely to come under Soviet influence because of its geographical proximity to the Soviet Union, according to U.S. government documents. Although tiny Kuwait had substantial oil reserves, the fear in the George H. W. Bush administration was that Saddam would go farther and also threaten or actually invade Saudi Arabia—the oil prize of the Persian Gulf. Maybe the administration should have thought two moves ahead toward this unlikely scenario before saying—before Saddam invaded Kuwait—that it declined to get involved with "inter-Arab territorial disputes." The administration alleged that after taking Kuwait, Saddam Hussein was massing Iraqi troops on the Saudi border for a possible further invasion. Yet Soviet satellite images and a Saudi investigation of the Iraqi-Saudi border area observed no Iraqi troop build up.[5] This allegation could have just been hype to justify the stationing of hundreds of thousands of U.S. troops in Saudi Arabia during Operation Desert Shield.

The first Gulf War was the first conflict in world history that was solely about oil—both in Saddam's motivation for invading Kuwait and the United States' reason for counterattacking.[6] In contrast to his son's avoidance, twelve years later, of an economic rationale for the invasion of Iraq, the blatant objective of George H. W. Bush's intervention in 1990 and 1991—much like the main goal of the Imperial Japanese during World War II—was to use military power to ensure "energy security" for economic and "strategic" reasons. Bush even admitted as much: "Our jobs, our way of life, our own freedom and the freedom of friendly countries around the world would all suffer if control of the world's great oil resources fell into the hands of Saddam Hussein."[7] In 1991, as Iraqi forces occupied Kuwait, Bush argued to Congress that war was needed because: "[vital] economic interests are at risk . . . Iraq itself controls some 10% of the world's proven oil reserves. Iraq plus Kuwait controls twice that." Later, Brent Scowcroft, Bush's national security adviser, recounted that " . . . what gave enormous urgency to [Saddam's invasion of Kuwait] was the issue of oil."[8] Similarly, then–Secretary of State James Baker noted, "The economic lifeline of the industrial world runs from the Gulf and we cannot permit a dictator such as this to sit astride that economic lifeline." Also, the day before he launched the first U.S. war on Iraq, Bush signed National Security Directive 54, which stated, "Access to Persian Gulf oil and the security of key friendly states in the area are vital to U.S. national security."[9] Although they were all Republicans, they were following the Carter doctrine, as Bush's son would also do in his invasion of Iraq in 2003.

The First Gulf War Was about Saudi Arabia, Not Kuwait

The clear purpose of moving U.S. troops to Saudi Arabia was to secure Saudi oil reserves, which were the largest in the world. George H. W. Bush even said so in his address announcing the sending of U.S. troops to the kingdom in Operation Desert Shield, "Our country now imports nearly half the oil it consumes and could face a major threat to its economic independence." Thus, "the sovereign independence of Saudi Arabia is of vital interest to the United States." Then–Secretary of Defense Dick Cheney went even further, implying that just by occupying Kuwait, Saddam could intimidate the Saudis: "Once [Saddam] acquired Kuwait and deployed an army as large as the one he possesses," he would be "in a position to be able to dictate the future of worldwide energy policy, and that [would give] him a stranglehold on our economy."[10] Of course, defending Saudi oil from intimidation or invasion using U.S. forces could have been done without going to war with Iraq to liberate Kuwaiti oil. Ironically, all of this happened less than three years after the United States had fought a major naval battle with Iran on Iraq's behalf. This is one of the many examples in U.S. history of reckless U.S. interventions causing worse future consequences.

Even with Saddam's forces in occupied Kuwait, the Saudis were less concerned about an Iraqi invasion than they were about domestic unrest that could be caused by a large U.S. military presence on their territory. Cheney had trouble convincing King Fahd to allow U.S. troops to defend the kingdom until he showed him the satellite photos that allegedly showed Iraqi armor moving toward the Saudi-Kuwaiti border.[11] As noted earlier, however, other sources cast doubt on such a massing of Iraqi troops.

But even in this worst case, were the president and secretary of defense right? Was it necessary for the United States to defend Saudi oil from an Iraqi invasion of Saudi Arabia? Even before the first Gulf War started, an economic analysis by David Henderson of the Naval Postgraduate School and conservative Hoover Institution cast doubt on the need for this action.

Even under Henderson's worst-case analysis—an Iraqi invasion of Kuwait, Saudi Arabia, and the United Arab Emirates—Saddam would have garnered a share of the world oil market large enough to raise the oil price only enough to amount to a loss in U.S. GDP of less than one half of one percent.[12] Like other Persian Gulf oil producers, which get between 65 and 95 percent of their external revenues from petroleum exports, oil was overwhelmingly Iraq's leading export and was valuable at that. Saddam had every incentive to sell into the market most or all of the additional oil he could have potentially conquered. In fact, the reason Saddam invaded Kuwait in the first place was because he needed money after the expensive long war with Iran. Even if Saddam had cut back production somewhat to increase the price, Henderson noted that his estimate of U.S. GDP loss was overstated, because other producers, trying to take advantage of the higher price, would have likely increased production. This increase would have at least partially offset Saddam's production cutback, and therefore would have moderated his price increase.[13]

Ironically, often when the U.S. intervenes militarily in the Middle East in attempt to secure oil, it makes things worse. Any war or conflict in the Middle East makes the price of oil go up, which is contrary to a policy of using military force to ensure supplies of cheap oil. In the case of the first Gulf War, in order to try to get Iraq to pull back from Kuwait, the United States got the U.N. Security Council to adopt the most comprehensive and grinding economic sanctions in world history. Initially, this involved a complete embargo on Iraq's and occupied Kuwait's oil exports—taking off 8.8 percent of world supply before higher prices led to increased production from other countries to take up some of the reduction.[14] The embargo failed to move Iraqi troops out of Kuwait but did remove more oil from the world market than Henderson had calculated Saddam would have held back if he had invaded Saudi Arabia, Kuwait, and the United Arab Emirates.

Even more oil was taken off the world market when the fighting started and Saddam torched Kuwait's oil wells and infrastructure as his troops withdrew from that country. Thus, the world market lost more petroleum from economic sanctions and a war to save oil than the amount Henderson estimated would have been lost to it under the worst case scenario of Saddam's potential aggression (which no credible evidence was ever produced to show that he was planning). Furthermore, although U.S. allies paid most of the costs of the first Gulf War, most wars in the Middle East would likely cost more than one half of one percent of U.S. GDP, $65 billion, according to Henderson.[15]

The loss to the world market from the disruption and economic sanctions was about the same amount as was lost during the 1973 and 1979–1980 oil crises and during the Iran-Iraq War (that is, not that much), but the oil price spiked on fears of war. This time, however, the United States had no price controls or petroleum allocation system to interfere with the market, thus avoiding shortages, supply disruptions, and gas lines. Almost all other producers increased production, especially Saudi Arabia, the United Arab Emirates, and Venezuela, which almost completely compensated for lost production, while at the same time worldwide demand weakened—thus averting a "crisis."[16] So like the slack petroleum market during the Iran-Iraq War during the 1980s—and unlike the tight market during the 1973 and 1979–1980 oil crises—loose conditions allowed the world market to absorb the loss in exports without a major calamity.

David Yergin, oil historian and author of *The Prize,* best summarizes what was learned through all the oil "crises":

The years of past oil crises have demonstrated that, given time, markets will adjust and allocate. Those years also provided evidence that governments do well to resist the immediate temptation to control and micro-manage the market. Of course, it is hard for governments to resist action when uncertainty is high, panic is building, and accusations are mounting. Yet the course of the six major disruptions from the early 1950s through 1991 [Iran's Prime Minister Mossadegh nationalizes Western oil interests in 1953; the 1956, 1967, and 1973 Arab-Israeli Wars; the 1979–1980 Iranian revolution; and the first Gulf War in 1990–1991] has revealed that the logistical and supply system can adapt to such an extent that the shortages ended up being less dire than had been expected. Indeed, the real problem in the 1970s turned out not to be an absolute shortage, but the disruption of the supply system and the confusion over ownership of oil, with the consequent rush to reorder the system under conditions of high uncertainty. And in 1990 and 1991, the lessons of previous crises, along with the mechanisms developed since the 1970s and improved information, made the impact of the disruption that came with the Gulf Crisis less serious than it might otherwise have been.

Yergin also concluded that, "As oil has become 'more like other commodities' so the oil industry has become 'more like other businesses.'"[17]

Yergin is essentially saying that the market for oil—as for other commodities and products—will provide adequate supplies at competitive prices as long as governments don't gum up the works.

The Continuing War Against Iraq

In addition, the first Gulf War, like most wars, gave the world dramatic unintended consequences that just keep on giving. Despite the first Gulf War's blatant "war for oil" motif, the security of oil grew no better as a result of the conflict (for example, instability grew in Saudi Arabia). Even in Iraq, war continued at a low level.

Although George H. W. Bush and Brent Scowcroft, his national security adviser, were criticized for not going on to Baghdad to remove Saddam from power while U.S. troops were in Iraq, the ill consequences of Bush's son's later full-blown invasion of Iraq retrospectively showed this to be a wise decision. The elder Bush and Scowcroft believed in 1991 that destroying Saddam's army and removing him from power would allow Iran to take advantage of a vastly weakened Iraq and the likely chaos in that fractious country that might ensue. The elder Bush did, however, unconscionably encourage the Kurds and the majority Shi'i in Iraq to revolt against Saddam, implying that the United States would support them, and then stood by and watched them be massacred. Henry Kissinger had done the same to the Kurds in the 1970s.

Most important, although Saddam was a brutal dictator—of which there were many in the world—he posed no direct threat to the United States and, as already noted, the market would have provided the United States oil even under the unlikely worst case scenario of Saddam's potential aggression. When going to war against a country, the U.S. government's modern propaganda machine demonizes the enemy so much that it is often hard to stop military action after having obtained limited objectives. This proved to be the case in Iraq and is proving to be the case with Muammar Gaddafi of Libya.

The excessive buildup of the threat Saddam posed also built up pressure for continuing measures to contain him, even though his military had been drastically smashed in the first Gulf war. Between the end of hostilities in the 1991 war—which destroyed half of Saddam's ground forces but allowed Saddam's elite units to get away (probably on purpose so that he would have something left to defend Iraq against Iran)—and the younger Bush's invasion of Iraq in 2003, the hostilities against Saddam's Iraq never stopped. Grinding economic sanctions remained in force and U.S.- and British-enforced "no-fly" zones prevented Saddam from attacking by air the Kurdish region in the north and the Shi'i region in the south.

Bill Clinton continued the elder Bush's policy under a new name—"dual containment" of Saddam's Iraq and the still fundamentalist Shi'i regime in Iran. This containment policy required an increase in post–Gulf War U.S. military presence in the Persian Gulf, despite the pronouncement in *Foreign Affairs* journal in 1994 by W. Anthony "Tony" Lake, Clinton's national security advisor, that "the end of the Cold War simply eliminated a major strategic consideration from our calculus. We no longer have to fear Soviet efforts to gain a foothold in the Persian Gulf."[8] With the main threat gone and a lesser threat—Saddam's Iraq—severely debilitated from the first Gulf War, a sober reassessment might have pointed toward reducing or eliminating U.S. military presence from the Gulf region. But neither Bill Clinton, from the liberal Wilsonian (interventionist) wing of the Democratic Party, nor his successor George W. Bush, from the neoconservative Wilsonian wing of the Republican Party, could pass up the mercantilist impulse of dominating the oil fields of the Gulf.

In 1998, Bill Clinton temporarily moved from containment to preventive strike by ratcheting up the already continuing air attacks under Operation

Desert Fox. These attacks ostensibly were to destroy sites associated with weapons of mass destruction that Saddam wasn't even developing or producing. Even at the time, leaks from the Pentagon indicated that the U.S. military didn't have a good idea where such sites were (now we know that there weren't any).

In addition to multilateral sanctions on Iraq, the U.S. placed sanctions on the Iranian and Libyan oil in the 1990s, and Russian oil exports were down because of the turmoil involving the fall of the Soviet Union. Yet world production still exceeded demand in the 1990s, keeping the price low and alternative oil investments restrained in Brazil, West Africa, the Caspian Sea, and deep offshore in the Gulf of Mexico. Also, during the 1990s oil glut, the OPEC cartel showed its lack of discipline when its members tried to make up revenues by increased volume. Only in 1999, prices sank so low that both OPEC and non-OPEC producers finally reached an agreement to cut production. (When oil prices are high, even less discipline exists, because producers have an incentive to cheat on their production quotas.)[19]

Blowback From the First Gulf War

The elder Bush's war set up the continuous chain of sanctions and hostilities that led to his son's disastrous invasion of Iraq more than a decade later. In addition, after the first Gulf War's end, the United States left forces in Saudi Arabia, which exacerbated one of the biggest threats to low priced oil—instability in the desert kingdom. Paying some of the bills for Iraq in the Iran-Iraq War from 1980 to 1988 and for U.S. forces in the first Gulf War against Iraq in 1990 and 1991—while Saudi oil revenues were reduced because of a long slump in the oil market—helped deplete finances the Saudi government normally used to pay off the domestic fundamentalist Islamist religious establishment. Also, that same establishment criticized the Saudi monarchy for relying on non-Muslim U.S. "mercenaries" to defend the country.

Saudi Arabia is home to the holiest places in the Islamic religion. Osama bin Laden came home from fighting in the Islamist victory that expelled the "infidel" Soviet superpower from the Muslim land of Afghanistan, only to find another "infidel" superpower's military forces in the most sacred country in Islam. Despite a U.S. pre–Gulf War I promise to a King Fahd, who was reluctant to have U.S. forces defending the kingdom in the first place, U.S.

forces did not leave after the war ended. About five thousand U.S. pilots and ground personnel continued to be based in Saudi Arabia to enforce the no-fly zone over southern Iraq, a permanent U.S. military presence was established in Kuwait, and pre-positioned U.S. military equipment in depots was stored in Kuwait and Qatar.[20]

In the Muslim religion, even moderate Muslims must do all they can to eject non-Muslims from Muslim soil (this also drives the conflict in Palestine, Chechnya, Iraq, and Afghanistan during both the U.S. and Soviet occupations). Bin Laden was no moderate, and he used this belief to recruit followers and urge them to violent action. Also, he adopted, as a model for his worldwide terrorist campaign against the United States, the use of terror tactics that had expelled the non-Muslim United States from Lebanon in the early 1980s during the Reagan administration and from Somalia in the early 1990s during the Clinton administration. His primary goal was to evict U.S. forces from the Arabian Peninsula and other Muslim lands.

The last straw for bin Laden was the broken U.S. promise to withdraw militarily from Saudi Arabia. In 1998, he declared,

> For over seven years, the United States has been occupying the lands of Islam in the holiest of places, the Arabian Peninsula, plundering its riches, dictating to its rulers, humiliating its people, terrorizing its neighbors, and turning its bases in the Peninsula into a spearhead through which to fight the neighboring Muslim peoples.

He then charged that it was "an individual duty for every Muslim" to "kill the Americans" and drive their military "out of all the lands of Islam."[21] Note that bin Laden has repeatedly said that he regards the use of U.S. military power to ensure the flow of the Arabian Peninsula's oil to the West as plundering Muslim riches. For example, in a March 1997 interview with CNN's Peter Arnett, bin Laden accused the U.S. of wanting to "occupy our countries, steal our resources." In a 1998 interview with al-Jazeera, bin Laden said that it was "not acceptable" that the U.S., Britain, and Israel "should attack and enter my land and holy sanctuaries and plunder Muslims' oil."[22]

Rich individuals and charities in Saudi Arabia were the main source of funds for bin Laden and al Qaeda, while the Saudi government turned a blind eye until January 2004 (long after 9/11). At this time, after a series of suicide bombings in the kingdom by homegrown terrorists, the Saudi government began to see a threat to the regime from Islamist extremists and cracked down on such domestic militants and Saudi funding sources for them. Even after the crackdown, the Saudi government was less than assiduous in stanching Saudi funding for Islamist militants overseas. In classified U.S. documents published by Wikileaks in 2010, the State Department confirmed that donors from Saudi Arabia were still the biggest funders of al Qaeda.[23]

But before the 9/11 attacks, during the Cold War, the U.S. government had no problem with, and even encouraged, Saudi funding of Islamist extremists at home and abroad in order to fight godless communism.[24] Even after the Cold War ended, but prior to 9/11, the Clinton and George W. Bush administrations also foolishly looked the other way on Saudi financing of al Qaeda and other radical Islamists, largely because of the kingdom's oil riches. Again politicians of both parties failed to understand the oil market.

In late 1995, bin Laden's followers bombed a U.S.-Saudi installation, which contained a U.S. military group that was training the Saudi National Guard. In early 1996, Hezbollah of Saudi Arabia, a Shi'i fundamentalist Muslim group, bombed the Khobar Towers apartment building, which housed U.S. military people; the blast killed 19 Americans and injured 372 more. The U.S. 9/11 Commission later speculated that bin Laden and his Sunni fundamentalist followers had some unknown involvement in that attack.

Bin Laden was not only was successful in eventually motivating the Saudi government to ask that the vast majority of U.S. forces and bases be removed from Saudi soil, but his attacks on 9/11 created one of the few threats to the relatively secure American homeland in the nation's history. Bin Laden and al Qaeda continued their terrorist attacks in order to evict the United States from many other Muslim nations in the Gulf and beyond. Wars usually beget unfavorable unintended consequences, and the questionable 1991 war for oil is still providing them.

After 9/11, instead of using law enforcement, intelligence, drones, cruise missiles, and Special Forces assets to covertly pursue and target bin Laden, the U.S. decided to engage in military social work by conducting a nation-building invasion and occupation of Afghanistan, which has turned into a quagmire.

Antonia Juhasz alleges that one of the goals of this war might have been to solve the problem of getting petroleum out of the oil-rich Caspian Sea basin. Had the Taliban not become resurgent in Afghanistan, she asserts, U.S. companies could have built a pipeline from the Caspian region through Afghanistan and Pakistan to transport oil to Indian Ocean ports.[25] This analysis may be going too far in attributing ulterior motives connected to the U.S. war, but it is at least plausible.

Even if the U.S. government believes that it needs to use military force to secure oil—a policy of which free market economists should be skeptical—the first Gulf War and its aftermath have shown that substantial forces do not have to be based in the Persian Gulf region to do so. They can be brought in as needed. It is true that this lighter footprint requires more work for the military in time of conflict. But if quietly withdrawing from or reducing U.S. military presence in Islamic countries can reduce the fuel firing Islamist terrorist attacks on U.S. targets worldwide, including the American homeland, it would help U.S. security to at least have a more discreet presence on the ground in such places.

The 9/11 tragedy and its aftermath once again demonstrated OPEC's lack of discipline and inability to control the long-term price of oil. The terrorist attacks led to fears of a worldwide supply disruption, resulting in a price rise of 30 percent. Yet there were plenty of supplies on the market. Kuwait, Nigeria, and later Russia began pumping at maximum capacity in order to take advantage of the higher prices. Prices went back down, only to be revived months later by angst over the likelihood of a second Gulf War.[26]

The Invasion of Iraq

The ultimate underlying reason for the invasion of Iraq, as in the first Gulf War, likely was oil. Because war for oil is unseemly—and as noted earlier, similar to Imperial Japanese behavior prior to and during World War II—officials of the George W. Bush administration emphasized other objectives. The media seemed to let them off the hook, even though Bush's father had been more honest about the reasons for conflict during the first Gulf War.

As Michael T. Klare, professor at Hampshire College, says in his ridicule of the George W. Bush administration's denials about the true reason for the invasion of Iraq:

. . . . Politicians and pundits regularly deny that there is any connection between blood and oil. "The only interest the United States has in the [Gulf] region is furthering the cause of peace and stability, not [Iraq's] ability to generate oil," President Bush's spokesperson, Ari Fleischer, avowed in late 2002. As the drive to war accelerated, Secretary of Defense Donald Rumsfeld declared, "This is not about oil, and anyone who thinks that, is badly misunderstanding the situation." We *know* that such statements cannot be true—the entire history of U.S. intervention in the Persian Gulf discredits them. . . . (emphasis in original)[27]

Energy journalist Paul Roberts agrees, ". . . we Americans (and most of our media) are largely untroubled by Secretary [of Defense Donald] Rumsfeld's absurd claim that the Iraqi war was 'not about oil.'"[28]

The real reason for the invasion was and still is murky, but occasional candid statements by Paul Wolfowitz, then the deputy secretary of defense and architect of the invasion, indicated that oil was a prominent factor. There is reason for suspicion, because all of the stated reasons for invading a country that had nothing to do with 9/11 didn't add up to a good case for such a drastic action. The two primary reasons were that Saddam had weapons of mass destruction that he could give to terrorists and the implication that Saddam had some role in 9/11 or links to al Qaeda. On March 17, 2003, President Bush gave several reasons for war: "Intelligence gathered by this and other countries leaves no doubt that the Iraqi regime continues to possess and conceal some of the most lethal weapons ever devised." He cited the threat that Iraq would give "chemical, biological, or, one day, nuclear weapons" to terrorists who could "fulfill their stated ambitions and kill thousands or hundreds of thousands of innocent people in our country or any other." He then linked Iraq to the specific terrorist group that perpetrated the 9/11 attacks by the accusation that Iraq had "aided, trained, and harbored terrorists, including operatives of al Qaida."[29] When these two main justifications for the Iraq War were discredited, the Bush administration fell back on the removal of a vile dictator and the democratization of Iraq.

In fact, many countries were working on chemical, biological, and nuclear weapons (all lumped into the questionable category of "weapons of mass destruction") at the time of the invasion of Iraq. No one in the U.S. intelligence community believed Saddam was ahead of North Korea and Iran in the most dangerous category and the only true weapon of mass destruction—nuclear weapons—and the long-range missiles that could deliver them to the United States. Even Bush's own intelligence community contradicted the "weapons of mass destruction" rationale for the invasion when it concluded that Saddam would be unlikely to use "weapons of mass destruction," or give them to terrorists, unless he had nothing to lose in the face of an invasion.

In the very worst case—Saddam possessing nuclear weapons and ballistic missiles with long enough range to hit the United States, which no one in the intelligence community believed he had—the United States could deter any Iraqi nuclear attack, consisting of only a few warheads, with the thousands of nuclear weapons in the most capable nuclear arsenal in the world.

Of course, in a September 2000 letter to President Clinton, the Project for the New Century—a group of future George W. Bush administration officials, including Don Rumsfeld, Paul Wolfowitz, and Richard Perle, who all advocated military action against Iraq—noted that Iraq, along with North Korea and Iran, was developing nuclear weapons and ballistic missiles as a deterrent to American intervention in their regions. So perhaps the Bush administration was less scared of a nuclear Iraq's threat to the United States and more frightened of its threat to U.S. interventionism and empire.

The 9/11 Commission later said that Saddam Hussein had no operational relationship with Osama bin Laden or al Qaeda. Richard Clarke, the White House's counterterrorism adviser under both Presidents Clinton and Bush, claimed that Bush personally implied that Clarke should find such a relationship that Clarke had told the White House didn't exist. In fact, the terrorist groups that Saddam supported focused their attacks on Israel, not the United States.

Iraq was always a long shot to have a unified democracy because it is an artificial country with three main ethno-sectarian groups. It did not have the unity, experience with democracy, or the advanced first-world industrial economy of post–World War II Japan or Germany. Moreover, there were many bad dictators in the world, so why single out Saddam for ousting with military force?

Because these three repeatedly stated reasons for the invasion all fell through, even Bush, when all else failed, was trapped into implicitly revealing the truth about oil being the original reason for the invasion. During an October 2006 press conference, Bush noted that the United States could not "tolerate a new terrorist state in the heart of the Middle East with large oil reserves that could be used to fund its radical ambitions or used to inflict economic damage on the West." A month later, Bush alleged that if the United States withdrew from Iraq and hostile groups took over that nation, they could "use energy as economic blackmail" and, in a future oil embargo, would be "able to pull millions of barrels of oil off the market, driving the price up to $300 or $400 per barrel."[30] Although Bush, a former oilman, seems either disingenuous or extremely naïve in believing that any radical regime in Iraq would refuse to sell oil for very long, Bush's original intent to control Iraq's oil is clear from these telling statements.

Paul Roberts, a reputable energy journalist, noted that even months before the 9/11 attacks, when then–Vice President Dick Cheney was promulgating a new national energy policy, he and other administration officials scoured maps of Iraq in order to deduce how much oil the country could quickly export to the world market. Many administration and oil industry officials believed that Iraq's output could be doubled. Roberts concluded that the falling prices from such a large dump of oil would have broken OPEC and its ability to set prices (in reality, as this book demonstrates, this ability exists only in the short term). Roberts also argued that when confronted by falling petroleum income and increasing debt, even the Saudis would be forced to open their oil fields to Western oil companies, as would other OPEC producers. (Yet the invasion of Iraq in 2003 began a long rise in oil prices that ended only with the global economic meltdown in late 2008, and the war caused Iraqi oil production to decline from prewar levels, thus negating both of Roberts's assumed Bush objectives.)

Also, lending credence to the "war for oil" thesis were Cheney's prewar comments about Saddam's threat to Persian Gulf oil and the U.S. invasion force's high priority on securing the rich northern Iraqi oil fields in Kirkuk and the oil ministry, while looking the other way as the rest of Baghdad degenerated into chaos and looting.[31] Moreover, the very first tasks during the U.S. invasion were to secure the oil fields and refineries in southern Iraq and Iraq's two tanker terminals for exporting petroleum to the world.[32] When all of the Bush administration's stated reasons for invading Iraq were demonstrated to have little credibility, busting OPEC and forcing producing nations to re-admit Western oil companies seem like very plausible—but imperial and unnecessary—real motivations.

Another hidden reason for the U.S. invasion of Iraq may have been that the U.S. military had been asked to leave its bases in Saudi Arabia, which were "safeguarding" Persian Gulf oil; the United States did so in 2003, right after the invasion of Iraq was complete. The Saudis were scared that the non-Muslim military presence in the land of the holiest Islamic sites was causing Islamist extremists to target the Saudi regime.

Being accustomed to having bases around the Gulf—and not focusing on the fact that the U.S. had defended oil in the first Gulf War with little prior presence on land—the U.S. seemed to be looking to replace these Saudi installations. Also, if the U.S. invaded Iraq, the administration's thinking might have been that the U.S. would no longer need the Saudi air bases to enforce the no-fly zone over southern Iraq to keep Saddam in his box.[33] In reality, Saddam's military, smashed during the first Gulf War, hardly needed to be contained.

Nearly 50 percent of the world's oil reserves are in Saudi Arabia (alone 25 percent of the global total) and Iraq and Iran (combined, another 25 percent of the world total). But compared to other oil regions of the world, Iraq's oil reserves have been underexplored and underdeveloped, because of years of autocracy and violence. At least one industry source estimates that Iraqi reserves could be as large or larger than Saudi Arabia's.[34] The U.S. Department of Energy estimates that undeveloped Iraqi oil deposits could be the largest in the world.[35]

Paul Wolfowitz even once stated, before the invasion, that U.S. bases in Iraq wouldn't gin up as much anti-U.S. Islamist terrorism as U.S. bases in Saudi Arabia. Also, when asked why the United States was going to invade Iraq instead of North Korea or Iran, which were farther along in getting nuclear weapons and long-range missiles, Wolfowitz responded that, "Iraq floats on a sea of oil."

In 1991, at the time of the first Gulf War and twelve years before the U.S. invasion, Wolfowitz opined, "The combination of the enormous resources of the Persian Gulf, the power that those resources represent—it's power. It's not just that we need gas for our cars, it's that anyone who controls those resources has enormous capability to build up military power." Such a threat, Wolfowitz noted, could come from Iran or a rebuilt Iraq.[36] What Wolfowitz and other advocates of the invasion failed to realize was that, compared to the rich U.S. superpower, these two countries were still small, relatively poor even with their oil revenues, relatively weak militarily, and half a world away—posing little direct threat to the United States. In the case of Iraq, more than a decade of grinding international economic sanctions had impeded Saddam from reconstituting his shattered military, which was demolished by the United States during that first Gulf War. But why didn't the U.S. invade Iran, another hostile oil-producing nation? Iran was much larger in population and area than Iraq, much more mountainous than the Mesopotamian flatlands, and therefore much harder to conquer.

In another portent of future U.S. policy, in 1999, then–chief executive officer of Halliburton oil-services company, Dick Cheney noted, "The Middle East, with two-thirds of the world's oil and the lowest cost, is still where the prize ultimately lies."[37]

In 2007, Alan Greenspan, former Federal Reserve chairman during the George W. Bush administration, lamented: "I am saddened that it is politically inconvenient to acknowledge what everyone knows: the Iraq war is largely about oil." That same year, an even more authoritative source admitted as much. General John Abizaid, the retired head of the U.S. Central Command and military operations in Iraq, speaking about the war, said, "Of course it's about oil, we can't really deny that."[38] Similarly, in 2003, David Frum, a former White House speechwriter, wrote, "the war on terror" was designed to "bring a new stability to the most vicious and violent quadrant of the Earth—and new prosperity to us all, by securing the world's largest pool of oil."[39] He was not referring to the war in Afghanistan, because that country had no oil.

If those are not blatant enough statements of the importance of oil to the reasons for the invasion, then the narrative of Paul O'Neill, Bush's first Treasury secretary, on the Bush administration's early days is instructive. Long before the 9/11 attacks, high levels of the administration discussed how to occupy Iraq, with specific plans on the disposition of Iraq's oil fields.[40] Upon actual occupation, without approval by the Iraqi people, the U.S. occupiers eliminated state-owned enterprises and abolished tariffs and laws that banned foreign investment. All foreign investors had the same rights as Iraqi investors and could repatriate without restriction all profits and dividends outside the country. Although in Saddam's day, Iraq had dealt mainly with Russian and French oil companies, the U.S. occupation banned these companies from winning Iraqi reconstruction contracts. Because 95 percent of Iraq's GDP is oil related, all of these actions effectively abolished Iraqi state-owned oil companies and gave control over Iraq's oil to private U.S. and British companies. Such an oil company–friendly arrangement had not been seen in the Arab world in many decades and could be done quickly because of the pre-9/11 planning cited by Paul O'Neill.[41]

Also, the massive resources that the U.S. has put into certain Iraq bases, implying their permanence, and the reluctance and slow pace of the Bush and Obama administrations' plan to pull all troops out of Iraq, should be indicators that the United States plans to stay a long time. Even the ostensibly pro-withdrawal Obama administration may leave thirty-five to fifty thousand troops in Iraq, and, according to an agreement reached between the U.S. and Iraqi governments, they can stay past the end of 2011, if the Iraqi government consents. Iraqi Prime Minister Nuri al-Maliki has thrown open the possibility that some U.S. forces might be permitted to stay past that milestone.

Implications of the U.S. Invasion

Given that anti-U.S. Islamist terrorism is driven primarily by the non-Muslim occupation of Muslim land—the continued U.S. military presence in the Islamic holy land of Saudi Arabia originally spurred Osama bin Laden to declare war on the United States—using the tragedy of 9/11 to justify invading an unrelated Muslim country was the worst possible thing that George W. Bush could have done. And it was exactly the type of overreaction that bin Laden and other terrorists want in order to generate funds and more Islamist militant volunteers. Wolfowitz's prewar statement that U.S. bases in Iraq would be better than American bases in the holiest nation in Islam—Saudi Arabia—because they would generate less Islamist blowback indicated that he recognized the main cause of anti-U.S. Islamist terrorism; but he failed to appreciate that there were also Shi'i Islamic shrines in Iraq that would make a U.S. occupation there a flashpoint.

More generally, Paul Roberts succinctly summarized the cogent argument that decades of Western—that is, U.S.-led—efforts to militarily secure oil have led to violence, instability, and blowback terrorism against Western targets:

Unstinting efforts by the United States, Europe, and other industrial-ized powers to ensure access to Middle Eastern oil—by any means nec-essary, and often with the help of Israel—have helped foster a perpetual state of political instability, ethnic conflict, and virulent nationalism in that oil-rich region. Even before American tanks rolled into Baghdad to secure the Iraqi Ministry of Petroleum, leaving the rest of the ancient city to burn, anti-Western resentment in the Middle East had become so intense that it was hard not to see a connection between the incessant drive for oil and the violence that has shattered Jerusalem, the West Bank, Riyadh, Jakarta, and even New York and Washington.[42]

One other factor in the decision to invade Iraq may have been the eroding international economic sanctions against Iraq. Saddam was using enticing oil contracts as a way to get countries to vote an end to the sanctions—the best ones given to companies in Russia, China, and France, which held seats on the U.N. Security Council. No U.S. companies were on the list. Thus, if sanctions were lifted, all of Iraq's oil would go to foreign companies. The U.S. invasion altered this outcome. Now U.S., British, Spanish, and French oil companies are in the best position to exploit Iraq's oil resources, using corporate-friendly exploration and production terms.[43] Note that the first three countries were the principal nations involved in the invasion.

Wolfowitz and other neoconservatives planned to use increased Iraqi oil production after the war to fund war reconstruction. But Iraq's oil infrastructure had been badly damaged by years of economic sanctions, wars, and neglect. Also, an Iraqi insurgency was attacking oil pipelines and other petroleum infrastructure. After Iraq was occupied by American forces, the U.S. had trouble even getting Iraqi oil production back up to the anemic prewar levels, which had dropped 85 percent as a result of the war.[44] The postwar quantity of oil produced was less than even the constrained amount produced during the last five years of U.N. sanctions from 1998 to 2002.[45]

Not only did the U.S. invasion reduce Iraqi oil production, but it destabilized the entire Persian Gulf region, made these nations less reliable suppliers, and thus rendered U.S. oil supplies less secure. Furthermore, the second Iraq War showed the world that military power—U.S. or otherwise—can never make oil supplies safe.[46] After all, it requires the cooperation of many people to get oil out of the ground, transport it, refine it, and ship it to consumers, and if even one small group of people doesn't want this to happen, oil supplies can be disrupted. Fortunately, under normal peacetime circumstances, the vast majority of actors have a financial incentive to get oil on its way to users, and disruptions are usually temporary or localized.

In addition, Kurds and Shi'a have most of the known reserves in the north and south of Iraq, respectively, with few known reserves in the central Sunni regions. This reality has prevented agreement on an oil revenue sharing law between the central government and the provinces.

Yet of the major Persian Gulf oil-producing nations, Iraq is the least explored and may contain oil not yet found. A Canadian oil-consulting firm has claimed to have discovered substantial oil reserves in Sunni areas, but the find has not been confirmed.

War in Iraq and High Fuel Prices

If Iraq had been able to turn around and increase production faster under American tutelage, it might have somewhat eased the high oil prices during the first decade of the millennium. These higher prices culminated in a record real $147 per barrel price in the summer of 2008 (the previous inflation-adjusted record was roughly $101 per barrel in April 1980—after reduced production because the Iranian revolution coincided with a tight world oil market).[47] The 9/11 attack didn't begin a sustained price increase, but the invasion of Iraq 2003 began a rapid march to the oil price stratosphere, which culminated in the $147 price.[48]

Memories of two oil crises, gasoline price increases, and gas lines of the 1970s embedded themselves in the nation's subconscious mind to a surprising extent, despite all of these issues going away with the cheap fuel prices for most of the 1980s and 1990s. (Those low prices led to almost a tripling of U.S. net oil imports as a share consumption from a little more than 20 percent in 1982 to about 60 percent in 2005.)[49] With the rising fuel prices at the start of a new millennium, these memories all came flooding back.

Pundits claimed that new oil discoveries and exploitation were not matching rising world demand caused by the rapidly growing economies of China and India. The record real oil prices seem to demonstrate that oil would never again go down in price. Yet historically, such Malthusian predictions have repeatedly proved false. For example, in the late 1800s, the problem for producers came in trying to keep the price up—because, from their viewpoint, there was too much oil, not to little. The demand for oil went up to fight World War I. The tight oil market in the early 1920s generated predictions of draining the world's supply. By the late 1920s, however, the world was again awash in oil. The cycle of tight oil markets, high prices, and gloom-and-doom predictions, followed by a gusher of oil and low prices keeps repeating itself. In the 1940s, because of the huge petroleum consumption needed to conduct World War II, analysts again predicted world supplies would exhaust themselves. As noted earlier, declining U.S. production caused Franklin Delano Roosevelt to meet with King Abdul Aziz al-Saud of Saudi Arabia to offer an implicit protection for oil trade. But by the 1950s and early 1960s, the world was floating on a sea of oil.

The industrialization of the world during the late 1960s and early 1970s increased the demand for petroleum and caused a tight market during the 1970s. Again, as in all other times, high prices brought conservation, switching to alternative fuels, and exploration and exploitation of new sources of oil (in this case, new non-OPEC sources of production). Once again, such developments led to a slack oil market in the 1980s and 1990s. Because of lag time between investment in new oil exploration and development projects and salable oil is long, this slack market and consequent low investment by producing countries are main reasons why today new discoveries are not keeping pace with increasing demand.

As the Chinese and Indian economies heated up, the demand for oil again began to grow and oil prices again began to rise in 1999 and into the new millennium. The invasion of Iraq began the rapid trend toward higher oil prices. Ironically, any war to safeguard Persian Gulf oil, or any war in the Middle East for that matter, causes fear of oil supply disruptions to push up petroleum prices. Despite the fact that most of the 9/11 hijackers were Saudis, the Saudi government—not happy with the U.S. invasion of Iraq—refused to increase oil production to reduce the world price (as it had during the Iran-Iraq war and the first Gulf War). Although in the last couple years of the twentieth century, the inflation-adjusted oil price had been at record lows in the history of the automobile, after only a decade, in July 2008, the price hit the record high level of $147 per barrel.

After the nationalization of most oil in the world, private companies control no more than 8 percent of global reserves, and state-owned companies invest less in new fields than private companies. Yet after 2001, new discoveries once again began to increase worldwide.[50] Higher prices likely had something to do with that development.

True to form, however, the price of oil continues to be volatile over time. The worldwide financial and economic meltdown caused the demand for petroleum to plummet dramatically—less than six months later, the oil price was $32 a barrel in December 2008. In 2009 and 2010, it was still fairly low in comparison to the peak in mid-2008.[51] By early 2011, however, the revolts in the Arab world, especially Libya, had begun to push the price back up.

11

The Oil Market Today

THE NATIONALIZATION OF oil resources in the developing world has left more than 80 percent of global oil reserves in government hands. Eighteen of the world's twenty-three largest oil companies are now state-owned.[1] (See Table 1.) Although the behavior of the OPEC cartel and the big private international oil companies—such as Exxon, British Petroleum (BP), and Shell—get all the publicity, the major development in the world oil market during the last thirty years has been the inefficiency and reduced exploration and development induced by socialism in the global oil industry.

In recent years, the wave of governments reacquiring oil assets on their soil has continued. Russia and Venezuela have effectively renationalized oil assets, and African countries—such as Libya, Algeria, and Angola—have increased their governments' take vis-à-vis the share of Western oil companies past the 90 percent barrier (the worldwide average, excluding Western oil producing nations, at the beginning of the twenty-first century was between 70 and 80 percent).

Once oil was nationalized worldwide—by the mid-1980s—the giant U.S. oil corporations, no longer dominant in the international market, returned home to the U.S. market. The majors had formerly ceded the domestic market to smaller, independent companies when the U.S. government began in 1950 giving tax breaks and antitrust exemptions for oil companies' production overseas—back when developing Middle Eastern oil and saving domestic deposits were in vogue. Then the majors started gobbling up each other beginning in 1999. Access to producible oil reserves is the name of the game; after nationalizations overseas blocked off the largest and cheapest reserves (in the Persian Gulf, Russia, and other places), and increased competition from state-owned companies in consuming nations (for example Chinese oil companies) sopped

Table 1: World's Largest Oil and Gas Companies

Company	Private or State-owned	Total Oil & Gas Reserves
Saudi Arabian Oil Co.	State-owned	303,285
National Iranian Oil. Co.	State-owned	300,485
Qatar General Petroleum Corp.	State-owned	169,959
Iraq National Oil Co.	State-owned	134,135
Petroleos de Venezuela	State-owned	128,594
Abu Dhabi National Oil Co.	State-owned	126,132
Kuwait Petroleum Corp.	State-owned	110,990
Nigerian National Petroleum Corp.	State-owned	67,671
National Oil Co. (Libya)	State-owned	50,028
Sonatrach (Algeria)	State-owned	39,379
Gazprom (Russia)	State-owned	29,261
OAO Rosneft (Russia)	State-owned	21,805
PetroChina Co.	State-owned	21,469
Petronas (Malaysia)	State-owned	19,547
OAO Lukoil (Russia)	State-owned	15,720
Egyptian General Petroleum Corp.	State-owned	13,700
ExxonMobil Corp. (United States)	Private	13,318
Petroleos Mexicanos	State-owned	13,198
BP Corp. (United Kingdom)	Private	12,523
Petroleo Brasilerio	State-owned	11,578
Chevron (United States)	Private	10,870
Royal Dutch Shell (Netherlands/UK)	Private	10,767
ConocoPhillips (United States)	Private	10,668

Reserves in millions of oil equivalent barrels in 2007.
Source: "OGJ 200/100," *Oil & Gas Journal*, Vol. 106, No. 37 September 15, 2008.

up some more, mergers to acquire harder-to-get deposits became paramount. The majors also began buying up domestic refineries and gasoline marketing operations. But even in these "downstream" realms, they face increased competition in Europe and the United States from state-owned oil companies from Venezuela, Saudi Arabia, and other producing nations, which now have their own refineries and gas stations.

Of the Seven Sisters, Exxon merged with Mobil (ironically, the two biggest remnants of the Standard Oil Trust that was broken up in 1911), Chevron with Texaco and Gulf, BP with Amoco (formerly Standard Oil of Indiana) and ARCO. Shell bought several other Standard Oil Trust remnants. Also, Conoco merged with Phillips. The merged companies were the largest in world history. Combined, these top five private companies have oil reserves that would make the top ten if ranked with oil producing countries. Yet the oil companies with the world's largest reserves are all now government-owned.

Despite the nationalization of many of its assets overseas, the oil industry is still the most profitable in the world. ExxonMobil, the world's largest private oil company, is the most profitable private corporation globally and in human history—with profits greater than the GDPs of each of ninety-three countries. Six of the top ten private corporations worldwide are oil companies. In rank order among the oil giants, they are ExxonMobil, Shell, BP, ChevronTexaco, ConocoPhillips, and TotalFinaElf. The first five all contain remnants of the old Standard Oil Trust. But the six companies plus Italian energy giant Eni—supermajors ExxonMobil, Shell, BP, and the rest being international majors—control only 15 to 18 percent of global production and only 5 percent of the world's reserves and have nowhere near the dominance of the original Seven Sisters.[2]

Moreover, the international companies try to find and exploit conventional oil in difficult-to-develop areas (such as the Arctic or in deep water) and unconventional petroleum deposits (such as heavy oil fields in Venezuela, the tar sands of Canada, or oil shale deposits in the Rocky Mountain West). In addition, the majors are getting into natural gas and even a little into alternative fuels (for example, hydrogen and solar power). Finally, they provide technological expertise to explore and produce oil in difficult geography that nationalized oil companies in various countries lack. Even here, international oil service companies from the West, such as Halliburton and Schlumberger, are taking over these tasks from the super majors and international majors.

Unfortunately, state-owned companies, including in the twelve OPEC nations, usually underinvest in future production.[3] This is the biggest problem in the world oil market, not temporary supply disruptions in certain countries because of a war or political instability. The West still holds the best technology for oil exploration, development, and production; that is, OPEC's weakness in this area is the West's leverage.[4]

OPEC No Longer Sets the World's Oil Price

Despite the fact that more than 50 percent of the world's known conventional oil reserves are found in five countries around the Persian Gulf (Saudi Arabia, Iran, Iraq, Kuwait, and the United Arab Emirates) and that a rising percentage of the world's oil extraction will come from the Middle East—as oil production is now predicted to peak later in that region than elsewhere in the world—OPEC has been undermined by the fact that it now has less power to set the world oil price. In 1983, the New York Mercantile Exchange (NYMEX) began to sell oil futures contracts, which established global oil prices. London also has an important oil futures market.[5] Thus, before the NYMEX and London set world oil prices, a near monopoly (Standard Oil), the Seven Sisters cartel of international oil companies (from 1928 to 1973), and the nationalized cartel OPEC (1973–1983) tried to do so via long-term contracts.[6]

Even when these monopolies and cartels tried to set prices, the market forces of new technology and additional competitors undermined their efforts. With the ascent of NYMEX and London, the market mechanism has become so efficient that any attempt by any one country, company, or group to set world prices can be attenuated. In addition, such markets have made oil-producing countries lose even the weak control they had over where oil shipments went—thus making embargoes against particular consuming countries very difficult.

Rather than the oil market being dominated by long-term contracts, this futures market and the spot market (dealing in oil shipments for one-time, quick delivery) now dominate the world's oil stage. Moreover, today, production is split among OPEC (40 percent of world production), the largest international private oil companies (13 percent, which is larger than Saudi Arabia's production), and state-owned oil companies (47 percent)—led mainly by those of China and Russia—that don't coordinate their production or pricing decisions with other parties.[7]

Oil Gloom and Doom Once Again?

Even with the decline of OPEC's perceived power (it was never really all that powerful), however, gloom-and-doom scenarios are back in vogue. As in the two oil crises in the crisis-prone 1970s, the oil price rose rapidly for most of the first decade of the twenty-first century. Demand for oil from industrializing nations, such as China and India, has been increasing. And since 1960, the rate of discovery for new fields has fallen behind the rate of oil consumption—now the world finds one new barrel of oil for about every four that it uses.[8]

Yet, as noted earlier, dire forecasts of running out of conventional oil reserves have been proved wrong in the past. The exploration and development of hard-to-reach deposits with new technology will put more oil on the market; and future world oil demand may be constrained by efforts to reduce global warming. Although the United States is twice as energy efficient as it was during the 1970s, the push to reduce warming gases in the atmosphere has placed more emphasis on energy efficiency than ever before.[9]

Even if the gloom-and-doom forecasts are correct this time, there is no reason not to believe that the market won't do what it did when the last type of fuel, whale oil, ran out: transition to a new fuel source. For centuries, whale oil was used for candles and lamps, but whales became "overfished," and the price of their oil rose as dwindling supply coincided with increased demand. Conservationists and consumers demanded better, and higher whale oil prices gave it to them. Technology was developed and perfected to drill for rock oil (crude petroleum) out of the ground.[10]

The same is likely to be true if the world is genuinely past its peak of conventional oil production. As the petroleum price goes up, new technology is and already has been used to discover and produce more oil from hard-to-reach deposits. Even oil derived from unconventional sources—for example, oil shale in the western United States and in Canada's vast tar sands—may be made economical by higher oil prices. When the oil price rises, conservation increases and so does the switching to alternative fuels. For example, high oil prices make research into hydrogen, solar, wind, nuclear, geothermal, biomass, and other alternative fuels more viable economically. And, of course, higher prices and accompanying better technology allow much better odds of finding oil, a greater percentage of crude oil to be recovered from existing fields, and more refined products—for example, gasoline and diesel fuel—to be gleaned from each barrel of oil.

To prevent what could be such long-term permanent reductions in demand for oil, the Saudis usually try to keep price increases within bounds; in 2005, when the oil price was increasing, but had not yet reached record levels, the

Saudis undertook a new oil investment program designed to restrain prices and also simply to take advantage of predicted future high prices.

In 2007 and 2008, the oil price soared to the record level of $147 per barrel. Only during the 1973 and 1979 oil crises did the price rise as rapidly. And when oil prices are high, public fury usually pressures the president and Congress to add inefficient or counterproductive requirements on top of the market's natural tendency to promote consumers' oil conservation when the price rises. For example, as a result of high oil prices in 2007, the Congress passed and President George W. Bush signed and praised the Energy Independence and Security Act of 2007 for taking "a major step toward reducing out dependence on oil. . . ." The act established minimum percentages for ethanol in transportation fuels; increased auto miles-per-gallon standards for the first time since 1975; enacted efficiency standards for equipment, buildings, and lighting; and even legislated the end of incandescent light bulbs.[11]

So in contrast to the 1970s, nowadays even oil producers don't want the price to get too high (or too low). They believe that stable prices should be the main goal, because excessively high prices ultimately lead to a long-term drop in demand for oil, either through conservation or the development and use of alternative energy sources. In other words, according to energy journalist Paul Roberts, for producers and consumers, "the oil weapon itself was seen more and more as a suicidal option." Although Roberts overstates the real effects of oil price shocks on the world economy (they have been illusory), he convincingly noted:

> Oil states have tried to use price as a weapon, by withholding supplies in order to drive prices up—or, alternatively, flooding the market to bring prices down—although these tactics almost always backfire. Pushing prices too high or too low invariably sets off a destructive chain of events that has, on several occasions, started wars and come disturbingly close to wiping out the world economy. This is why, after fifty years of painful experimentation and catastrophe, price stability has become the overriding goal for countries as politically divergent as Saudi Arabia, Russia, and the United States.[12]

Forecasters, including those in OPEC, were predicting high prices for the future beyond the record prices in 2008. Yet as we have seen before, forecasting the oil market can be hazardous. For example, in April 2008, Jeff Rubin, the chief economist for CIBC World predicted the following:

> Despite the recent record jump in oil prices, the outlook suggests that oil prices will continue to rise steadily over the next five years, almost doubling from current levels.[13]

Needless to say, shortly thereafter, Mr. Rubin's prediction was thrown onto the ash heap of history when the global economic and financial meltdown caused the price of oil to plummet into the $30 a barrel range. It was déjà vu all over again.

In 2011, oil prices rose again after the long recession, but predicting future prices is still as difficult as ever.

PART II

Myths about Oil and Its Market

12

Myth 1
No Viable Market Exists for Oil

SOME ALLEGE THAT a completely free market for oil does not exist because of historical subsidization and protection of the industry by the U.S. and other governments, the politicization of oil through producers being organized into cartels, embargoes and attempted price collusion on the sale of oil by those oil producing nations, and the nationalization of the oil industry in many producing countries.

Although the industry has received unneeded and costly federal and state subsidies in the form of preferential tax breaks and government protection from imports and domestic overproduction, a viable market for oil has always existed. Besides, other industries receive lavish government benefits, and we don't say that a viable market does not exist for those products.

Internationally, the OPEC cartel accounts for about 35 percent of the world's oil exports.[1] (See Table 2.) As for reserves, it accounts for roughly 70 percent. (See Table 3.) As we saw in the history of the oil market, however, cartels don't have much success holding the oil price artificially high in the long-term because of incentives to cheat on production quotas. In fact, Jay Hakes, the former head of the Energy Information Administration, the office that is the center for tracking worldwide energy data for the U.S. government, said that the EIA routinely disregarded OPEC claims of production cuts because of a history of rampant cheating on such cuts by its members. Incentives for such cheating are many when the price is high and huge revenues can be had, but such devious behavior acts to eventually reduce that price. In contrast, OPEC's unity increases somewhat when the oil price is low because fewer incentives exist to cheat—as in the late 1990s when inflation-adjusted oil prices were the lowest in the history of the automobile—making production cuts and resultant price increases more

Table 2: Top Net Oil Exporters in the World for 2009

Rank	Country	Net Exports (Thousand Barrels Per Day)
1.	Saudi Arabia	7,322
2.	Russia	7,194
3.	Iran	2,486
4.	United Arab Emirates	2,303
5.	Norway	2,132
6.	Kuwait	2,124
7.	Nigeria	1,939
8.	Angola	1,878
9.	Algeria	1,767
10.	Iraq	1,764
11.	Venezuela	1,748
12.	Libya	1,525
13.	Kazakhstan	1,299
14.	Canada	1,144
15.	Qatar	1,066

Source: Energy Information Agency, Department of Energy,
http://www.eia.doe.gov/countries/index.cfm?topL=exp

enforceable until the price rises and more cheating commences.[2] Sometimes, however, even when prices are low, countries desperate for revenue make up lost earnings by increasing production. In any event, OPEC's actions may alter the long-term price of oil only on the margins.

Also, in a global oil market for a largely fungible product, the ability to embargo specific nations is illusory. The market simply adjusts as it did in the 1973 oil embargo—with different suppliers taking over for the embargoing exporters as sellers to the embargoed country or countries, and the sanctioning nations selling to non-embargoed buyers. Future embargoes are even more unlikely with the creation of the New York and London oil futures markets, because oil-producing nations no longer have control over who buys their oil.

Furthermore, the Arabs will probably never attempt another such embargo because of the disastrous effect on the long-term demand for oil. Regardless of the actual marginal effects on the world oil market, the threat of a supply disruption did lead to long-term government encouragement in consuming nations for conservation and switching to other fuels—thus helping to depress demand

Table 3: Countries with the Largest Proved Oil Reserves in 2010

Rank	Country	Proved Reserves (Billion Barrels)	Share of World
I.	Saudi Arabia	264.6	19.0%
2.	Canada	175.2	12.6%
3.	Iran	137.6	9.9%
4.	Iraq	115.0	8.3%
5.	Kuwait	104.0	7.5%
6.	United Arab Emirates	97.8	7.0%
7.	Venezuela	97.8	7.0%
8.	Russia	74.2	5.3%
9.	Libya	47.0	3.4%
10.	Nigeria	37.5	2.7%
11.	Kazakhstan	30.0	2.2%
12.	Qatar	25.4	1.8%
13.	China	20.4	1.5%
14.	United States	19.1	1.4%
15.	Angola	13.5	1.0%
16.	Algeria	13.4	1.0%
17.	Brazil	13.2	1.0%

Proved reserves are estimated with a high degree of confidence to be commercially recoverable from known resevoirs and under current economical conditions.
Source: U.S. Central Intelligence Agency, World Factbook, January 1, 2010, http://en.wikipedia.org/wiki/List_of_countries_by_proven_oil_reserves.

for oil in the 1980s and 1990s. Although the United States lags behind Japan and northern Europe in efficiently turning energy into GDP, even with U.S. government policies that have encouraged the excessive use of energy, between 1970 and the present, three-fourths of the United States' additional energy demand has been met by rising energy efficiency rather than new production.[3]

Persian Gulf countries need to preserve the long-term demand for oil, because the commodity accounts for an average 40 percent of their respective GDPs and more than 85 percent of their respective exports.[4] To be blunt, the undiversified economies of most oil-producing nations make selling oil critical for them. In fact, in the long term, with rising populations and declining per capita GDPs, oil producers are more dependent on oil consuming nations than vice versa.

The greatest distortion of the world oil market is the nationalization of many countries' oil companies. State oil companies are inefficient, invest too little in exploration and added production, and therefore cannot develop oil exploration and production technology as fast as private companies can. Thus, state-owned and controlled oil companies often seek help from private transnational oil and oil services companies in order to adopt their technology or to get those companies to show them how to undertake a technically challenging operation. Instead of having rights to develop the foreign deposits, as they did in the old days, the companies sometimes get kicked out when they are no longer needed. Because of nationalization, which has been happening since the 1930s, the private companies have fewer and fewer oil deposits open to them for exploration and production. Nationalized oil companies own all but 10 percent of the world's reserves.[5] The deposits the companies do get are usually in nations that are politically risky or when countries don't have the technology to extract oil from hard-to-reach areas.[6]

Such nationalization is inefficient from the perspective of even the countries doing it, but the governments in those countries benefit financially. Nationalization also raises the price of oil somewhat from what a free market would produce. But bad decisions by foreign governments of oil-producing nations shouldn't be compounded by bad policies on the part of governments of consuming nations, especially the largest consumer—the United States. Even under imperfect conditions, the best course of action for the U.S. government still is to let the oil market deliver oil at the cheapest price obtainable.

Even in times of crisis-induced disruptions of petroleum supplies, the oil market has bounced back quickly and restored supplies and ex ante prices. Eugene Gholz and Daryl G. Press present convincing data that during four out of five major oil supply shocks in the last thirty years—that is, strikes in the Iranian oil industry in 1978, the beginning of the Iran-Iraq War in 1980, the Iraqi invasion of Kuwait in 1990, and strikes in the Venezuelan oil fields in 2002–2003—the world market rapidly increased production and either held prices constant or reduced them back to pre-crisis levels. During the four episodes, because of crisis-induced price increases, lost production in one country was compensated for augmented output elsewhere. Also, higher prices induced furious efforts in the affected country to restore production. The only case in which the pre-crisis production and price levels were not restored rapidly was during the collapse of the Iranian oil industry in 1979. Gholz and Press also note that since the 1970s, new investment and financial tools have allowed the oil spot and futures markets to adjust quickly. In other words, the oil market is now more efficient than it has ever been and much more so than it was back then.

Gholz and Press answered hypothetical criticism that the four episodes all occurred when the market had the slack capacity to produce more during a crisis. The criticism would be that now rising demand from China might make the market so tight that producers could not increase output in time of supply disruption. However, Gholz and Press assert that a cartel (OPEC), by definition, is trying to restrain output below what the market would produce to generate a world price higher than the market price. To do that, and also to threaten increased production when other cartel members cheat and produce in excess of their quotas, requires members always to maintain some excess capacity. Also, when the likelihood of supply disruptions increases, such producing countries, large oil companies, and oil wholesalers have an incentive to expand potential supplies (slack capacity or inventories) in order to be ready to take advantage of the crisis-induced higher prices.[7] This argument works best for short and medium-term crises—when Saudi Arabia, the cartel's traditional enforcer, has excess capacity—but is less explanatory in the long term, when cheating is likely to negate any Saudi production restraint.

13

Myth 2

*"Big Oil" Colludes with OPEC
to Stick Consumers with High Prices*

THE WORLD'S MEDIA loves to cover oil. All the elements for a good story are there. Some of the largest companies in the world are making substantial profits in exotic places—both domestic and abroad. There are rich oil sheikhs, a murky cartel, billionaires here at home, and a commodity that almost everyone consumes—either when driving their car or enjoying consumer goods (oil is used in manufacturing them and transporting them to market). And gasoline and diesel fuel prices are more visible to the public than the prices of other consumer items because you can see them posted in bold letters when driving along the highway. For a price check, you don't even have to leave your car. Most important, since before World War I, governments have deemed— incorrectly for the most part, as this book will show—that oil is a strategic commodity that needs to be publicly managed. Thus, the oil industry is one of the most watched, misunderstood, and political businesses in the world.

The industry, with its episodic huge disastrous spills and occasional barometer-like high gasoline prices, finds it almost impossible to shed its bad public reputation. When the price of oil is high, the oil companies are usually pilloried in the media, as when record real price levels occurred in 2008. It is often insinuated that oil companies and/or foreign oil-producing countries hike prices to take advantage of innocent consumers. Repeated government studies—including one in 2006 by the Federal Trade Commission—have found no indication that oil companies artificially raise prices.[1]

Concurring, Jay Hakes, former head of the Energy Department's Energy Information Agency, who studied the oil calamities of the 1970s, has concluded:

During the oil crises of the 1970s, politicians and the public widely condemned the oil companies for causing the shortages. . . . I have studied that period carefully and concluded that the problem of gasoline lines was caused mainly by the Arab production cuts and inept allocation by the federal government. Based on my research, I concluded that the oil companies stretched out the oil available about as well as possible.

. . . . Accusations that oil companies illegally ignore antitrust laws and fix prices have produced scant evidence to support them over the years. On the whole, the major energy companies have obeyed the law.[2]

Of course, the media spotlight evaporates when the price goes back down—as it often has in a cyclical fashion—and the profits of oil companies are down.

The public perception that unscrupulous rich men, who operate in the shadows, populate the industry probably originated with the secretive John D. Rockefeller. Rockefeller started the Standard Oil Trust in the late 1800s and built it into one of the first transnational corporations. He used ruthless business tactics in an attempt to destroy his business competitors. It didn't always work.[3]

Even at the zenith of Standard's wealth and power, well before the much later U.S. government antitrust action in the courts broke the company into pieces in 1911, it had competitors overseas—for example, Royal Dutch Shell and the Nobels and Rothschilds in Russia—and the price of kerosene (what oil was refined into before the automobile and gasoline became popular) dropped. So domestic antitrust action against the company was unneeded and came, as is usual in such government actions, much after Standard's peak in market dominance. The market power of most monopolies erodes over time because of changes in technology and new market entrants. Standard certainly did not have an enduring global monopoly in oil production, transportation, refining, or marketing.

And although throughout the history of the oil industry, various cartels—the Seven Sisters transnational oil companies, the Texas Railroad Commission, and OPEC—have tried to keep prices artificially high, they have not been very successful in the long term. As Leonardo Maugeri, a top executive for Eni, an Italian energy company, best sums up historical efforts to control the oil price, "Those who thought they could control it for their own benefit have been thwarted time and again by oil's boom and bust production cycles, its frequent market crises and often uncontrollable price fluctuations, as well as political explosions in which it has played a crucial role."[4] More specifically, Maugeri concludes:

> The impossibility of specific forces—companies or countries—to command thoroughly oil supply and prices clearly emerged also when the world oil market was characterized by powerful oligopolies.
>
> The Seven Sisters were only partially successful in restricting production in order to sustain prices form 1950 to 1970, because they did not succeed in avoiding either the destructive competition of independent companies or the rising tide of producing countries' reactions. By the same token, OPEC was incapable of managing its apparent success after the 1973 shock, which was by no means the outcome of a plan devised by the organization. The cartel's producers only exploited consumers' anxiety, which boosted prices higher and higher even if supply was wide and growing. The final result of that mismanagement was the countershock of 1986. Since then, the era of oil oligopolies has ended, and this has further made the control of oil an impossible dream.
>
> . . . . The organization [OPEC] is far from being a monopolistic body. Its members have different ideologies, policies, and economic targets, so that their discipline tends to be driven by self-interest rather than by a sense of common purpose. In their turn, international oil companies are driven by targets that structurally collide with OPEC's. . . . Every year, they need to replace reserves in order to sustain their future production, so that their main interest is to open new frontiers and experiment with new technologies in their quest for survival. Naturally, the more OPEC limits its own production to raise oil prices, the more international oil companies have an incentive to spend money to develop new resources outside the OPEC realm. . . . The consequence, then, is that oil *can* be a weapon, but only for brief periods. And its use as such can backfire, inflicting serious damage on the weapon wielder—as the Arab oil producers learned the hard way in the 1980s.[5]

In the short term, at times when the market is tight anyway (for example, the 1970s), commodity cartels probably have some upward effect on the price, but when the market is slack (for example, the 1980s and 1990s), the cartel will likely struggle to push up the price artificially. In the long term, cartels are intrinsically unstable, because potent incentives exist for members to pledge to restrict production and then cheat to take advantage of the rising prices; this furtive increase in supplies eventually leads to a drop in the price. Even when prices are low, it is sometimes difficult to get cartel members to cut production, because they try to maintain revenues in hard times by increasing the volume sold.

So the alleged intrigue in the oil industry has been vastly exaggerated. In short, a market for oil exists and, with the addition of oil futures and spot market trading, has never been more open and efficient. Unlike the market for natural gas, which is more difficult and expensive to transport over oceans than seagoing oil, the oil market is truly a single global market. Oil supplies readily and cheaply move in tankers from where they are produced to wherever they are needed. On the other hand, most natural gas is marketed within the region of the world in which it is produced, because it usually depends on land pipelines. Facilities for compressing or liquefying the gas and putting it on special tankers—and reversing the process when it reaches the destination—are still expensive. No such processing is required for transporting oil, because it is liquid at normal temperatures.

Repeated cycles have shown that the global oil market does work. When the price of oil goes up, as did in the 1970s, people conserve more and alternative energy sources become more viable in the market; producers, predicting greater profits, explore for and produce more oil and also develop more technologies for doing so. The lessened demand and greater supply for oil then brings the price back down—as happened in the 1980s and 1990s as a result of increased prices in the 1970s.

14

Myth 3

*Global Oil Production Has Peaked
and the World Is Running Out of Oil*

U.S. OIL PRODUCTION is reported to have peaked in 1970 at 10 million barrels of oil per day. U.S. production is now about half that at 5.1 million barrels per day. Yet 85 percent of the U.S. outer continental shelf off the American coastline and parts of Alaska are excluded from exploitation (the U.S. Department of Interior estimates that the Arctic National Wildlife Reserve alone may have more oil than Texas[1]). Also, the U.S. has oil in shale rock in Colorado, Utah, and Wyoming that is estimated to be three times the oil in Saudi Arabia's reserves. Of course, much of these three types of oil are expensive—and currently illegal—to extract, but the political winds and technology march on; so even the seemingly obvious peak of U.S. oil production may not be so in the long run.[2] For example, in 2006, a huge oil field was found in the deep water of the Gulf of Mexico less than three hundred miles southwest of New Orleans. The Jack, as it is called, could increase U.S. oil reserves by 50 percent and was drilled to more than twenty thousand feet below the sea floor in seven thousand feet of water.[3] That combined depth is almost equivalent to the height of Mount Everest. In sum, it is still unclear whether the economics of extracting oil from all of these potential future sources will allow U.S. production to reverse course and top its 1970 peak.

Similarly, some analysts claim that global oil reserves will soon peak, or already have reached their apex. Those neo-Malthusians predict that world consumption will rise 50 percent by 2030, while arguing that the oil industry is currently living off past success—with the last big oil finds occurring in the late 1960s in Siberia, the North Sea, and Alaska's North Slope.[4] The peak oil analysts routinely assume that oil consumption is indifferent to price increases, but demand has been price-sensitive in the long term—as was proved by the price hikes of the 1970s leading to conservation in the 1980s.

Even with modern geological knowledge and probability and statistical models, however, no one knows how many oil deposits the planet holds or what percentage of known reserves are ultimately recoverable; technology keeps increasing that percentage. In fact, resource estimates cannot even be made within an order of magnitude because of difficulty in predicting price trends, political decisions, changes in propensity to consume, and technological changes in production and consumption.

According Vaclav Smil, a professor at the University of Manitoba in Canada,

> Values of EUR (estimated ultimate recovery) are not at all certain and tend to rise with better understanding of petroleum geology, with frontier exploration, and with enhanced recovery techniques. Moreover, the proponents of an imminent peak of global oil extraction disregard the role of prices, they ignore historical perspectives, and they presuppose the end of human inventiveness and adaptability.[5]

Of the known sedimentary basins on earth capable of producing oil and natural gas, some of the 30 percent currently active need further exploration (for example, Iraq), the 39 percent that have tested negatively need more thorough examination, and the remaining 30 percent remain unexplored. In short, peak oil analysts don't admit that the knowledge of oil deposits is imperfect, and much evidence exists to be optimistic about future oil production.[6]

Predictions of "Peak Oil" Have Been Repeatedly Wrong

Wrong predictions of peak oil have been made before. In fact, such peak oil predictions usually occur when the market is tight and prices are high, and they then evaporate when the price goes back down. As was mentioned in Chapter 1, the peak oil craze coinciding with the high prices during 2007 and 2008 was the fifth time predictions have been made that the world was running out of oil—they started in the 1880s, and the penultimate episode was during the tight oil markets of the 1970s.[7] In between, World War I and World War II sucked up much oil and caused the U.S. government each time to predict that global oil supplies would soon peak. All four previous times, the peak oil predictions proved unfounded. Similarly, recent predictions of peak oil have a dearth of evidence to back them up. In fact, statistics show that the world's oil reserves are increasing in size.

Of course, the world ultimately has a finite amount of oil, but no one knows how much that is or when global production will begin to decline; the debate rages fiercely about when peak oil will occur. Proponents of the peak oil thesis have claimed that the planet has only 2 trillion barrels of recoverable oil. According to Michael Lynch, the former director for Asian energy and security at Massachusetts Institute of Technology, the consensus among geologists is that the earth has about 10 trillion barrels of oil. The percentage of economically recoverable oil as a percentage of total oil is always increasing over time and is now 35 percent, or 3.5 trillion barrels of recoverable oil on planet earth. This amount does not even include unconventional oil, such as that in tar sands, which eventually may be economically recoverable.[8]

Similarly, Daniel Yergin—an energy consultant who won the Pulitzer Prize for *The Prize,* a book on the petroleum industry—reported in 2009 that his firm's analysis of more than eight hundred of the largest oil fields globally indicated that the world had enough oil to meet demand for decades.[9]

Past tight markets for oil have brought gloom-and-doom predictions of exhausting global supplies and permanently higher prices. But then the higher prices made previously uneconomical oil deposits profitable to extract and brought forth new technology to get at previously unreachable deposits. Yet peak oil advocates always fall victim to the long lag time between higher prices and the time when such investments bear fruit, thereby perennially and falsely predicting the end of the world for oil.[10] Thus, such predictions of shortage have usually been followed by gluts.

Periodic and unfounded fears of oil shortages have driven governments to ill-conceived and unneeded action, as summarized by Leonardo Maugeri,

> It was the fear of oil shortages that moved the great powers to develop their first oil-driven foreign policies at the dawn of the twentieth century, leading to British control of what was then Persia (today's Iran) and to the establishment of today's Iraq (then Mesopotamia) in the 1920s. Later on, it was the perception of dwindling oil resources in the United

States that inspired the close links between the American government and Saudi Arabia's. And it was the fear that Arab oil would fall under the influence of the Soviet Union that largely shaped American foreign policy in the Middle East after World War II.

Yet, the obsessive fear of a world short of oil and the political analyses and responses it produced always proved to be inconsistent with reality. Over almost 150 years, the dominant characteristics of the oil market have been oversupply and low prices, sometimes temporarily interrupted by shocking reversals. Each period of dramatic expectation that the end of oil was near concluded with a major glut.[11]

How Much Oil Is Left?

According to Eugene Gholz and Daryl G. Press, over time, the world's ultimately recoverable reserves (URR) have been rising because oil fields usually contain more oil than originally estimated. New technology has allowed a greater percentage of oil to be extracted from the reserves. In 1980, only 22 percent of oil in the average field was recoverable, but now that number is the aforementioned 35 percent. New exploration and production technology has made it easier to locate new deposits, find new pockets of oil in existing deposits, and extract oil from previously uneconomic deposits or unreachable places— for example, under deep water, in the tar sands of Canada's Alberta province, or under permanently frozen tundra, such as found in Siberia. Advances in technology allow drilling off the coast of Alaska and north of the Arctic Circle, which a number of countries are doing. Siberia and deep water, such as in the Arctic, are predicted to be the next drilling frontiers.[12] Thus, such technology has allowed the average exploration and development cost of a barrel of oil to plunge dramatically. As for existing producers, Russia, Saudi Arabia, Iraq, and Kuwait are not believed to be currently producing to their full potential.

For all of these reasons, Gholz and Press note that the life-index of global oil reserves—the time that known reserves could support the current rate of production—has increased from thirty-five years in 1972 to forty years in 2003. Thus, they conclude that little evidence exists that global oil production has peaked and that the world's oil reserves are running out.[13] It is hard to declare credibly that the planet will soon run out of oil when the life-index of proven reserves is higher than it was thirty or sixty years ago.[14]

Even Paul Roberts, an energy journalist and pessimist about peak oil, uses the "respected"—but "optimistic"—U.S. Geological Survey's statistics on reserves to calculate that the world will reach peak oil in 2030. Roberts then cites the even more optimistic prediction by Energy Information Administration in the Department of Energy that large discoveries off the coasts of Latin America and West Africa will push peak oil to 2035. Roberts says that his fellow pessimists put the estimate the peak in oil reserves to occur somewhere between 2010 and 2016.[15]

However, as David O'Reilly, the Chief Executive Officer of Chevron, cogently concluded in 2006,

> People who think that peak oil will occur are just looking at conventional oil. You have to think beyond that. Think of all the other hydrocarbon sources, the oil sands in Canada. . . . Think of all the remote areas of the world that have not yet been explored. . . . [16]

Even Antonia Juhasz, one of the oil industry's foremost critics on the left, implicitly rejects the peak oil hypothesis and admits that there are trillions of barrels of oil in the Canadian tar sands of Alberta (which has reserves estimated to be second in size only to those of Saudi Arabia), in the American oil shale west of the Mississippi River (these reserves could be larger than those of Alberta, and Juhasz terms them potentially "staggering" in size), in the waters off all coasts of the United States (4.5 billion barrels in proved reserves and an estimated 86 billion barrels when yet undiscovered deposits are found), and in the deepest oceans of the world.[17] The "difficult" oil shale and tar sands deposits become more viable when the price of oil is $60 to $80 a barrel.[18]

Despite the dubious predictions of peak oil, oil markets can periodically become tight if rising world demand (for example, spurred by China's rapid economic growth during the years of the first decade of the twentieth century) exceeds supply. But the higher price doesn't indicate that the world is running out of oil. It only indicates that demand exceeds current supply, which is determined by investment long past. As noted above, in the longer term, the market usually responds to the higher price by increasing investment to discover new oil and extract petroleum better. Increases in consumption have recently outpaced new discoveries of oil because oil investments take a long time to produce oil.

Low oil prices in the 1980s and 1990s curtailed investments; with the higher prices after the new millennium, new discoveries have picked up again.[19]

Oil Is Relatively Cheap

Over the long term, because of technological advances and market-based allocations, most commodities have become more abundant during the last thirty years—and thus their prices have decreased in real terms. Although oil has its ups and downs, it has been no exception. When measured in work time at the average manufacturing wage, the price of gasoline has been declining since the 1920s, according to Donald Losman of the National Defense University. For all the hoopla about high gas prices, a gallon of gasoline is often less expensive than a gallon of milk or mouthwash.[20] Robert Bryce says much the same thing, but uses different statistics. Bryce says that gasoline expenses as a percentage of the cost of owning a car has decreased from about third in 1975 to about 12 percent in 2004 (a record low for the modern era) and 18 percent in 2005. Bryce says that gasoline is a bargain, even at $3-plus a gallon, when compared to Starbucks coffee at almost $23 a gallon and Budweiser beer at almost $11 per gallon.[21]

Even if the world is finally running out of oil, the market is still the best way to change over the economy to new fuel sources. This has been demonstrated by previous changeovers. People resisted adopting coal, because of the smoke, until the price of wood became high in the eighteenth century as a result of the deforestation of Europe for wood burning.[22] Similarly, petroleum-based kerosene replaced whale oil for illumination only after whale oil became expensive because whales had been slaughtered to near extinction in the Atlantic Ocean. Whalers had to travel to faraway seas to find catches, thus spiking the price of the huge mammal's oil.[23] Thus, in the past, the market, through the mechanism of rising prices, efficiently facilitates a gradual transition from one fuel to another. The world is hardly condemned to the alarmist's scenario of plummeting crude oil supplies, economic cataclysm, and wars over dwindling oil supplies.

Would Scarcer Oil Cause More Conflict?

Even if oil supplies are really becoming scarcer, academic research casts doubt on claims in security circles about the increased likelihood of conflict over this resource. Research indicates that scarcity of resources can be alleviated by globalization rather than by resorting to war. Ronnie Lipschutz and John Holdren noted that wars over scarce resources are unlikely, because in an interdependent world, trade is a more cost-effective way to get resources than waging war, technological advances have increased the substitutability of materials, and raw materials are less important to economic success.[24] Thus, as long as there exist markets with viable price mechanisms to reflect relative scarcity, the threat of conflict over resources will be lessened.

In fact, more conflict over oil may result from abundance rather than shortage. The violent bone of contention in developing countries is often not competition over scarce resources but control over the revenue stream from abundant resources. For example, rebellion in Nigeria's Niger Delta is caused by a portion of the population feeling left out of getting substantial revenues from the delta's plentiful oil reserves.[25]

Thus, even dwindling oil supplies need not cause increased conflict in the world.

15

Myth 4

Oil Is a Special Product or Even Strategic

ACCORDING TO THE media and politicians, oil is a special product because it is the "life's blood of the economy" and the military requires it to operate. Thus, it has been deemed "strategic"—that is, the government must get heavily involved in making sure U.S. supplies are secure and that the price doesn't go up too high. Yet, there are many products critical to the economy of which the market is allowed to provide ample supplies at efficient prices. Oil really should be no different. If governments avoid enacting counterproductive policies, industrial economies are fairly resilient to even significant oil price hikes. Furthermore, as was mentioned, enough oil is produced domestically, many times over, to run the U.S. military in time of war, and this supply can be augmented with petroleum from nearby friendly countries—for example, Canada and Mexico. Canada alone has the second largest proved oil reserves in the world, next in size to those of Saudi Arabia (see Table 3). Thus, contrary to conventional wisdom among the public, the media, and government officials around the world, oil is not strategic.

There is no need for the hysteria that seems to occur when oil prices are high. They always seem to go back down. The country doesn't go into hysteria when the price of coffee goes up because of blight in the crop in Central America, so why should the nation go berserk every time the price of oil goes up? Furthermore, Donald Losman, an economist at the National Defense University, asks why we are willing to send U.S. service personnel overseas into harm's way to ensure the flow of oil when we are unwilling to do so for access to coffee supplies, which are more valuable to U.S. society (he bases this conclusion on comparing the two products' unit prices).[1]

People make several arguments about why oil is not like any other good, such as coffee. First, they say that the world's oil can be depleted, whereas coffee plants are a renewable resource. Allegedly, the same applies to manufactured goods, such as electronic circuits, more of which can be made. Of course, producing many manufactured goods requires non-renewable inputs. Just because the world has fixed reserves of oil, that doesn't mean they will be near exhaustion any time soon. As noted earlier, the quantity of the world's known exploitable reserves has increased.

Second, many people argue that oil has so many uses in the economy that it is special as a product. Of course, electronic chips are used in many products (including weapons used by the Pentagon) and employed heavily in manufacturing, assembling, storing, and transporting many other goods, but no one speaks of using military force to safeguard supplies of the 80 percent of imported semiconductors that come into the U.S. from East Asia. That region is also unstable and contains regimes hostile or potentially hostile to the United States.[2] Also, the United States is heavily dependent of foreign sources for critical minerals other than oil, such as copper and cobalt, but few people advocate using force to protect them.

In contrast, Table 4 shows that the United States doesn't get most of its oil from the Persian Gulf. Although it is true that oil is used to make petrochemicals and also to transport most other goods and the people who buy them to market, there is no reason to believe that oil price spikes induce economic recessions and that the market is not still the best mechanism for allocating this resource.

Industrial Economics Are Resilient to Oil Price Spikes

Contrary to the conventional wisdom, modern industrial economies are actually fairly resilient to oil price spikes. The oil price increases of 1999 and 2000, combined with a decline in the value of the euro currency, subjected Germany to a 211 percent increase in crude prices from the fourth quarter of 1998 to the third quarter of 2000. Despite this hefty increase, the German economy experienced economic growth, dropping unemployment, and declining inflation.[3] In the United States, from 2002 until 2006, the oil price increased 245 percent,

Table 4: Largest Exporters of Oil to the United States and
Their Percentage of U.S. Imports

Rank	Country	Amount Exported	Percentage of U.S. Imports
1.	Canada	678.1	25.6
2.	Mexico	405.3	15.3
3.	Nigeria	331.3	12.5
4.	Venezuela	273.7	10.3
5.	Saudi Arabia	143.3	5.4
6.	Angola	141.4	5.3
7.	Columbia	114.3	4.3
8.	Algeria	77.9	2.9
9.	Ecuador	73.1	2.8
10.	Brazil	67.8	2.6
11.	Iraq	58.9	2.2
12.	Other	282.3	10.7

Total exported by country in millions of barrels for 2010
Sources: U.S. Census Bureau, 2010, http://en.wikipedia.org/wiki/United_States_oil_politics

but U.S. economic growth averaged 3.2 percent—at the high end of its normal range.[4] So high oil prices had little to do with the eventual economic meltdown at the end of the decade, which was caused by an excessively liberal monetary policy that caused an artificial housing boom and bust.

Industrial economies appear to be more resilient to oil shocks than they were in the 1970s for several reasons. As a percentage of GDP, U.S. oil consumption has declined from 6 percent in the early 1970s to 3 percent recently. Thus, oil is less important to the economy than it was in the 1970s because of conservation, switching to alternative fuels, and economic and productivity growth. Also, other things besides oil price increases contributed to the stagflation of the 1970s. During that decade, the prices of many raw materials were increasing, not just oil. In addition, unlike the 1970s, when the Consumer Price Index rises now, wages don't automatically increase. Thus, when the price of oil rises, workers now more readily accept lower real wages, leading to less unemployment. Finally, at least some lessons have been learned from the bad (read: profligate) monetary policy of the 1970s.[5]

Is Oil Really "Strategic"?

Third, governments—and as a result the world media—have deemed oil to be a "strategic" commodity. There is some truth to this in a limited sense, but the argument is usually blithely used to encourage U.S. government meddling in the world oil market.

Rather than being strategic to the economy, oil can be tactically important on the battlefield. Military tanks, trucks, aircraft, and some ships require gasoline, diesel, or jet fuel to fight and supply battles. Yet the U.S. military's daily consumption of oil is about 0.3–0.4 million barrels per day. The United States produces more than 13 to 17 times that amount of oil domestically (5.2 million barrels per day) and has domestic reserves of more than 21 billion barrels.[6] Also, in time of conflict, many friendly oil-producing countries—such as Canada (this nearby and friendly country alone has reserves in excess of 178 billion barrels), Nigeria, Norway, the United Kingdom, etc.—could and would sell the United States oil.

Although oil is important for battles, so are other supplies. A staple of military tactical thinking says, "Why fight the opponent's army when you can render it ineffective by destroying its supply train?" Yet, if critical food supplies, tank treads, spare tires, vital mechanical parts for vehicles, and so on, are destroyed, the opponent's military force may be rendered as ineffective as when its oil and gasoline supplies have gone up in flames.

Shortages of rubber and steel, critical for the war effort, occurred during World War II. Because natural rubber came primarily from Japanese-occupied East Asia, the United States had to synthetically produce it. Many critical items are needed for waging war, and the government cannot manage all of them effectively and efficiently.

If the government nevertheless declares that oil is strategic for the entire economy, we are back to the previous discussion in this chapter. But if the government chooses to intervene in the market to "manage" supplies to either ensure oil supplies for the military or for the general economy, it will have similar problems. Oil would not be the only "strategic" commodity that the government would need to manage. For example, platinum-group metals (platinum and palladium) are rare, expensive catalysts found in only a few countries. They are required to efficiently "crack" oil into smaller molecules in the refining process, which produces gasoline, diesel fuel, jet fuel, and so on. Although a big fuss arose when China wanted to buy UNOCAL, one of many U.S. oil companies, and the deal was nixed, a Russian company, without fanfare, bought Stillwater Mining, the only U.S. producer of platinum and palladium.[7] In fact, although the United States imports 60 to 70 percent of its oil needs, it imports 91 percent of its platinum, 81 percent of its palladium, 99 percent of its gallium (used to manufacture lasers, semiconductors, and photovoltaic cells), 88 percent of its tin, 76 percent of its cobalt, 72 percent of its chromium, 80 percent of its semiconductors, 83 percent of its uranium used in civilian nuclear power plants, and 100 percent of its bauxite, alumina, manganese, strontium, yttrium, and 13 other "strategic" minerals. As Robert Bryce, a Fellow at the Institute for Energy Research, asks facetiously, "Why should America stop at energy independence?"[8]

To transport oil from overseas to the United States requires tankers, but there have been shortages of these before. Platinum-group metals and tankers are only two examples of the other many critical items required to find crude oil, extract it out of the ground, transport it to a refinery, refine it, transport it to fuel stations, and distribute it to users. Will the government be able to correctly identify all bottlenecks in the system and manage them all? No, the web of products and services needed to produce any product is immense. Oil is no exception. Before long, the government would have to manage everything—leading to a socialist economic mess.

Besides, if oil is so strategic for the U.S. economy, why did Secretary of State Henry Kissinger, in 1975 during the Cold War, try to cut a deal with the United States' principal adversary to make America dependent on imports of oil from the Soviet Union? Although the deal fell through, Kissinger was attempting to swap Soviet oil for U.S. wheat. Yet, hypocritically, the United States, during the 1980s and under Reagan, imposed sanctions on America's Western European allies for becoming overly dependent on Soviet natural gas. The same fallacious "European reliance on Russian energy is strategically bad" complaint was more recently resurrected during the George W. Bush administration.

16

Myth 5

*A Strategic Petroleum Reserve
Is Needed in Case of Emergency*

PRIOR TO THE 1973 oil crisis, no Strategic Petroleum Reserve
(SPR) was needed. The Texas Railroad Commission, a government-facilitated
domestic oil cartel that tried to keep prices higher than the market value, had excess production capability. As world and U.S. oil consumption increased and
domestic production declined—creating the tight market conditions that made
the 1973 oil crisis possible—that excess capacity vanished. In 1975, after the
Arab production cutbacks and oil embargo toward the United States, Congress
authorized the SPR.

The SPR was a product of the Cold War mindset. This act was more about
demonstrating the U.S. government's intent to protect its economy from disruptions in order to deter foreign countries from shutting off supplies. The ninety-
day supply was to provide time for negotiations or a show of military force to
free up supplies from producers again.

Yet, Donald Losman, of the National Defense University, has cogently argued that if the U.S. government goes into hysterics over oil by declaring it as a
strategic commodity, when it's best allocated by the market, this type of thinking
will only tempt any potential U.S. adversary to strike at the perceived U.S. Achilles' heel.[1] Also, because the United States is a superpower, other governments
often imitate its alarmist thinking.

Moreover, by the time the SPR was up and running in 1984, oil embargoes
were a thing of the past because oil-producing nations were trading petroleum
on the New York and London markets, losing even the weak control they had
over who got what supplies—thus making supply cutoffs to particular countries
difficult. And as Sarah Emerson, an analyst at Energy Security Analysis, Inc.,

has said, "In a way, the SPR is an anachronism." Government policies, which are the result of slow processes, often come along too late to make a difference. Oil could still be released from the SPR to attempt to reduce high oil price when no "emergency" exists, but there is no clear policy to do that.[2]

Now, the U.S. and other governments have stored billions of barrels of oil in strategic reserves. World commercial reserves are several times these amounts. Countries have formed the International Energy Agency (IEA), which requires its members to maintain oil reserves equal to ninety days worth of net petroleum imports (reserves can be a combination of government and private stockpiles) and to coordinate during a major supply disruption by releasing such reserves, restraining consumption, increasing production, or changing to other fuels. The IEA and the expanding U.S. SPR are designed to deal with such supply hiccups in the short term by selling oil into the market. For example, they did so during the first Gulf War in 1991 and after the disruption of refining capacity after Hurricane Katrina and Rita hit the United States in 2005.[3] But the release in 1991 was a miniscule amount, designed just as a signal to the markets that the U.S. government would be willing to release more to stabilize the price. The increase in Saudi production vastly dwarfed this small release.

Problems with the SPR

Although the SPR has three times the amount of oil held in on-hand U.S. industry and refinery stocks and can pump about a third of what the U.S. consumes in a day,[4] some analysts claim that the stockpile is not big enough to compensate for a catastrophic production loss from the Persian Gulf. The SPR has never met its goal of storing a billion barrels of oil and maintaining enough of a reserve to replace ninety days of imported oil. Although George W. Bush enlarged the reserve slightly after 9/11, these analysts advocate significantly enlarging the stockpile, modernizing it, and modifying the rules for the release of oil. Advocates of the reserve contend that it makes less necessary the use of military force to ensure the flow of Persian Gulf oil. If that were true—a dubious proposition—it might be an improvement over current policy, but not as good as avoiding war for oil, eliminating the SPR, and letting the unfettered market provide oil.

With the SPR, it seems that the U.S. has the worst of all worlds. Despite the reserve, whether enlarged or not, U.S. policy to ensure the flow of oil—and U.S. foreign policy in general—is still heavily militarized. In the last two decades, two U.S. wars in the Persian Gulf have been fought over oil—both in Iraq. In addition, the reserve includes only crude oil and not refined products, such as gasoline and diesel fuel. After Katrina and Rita, the crude oil stockpile was less useful because the hurricanes knocked out refineries and pipelines.[5] All crude oil in the world won't help if there is a shortage of refining capacity.

What if the government added refined products to the stockpile, as some advocate? But then shouldn't the government stockpile tankers to transport the oil or platinum group metals—considered rare and "strategic" minerals—that are used to crack crude oil molecules into the smaller molecules of refined products. Where does government interference in the market end?

Also, the creation of government reserves tends to reduce private reserves, thus transferring the expensive inventory costs from industry to the taxpayer. Moreover, industry players with fewer reserves tend to bid up oil prices higher.[6]

If the government buys oil for storage when political support for expanding such reserves is strongest—that is, when the market is tight and the prices are consequently high—government interference in the oil market will make prices go up even further. There is a debate on the magnitude of such government-induced price increases. One analyst estimated that George W. Bush increased oil prices as much as 25 percent when he continued to fill the SPR during the Venezuelan political crisis in late 2002, when Venezuela's oil exports plummeted to almost zero.

U.S. government purchases for the SPR can also have a ripple effect in the world market. When Bush increased the reserves slightly to show he was doing something about 9/11, other countries became unnerved, believing that the United States might know something that they didn't; they began stockpiling oil too, thus magnifying the price increase from the crisis.[7]

Conversely, when oil prices are low, the government could get a better bargain for taxpayers and disrupt the oil market less when making purchases, but during these times, little political support for buying exists—as happened in the slack market of the 1990s. The old saying, "you can't fix your roof while it's raining, and you don't have to when it's not," seems to apply to the SPR.

Such politics intrude on any government program, and the SPR is no exception. The mere existence of the SPR makes it a player in the market, watched by all parties. Presidents already are pressured to release oil from the stockpile to combat mundane (non-crisis) rises in the oil price; and they may be tempted to do it before elections or to shore up a president's sagging popularity. For example, in 2000, after Bill Clinton released petroleum from the SPR during a heating oil shortage, he was criticized for playing politics in an election year. Because of such accusations, presidents sometimes have been reluctant to release oil from the reserves—for example, before the U.S. invasion of Iraq, George W. Bush asked the Saudis to produce more oil rather than dispense petroleum from the reserve.[8]

Moreover, the SPR is not really needed to safeguard the economy from oil price shocks. Industrial economies have reduced their vulnerability to those shocks—for example, the United States has reduced the percentage of its GDP accounted for by oil. Thus, given the government's history of doing the wrong thing during oil crises, much doubt should exist about whether it should interfere with the petroleum market at all—even to stockpile oil for emergencies.

Finally, the SPR could be a target for terrorists, especially the pipelines leading out of the SPR sites, all of which are on the Gulf coast. Much more likely is a natural disaster affecting the SPR. The Gulf coast, also where more than half U.S. petroleum supplies begin, is the area most prone to hurricanes in the country; thus U.S. oil supplies and the SPR emergency reserves are in the same vulnerable locale.[9] If one believes in the efficacy and efficiency of the oil market, this is not a problem, because new oil could be purchased from anywhere. But it is a problem for the SPR, which treats oil as if it were . . . well, "strategic."

Oil analyst Lisa Margonelli best sums up the mistake the SPR has become:

Originally built in reaction to the Arab oil embargo of 1973 and as a shield against OPEC's power, the SPR was supposed to be an emergency stockpile—like those 5-gallon jars of peanut butter survivalists keep in their closets—intended to insulate the United States from the politics of keeping foreign oil flowing, to make us self-reliant, and to cause any rogue to think twice about shutting off the nation's oil supply. But thirty years later, the SPR itself has become a political football, a security issue, and a possible hazard in the oil markets. Some economists even say its existence is inflating oil prices by 25 percent. Is it possible that simply by filling the reserve the United States was transmitting fear to the market instead of confidence?

Or more bluntly at the time the government chose to store SPR oil in salt caverns on the Gulf Coast, the governor of Louisiana cracked, "If the federal government is going to pour money down a rat hole, I'd just as soon it be a rat hole in Louisiana."[10]

17

Myth 6

The United States Should Become Independent of Oil, Foreign Oil, or Overseas Energy[1]

ARE THE POLITICIANS and public wrong about the need for the United States to become independent of oil and especially foreign oil? As I asked before, can so many people be wrong? Yes, they can.

The following misconceptions bear repeating before they are dismantled: that if the United States was independent of foreign oil, U.S. military personnel would not have to die in the Middle East, and the United States would not have to meddle in or be allied with nasty, corrupt Middle Eastern countries. In truth, market forces can bring us the oil we need, and we won't need independence from foreign sources of petroleum to achieve those objectives.

Even if the consensus on the desirability of being independent of foreign oil is valid (it's not), independence has been difficult to achieve. Although every president since Richard Nixon has endorsed independence from foreign oil, the percentage of America's oil consumption that is imported has risen from 34 percent in 1973 to more than 70 percent now.

Before the early 1970s, the United States had market power in petroleum as a producer, but now its market power is based on being the world's largest oil consumer. The United States contains only 5 percent of the world's population but consumes about a quarter of the world's oil. Since the United States is such a large market, it is closely watched for trends, and even anti-U.S. oil producers, such as Libya and Venezuela, court U.S. sales. Saudi Arabia even discounts oil to maintain its share of the American market. As business journalist Paul Roberts noted, ". . . . the sheer extent of American demand, coupled with the country's own booming production (the United States is still the number-three producer), gives Uncle Sam a degree of influence over world oil markets and world oil politics that goes well beyond anything the U.S. might achieve militarily."[2]

The United States is severely dependent on oil in only one sector—transportation. The fuel source for about 95 percent of all U.S. vehicles (and world vehicles) is oil, and U.S. transportation accounts for 69 percent of U.S. oil consumption and about 14 percent of world consumption. In contrast, only one percent of the nation's electricity is generated by oil. Coal, nuclear power, natural gas, and hydroelectric power satisfy the bulk of this demand.[3] Globally, oil satisfies about 35 percent of the energy demand, with coal in second place at 26 percent and natural gas in third place at 23 percent.[4] Even if these other members of the hydrocarbon family supplanted oil, they have their own problems—for example, coal is dirty and natural gas is hard to transport and, like oil, also comes from some politically unstable countries.[5]

All in all, the United States has the most energy resources and fossil fuels (coal, natural gas, and oil) of any country in the world;[6] however, it will not be independent of oil—produced domestically or abroad—for a long time. The Department of Energy projects that in 2025, oil will make up the same percentage of U.S. energy consumption that it does today—about 40 percent.[7] The International Energy Agency (IEA) estimates that during the next 25 years fossil fuels (oil and natural gas) will make up more than 90 percent of the *increase* in global primary energy demand. During that time, oil will still be the dominant primary energy fuel in the world[8] because oil's refined products—gasoline and diesel—have a high energy content, are abundant, are relatively cheap and easy to transport, produce less carbon dioxide than coal, and have a massive infrastructure that is already in place to get them to consumers. Other energy sources are scarce (hydropower), are too expensive (wind and solar), or generate detrimental waste (carbon dioxide from coal and radioactive waste from nuclear power).[9]

Although Americans grouse about the very visible price of gasoline, yearly consumption for the average household is only about 3 to 4 percent of its income.[10] Over the long term, the real price of energy has gone down, incomes and GDP have gone up, and thus energy consumes a smaller part of business and consumer budgets.

Even if viable new fuel technologies are developed, the U.S. vehicle fleet is replaced only every fifteen years, at a rate of 7 percent per year.[11] Thus, any new fuel technologies will enter the market only slowly.

Alternatives to Oil Are Not that Promising

Energy journalist Paul Roberts best summed up the state of research and development for alternative energy technologies:

> For all their huge potential, most alternative technologies really aren't ready for prime time. Despite decades of research and development—and despite recent growth rates that rival that of computers and cell phones—nearly every major alternative technology still suffers from serious engineering or economic drawbacks.[12]

Although some alternative fuels might be great for the environment—in terms of traditional air pollution or global warming—most cleaner alternatives are not now economically viable and will not be for quite some time. Although politicians, starting with Richard Nixon, have encouraged the government to undertake a new Manhattan-like or Apollo-like program to field new technologies to make the U.S. energy independent, energy technologies—unlike those two previous technological efforts—need to be viable in the private marketplace and require technical breakthroughs that have not emerged even after many decades of research effort. Even back in Gerald Ford's day, federal spending on energy research and development had exceeded that spent on each of these two other high-profile government efforts, but had very little to show for all of the government subsidies.[13]

As Robert Bryce, author of the best critique of the goal of energy independence, correctly points out, "The rhetoric of energy independence provides political cover for protectionist trade policies, which have inevitably led to ever larger subsidies for politically connected domestic energy producers. . . ."[14]

Like repeatedly erroneous predictions that global oil production had peaked and that the complete depletion of the world's oil resources was imminent, Nixon's implicit prognostication that new technology would liberate the United States from foreign sources of energy in a few years has proven wildly off the mark. Some alternative fuels that have been held up as a panacea are not so, and even if eventually realized, will take years to reduce the demand for oil—foreign and domestic. Paul Roberts, a journalist, concluded that the global economy "is nowhere even close to having alternative energy sources."[15]

Other Hydrocarbons

If the use of coal, which is abundant in the United States (which is often called the "Saudi Arabia of coal," with 27 percent of the world's total[16]), were increased, air pollution and global warming would probably worsen. Making the coal "clean"—that is, carbon capture and storage underground (sequestration) from burnt coal—is expensive and is probably not market viable. Carbonic acid from coal stored underground may pollute ground water.

In addition, plants to generate electricity from coal are expensive to build and are subject to stringent environmental regulations, thus discouraging utilities from building new ones. Besides, as a result of the oil crises of the 1970s, coal, in all but the transportation sector (see below for the prospects of liquefying coal), has already largely helped displace oil for industrial uses and electric power generation.

Another alternative that is potentially environmentally questionable is shale oil, which the United States has three times as much of as Saudi Arabia does conventional oil.[17] Yet such oil is expensive to get out of the rock and polluting to refine. The same expensive production and pollution problems apply to the tar sands of Alberta, Canada.

The most promising alternative fuel in the transportation, industrial, and energy generation sectors may be natural gas, but even it has drawbacks. Natural gas is an abundant fuel, and new deposits are being found at much faster rate than new oil reserves. Gas from Russia, Iran, Qatar, and Turkmenistan—countries with the largest deposits and that make up over half the world's reserves—would last the planet more than fifty years. Natural gas is the cleanest of the fossil fuels. Yet natural gas is much more expensive to transport and store than oil, and its deposits are far away from customers (for example, Japan, Europe, and the United States). Unlike oil, gas usually must flow through pipelines on land, unless expensive facilities are purchased to liquefy the gas, transport it on special ocean-going tankers, and re-gasify it on the other shore.[18] To date, natural gas has only broken into the transportation sector in a limited way via bus and taxicab fleets. But with modifications, most cars can be converted to run on natural gas. Natural gas could also be used to heat homes, to generate electricity, and as a feedstock for chemicals and other products. According to energy writer Robert Bryce, wood dominated the eighteenth century, coal the nineteenth, oil the twentieth, and natural gas will likely be the dominant fuel of the twenty-first century.[19] In the medium term, if any fuel replaces oil's dominance, it will probably be natural gas. But that may not make the United States more independent of foreign energy. U.S. natural gas production does not meet U.S. demand and is declining, and many of the remaining substantial reserves are under protected areas (for example, national parks or off the coast) or are uneconomical to extract and transport without government subsidies. Furthermore, because much of any natural gas that would displace oil would have to be imported, U.S. policymakers would probably be disappointed to learn that many of the same potentially unstable countries that produce the most of the oil also produce most of the natural gas—for example, Iran, Russia, Qatar, Nigeria, Algeria, and Venezuela.[20] New technology—either supercooled lique-fied natural gas (LNG) or compressed natural gas—which makes economical the shipping of natural gas from overseas in special tankers, will likely increase future U.S. imports of foreign natural gas.

Alternative Fuels

Another existing alternative entails hybrid gasoline-electric cars, which get higher gas mileage than normal cars and are on the road today. Plug-in hybrids could travel much farther solely on electricity than regular hybrids and could save even more gasoline by allowing people to commute daily to work on only a battery charged up at night by plugging into the electric grid. For longer trips, batteries could be swapped out at battery replacement stations, but this would require a huge investment in a new infrastructure. Plug-in hybrids, however, so far are not market viable because the appropriate battery technology is expensive and wears out quickly. Furthermore, the potential for plug-in hybrids to reduce greenhouse gases has not been confirmed. Of all alternative energy technologies, the plug-in hybrid probably has the most potential to substitute for oil. Yet even under the most optimistic scenarios, a vehicle fleet with 50 percent plug-in hybrids is several decades away.[21]

With the huge upfront capital costs to build plants, nuclear power, an existing and widespread alternative energy source, probably is not cost-effective without government subsidies or a very high carbon tax. In addition, even if the government subsidizes nuclear plants, people don't want one in their backyard after the Three Mile Island, Chernobyl, and Japanese accidents. Finally, although the increased use of nuclear power would reduce carbon emissions, the problem of what to do with the radioactive waste products has not been solved, and the fuel has to be properly safeguarded against theft by criminals or terrorists. Thus, even though the Bush administration advocated a "nuclear renaissance," only five countries (not including the United States) are expanding the number of nuclear power plants; most nations are phasing them out, making it a good bet that the portion of global electricity provided by nuclear power will decline. More nations may decide to discontinue nuclear power after the recent Japanese disaster. Even if the United States did increase the use of nuclear power, it wouldn't help reduce U.S. dependence on foreign energy; about 83 percent of uranium for civilian nuclear reactors is imported from abroad.[22] The portion of world energy provided by hydropower will probably not grow because dams are expensive and most of the good sites in the industrial world are already taken.[23]

Since Nixon's presidency, hydrogen has been hyped as an emerging panacea to revolutionize energy.[24] But this hydrogen breakthrough never seems to happen.

Hydrogen works in fuel cells. These cells combine that substance with oxygen to create electric current to continuously recharge small batteries, but they emit only water vapor instead of greenhouse gases and pollutants. Even if a massive and costly infrastructure to fuel hydrogen cars were perfected, developed, and installed, however, the problem of where to get the substantial energy needed to break hydrogen away from other atoms would remain. Hydrogen does not exist by itself in nature and is usually attached to some other atoms—as in coal, oil, natural gas, or water. Processes needed to bust these molecules and release hydrogen are currently costly or environmentally dirty. Likely, either these processes or raw materials to use in them will require fossil fuels. Thus, autos using hydrogen would probably not emit greenhouse gases any less than gasoline-powered or hybrid-electric cars.

According to the National Academy of Sciences in 2004, "Although a transition to hydrogen could greatly transform the U.S. energy system in the long run, the impacts on oil imports and CO_2 emissions are likely to be minor during the next 25 years."[25] Hydrogen has a low energy content per unit of volume (unless pressurized or cooled), thus making it difficult to transport and use, and can be explosive when under pressure. The substance is expensive to store. Now fuel cell cars only last about thirty thousand miles.

In short, small fuel cells for cars are expensive to build and require a costly infrastructure to provide a high-priced fuel. Initially ebullient about new cars powered by fuel cells, most auto companies are now much more cautious about their potential.[26] Yet despite hydrogen's low potential for extensive use in the coming decades, George W. Bush diverted government energy research and development dollars into hydrogen.[27]

Past Government Failures in Alternative Fuels

Most of the many alternative energy sources are not now—and are unlikely to be in the foreseeable future—cost-effective when compared with oil. Many are not viable in the energy market, and the government has had a bad track record of picking technologies to give a "leg up," via subsidies, toward market viability. The government could potentially bet its subsidy money on the wrong technologies, thus wasting the private energy sector's valuable time and resources too by furthering its wild goose chases.

For example, producing ethanol from corn, which has been heavily subsidized by the government, will likely increase dependence on foreign oil, which the government is supposedly trying to reduce. Corn ethanol may generate more greenhouse gases than it alleviates by taking massive amounts of land from and destroying carbon dioxide–absorbing forests and by heavily using energy from fossil fuels to plant, fertilize, and harvest the corn and turn sugar into alcohol. (Corn ethanol is not even the best form of ethanol; although most certainly over-hyped, cellulosic ethanol from switchgrass, crop waste, or forest residue uses less fossil fuel but is more expensive to make and also uses massive amounts of land.) Taking cropland for corn ethanol raises food prices, uses much water, and generates a fuel that is more expensive than gasoline. Nevertheless, the U.S. Congress has mandated that corn ethanol replace a significant portion of the demand for gasoline, and the U.S. government provides huge subsidies and a protective tariff for the corn ethanol industry largely because of the political power of corn farmers.

Similarly, since the Ford administration in the mid-1970s, the federal government has provided huge subsidies for solar power but has seen only modest progress in this industry. Solar technology remains expensive (it costs many times what coal-generated electricity costs[28]), is intermittent (generated only when the sun shines), and takes up much space for the amount of power generated. Wind power is plentiful in the Midwest and along the coasts, and it too has received government subsidies. But wind power too is intermittent and expensive to generate via the construction of many windmills; they also take up much space for the amount of energy generated. Intermittency probably condemns solar and wind power to be niche players in the future energy outlook. If solar and wind projects were to forfeit their government subsidies, the present boom in bringing new equipment on line would stop; thus, most of the projects are not currently economically viable.[29]

Another example of government pressure to adopt economically nonviable technology was California's attempt to mandate in 1990 that car companies ultimately manufacture some zero emission cars—that is, vehicles that ran solely on battery power. In 2003, California had to back off on the requirement because consumers wouldn't accept the cars.[30] They had heavy, inefficient batteries that took a long time to recharge and offered only a tiny vehicle with a short driving range.[31]

Finally, the government has tried twice, once in the 1940s and once in the late 1970s, to subsidize the production of synthetic fuels—converting coal to liquid fuel (CTL). Although both of these efforts ended up in utter failure, the U.S. government, including the military, is once again subsidizing this failed technology. Even if the expensive technology eventually pans out, it would displace expensive—that is, domestically produced—oil first, not cheaper foreign oil, thus failing to achieve even the dubious goal of making the United States less dependent on foreign oil. In addition, as noted earlier, even without CTL, the U.S. military will likely never run short of fuel during a conflict because domestic petroleum production and the large reserves of near and friendly Canada are many times the needs of the military, even with two wars going on simultaneously. Finally, CTL will worsen global warming, because it produces twice the greenhouse gas emissions of oil.[32] Yet, even though CTL technology is expensive, unneeded by the military, unlikely to reduce dependence on foreign oil, hazardous to the environment, and a repeated failure, the government continues to waste money subsidizing it to satisfy domestic interest groups.

Therefore, the corn ethanol, solar, electric car, and CTL cases illustrate that when the government intervenes in the energy business, political considerations will always severely warp efforts to achieve foreign oil or energy independence or reduce global warming. Jay Hakes, former head of the Energy Information Administration, admits, "I hesitate to put major emphasis on big technology advances. They often fizzle out when confronted with the realities of energy markets. They can often distract attention away from more practical things we can do in the short run to implement the technologies we already have."[33] Unfortunately, most of these technological energy get-rich-quick schemes are funded by taxpayer dollars going to the most politically powerful industries, thus taking societal resources away from the more valuable incremental progress being made in private energy markets.

Why the United States Shouldn't Want Independence from Foreign Oil

Most economists consider protectionism—restricting the home market to imports—to be bad. Free trade is considered more efficient because each country sells what it is more relatively suited to produce. For some reason, government policy makers throw such principles out the window when it comes to energy or oil. What they don't tell the consumer is that energy, or even oil, independence will likely result in them paying more for these items—as they would if the country were to become entirely independent of foreign sources for any other product. The only way this would not happen is if the United States replaced oil imports with cheaper domestically produced alternative energy sources—unlikely because, as noted earlier, such sources tend to be more expensive than oil. According to a Congressional Research Service report in 2002, "If an energy independent U.S. no longer participated in the world market, prices would become less volatile but would likely be higher than at their current peak."[34]

Compared to the United States, a host of other countries produce cheaper oil. Many U.S. oil reserves are aging or located in areas with high costs of production (production costs usually range from $15 to $20 per barrel), compared to nations with fresher reserves or more easily accessible oil (for example, Saudi Arabia has a production cost of only $2 a barrel). Proponents of opening the Arctic National Wildlife Reserve (ANWR) in Alaska or the Atlantic, Pacific, and eastern Gulf coast continental shelves (85 percent of waters on America's coastlines[35]) for oil exploration and drilling don't tell the consumer that the oil price might increase if the government put tariffs or quotas on cheaper imports, as it did quotas from

1959 until the early 1970s, and such higher-cost domestic oil is substituted for them in order to reduce U.S. dependence on foreign sources. In an unfettered market for oil, however, any new significant source of U.S. production would lower the world price somewhat (assuming demand would be held constant), but some or all of ANWR or continental shelf oil could end up being exported, thereby eroding U.S. efforts to lessen dependence on foreign oil.

Also, becoming independent of oil from unstable or terror-sponsoring Persian Gulf nations could clash with measures adopted to counter global warming. If the United States signed up for any cap-and-trade regime to put an overall limit on carbon emissions, but allowed companies to trade carbon emission credits, neither ANWR oil—expensive to extract and refine—nor even sludgy Canadian oil—with hefty refining requirements that create quite a carbon signature—would be likely to pass muster. On the other hand, light Saudi crude—which is easily accessible, cheap, and doesn't require much refining—would thrive under such a system, thus increasing U.S. oil imports.[36] Thus, being independent of imported oil could be expensive and would probably not allow promulgation of a cap-and-trade system.

In the end, unless the government adopts protectionist measures to reduce U.S. dependence on foreign oil, Americans will end up paying the world price for oil, no matter how much America produces domestically or imports. To illustrate the effects of a world market for oil, consider the following: In summer 2000, British truckers went out on strike because of the high oil price. British independence from imports of foreign oil—because of British North Sea oil deposits—didn't insulate the truckers from the world oil price.[37]

Ironically, with all the talk about the desirability of oil and energy independence, the largest producer of oil and natural gas in the United States is British Petroleum (BP), the United Kingdom's largest corporation, which shows that independence is a chimera in a globally interwoven market for oil.

Importing Petroleum Isn't That Bad

Sometimes imported oil or petroleum products can be a godsend. In September 2005, gasoline prices in the eastern United States jumped because of a temporary loss of refining capacity due to Hurricane Katrina's devastation of the U.S. Gulf coast. In response, imports of refined gasoline into the United

States helped lower prices at the pump until the refining facilities again became operational. Thus, imports of foreign oil and oil products can help manage such supply "crises."[38]

The world market for such oil products is actually becoming more interdependent. Previously, crude oil was usually shipped by tanker and refined near where it was consumed. But now India, OPEC countries, and other nations are rapidly expanding their refining capacity. At the same time, for environmental and other reasons, U.S. refining capacity has been constrained. Thus, the United States will likely import more refined gasoline via tanker from overseas, even in normal times when natural disasters are not occurring.

Let's try a thought experiment. If one believes that the world's oil reserves are depleting rapidly, that demand for petroleum will be soaring under normal economic conditions (excluding economic recession, meltdown, or depression), that high and increasing oil prices will be a constant in the future, and that oil is a strategic commodity needed for national security, one should drop the goal of independence from foreign oil. Instead, one should adopt the "conservationist" view common in America during the 1940s and most of the 1950s.

Triggering this view was the spiked demand for petroleum during World War II, which depleted known U.S. oil reserves quickly and increased prices. The reasoning was that if oil would become more valuable in the future because it was needed for national security reasons or because depletion would make the price go ever higher, it would be better to import and use other countries' oil and save our own. In fact, beginning in 1950, to control Middle East oil during the Cold War, the U.S. government even formally encouraged increased dependence on foreign oil by allowing the big international oil companies to subtract from their domestic taxes royalty payments to foreign governments for oil, thus effectively taxing imported oil less than that produced domestically. But there were also countervailing pressures from the U.S. domestic oil industry. The government promotion of overseas dependence attenuated in 1959 when import quotas were placed on foreign oil to prop up the domestic oil industry.[39] Also, tax breaks for the domestic industry accelerated the depletion of U.S. reserves.[40]

It is curious that reasoning opposite the earlier "conservationist" view holds sway at the beginning of the twenty-first century, even though many people believe that rapidly depleting world reserves, rising world demand, and slower increases in new supplies will make the price of oil go ever higher. Becoming independent of foreign oil requires depleting U.S. oil and other sources of energy in order to avoid importing, and thus depleting, foreign sources of oil.

Of course, leaving all U.S. oil in the ground for a rainy day and importing 100 percent of our requirements in the meantime also would be ill advised. A technological breakthrough could occur, possibly driven by a major push against global warming, which drastically reduces the demand—and the price—for U.S. oil still in the ground. Vladimir Putin, the prime minister and most powerful leader in Russia, worries that such a breakthrough could lead to plummeting future oil and gas prices and wants Russia to pump all the oil it can now for this reason.

Besides, the United States consumes about a quarter of the world's oil, which gives it market power. Oil-producing companies and countries have learned—as they did the hard way after the 1973 Arab embargo and production cutbacks— that if supplies are too unreliable or prices spike too often, the United States could adopt conservation measures or alternatives that could permanently lower the demand for their product.

This analysis takes us back to the best option for the U.S. and other governments to follow: allow the free market to set oil prices and the amount imported from other nations. As the last chapter showed, throughout the history of the oil industry, gloom-and-doom predictions about rising demand and dwindling supplies have always been proved wrong by new discoveries and technological advances making previously uneconomical deposits extractable. At the beginning of the twenty-first century, the narrative is familiar: increasing demand from China, India, and other developing countries will exceed slowing new discoveries. But in the past, as the oil market tightened and prices rose, the market naturally made the export of oil more profitable, which in turn triggered exploration for new deposits in harder-to-reach regions using newer technologies. For example, only at high prices are the oil sands of Canada economical to develop. Similarly, deposits under the Arctic ice cap could make up 25 percent of the undiscovered global oil and gas reserves; ironically, the melting of those caps from global warming could provide access to more carbon-emitting petroleum.[41]

As noted earlier, even in the event that the world finally physically runs out of oil (a dubious proposition given the vastness of the sparsely explored oceans and the tar sands and oil shale on land), the transitions from wood to coal and whale oil to kerosene show that the unfettered market is the best mechanism for such a transition. But what about market volatility? Being independent of oil would insulate the United States from gyrating oil markets. The markets for many commodities are volatile, but that's why futures markets were invented. Futures markets allow consumers and producers to lock in a certain future price in a volatile market. The NYMEX oil futures market made its debut in 1983 and revolutionized the oil market—mitigating the volatility problem and taking away the price setting mechanism from OPEC.

The Council on Foreign Relations, in 2006, best summarized clear thinking on energy independence:

> The voices that espouse "energy independence" are doing the nation a disservice by focusing on a goal that is unachievable over the foreseeable future and that encourages the adoption of inefficient and counterproductive policies.[42]

Myth 7

Oil Price Spikes Cause Economic Catastrophes

MOST BASIC oil price spikes—such as those in 1973, 1979–1980, and after the turn of the twenty-first century—are rarities in history. But it is human nature to remember and give more importance than warranted to such abnormal and spectacular events.

The myth that such oil shocks cause economic mayhem stems from the stagflation that followed 1973 oil embargo and production cutback. As noted earlier, however, other factors were responsible for this bout of simultaneous inflation and recession. To state it again, inflation—defined as increases in the general price level in the economy—is not caused by increases in the price of any one item, such as oil or gasoline. Increases in the price of one item mean that people have less to spend on all other items, thus lowering prices for those other items and putting offsetting downward pressure on the overall price level. Only when the government increases the money supply in the economy can people spend more money simultaneously on oil or gasoline and on other items too.[1] Thus, only increases in the money supply can cause general price inflation.

The stagflation of the 1970s was caused by the Vietnam War and by increases in the monetary supply by Richard Nixon (who wanted to pump up the economy artificially to get re-elected in 1972) and Jimmy Carter early in his presidency (in an attempt to buffer the economy from the oil price shocks of the 1970s). Carter eventually appointed Paul Volcker as chairman of the Federal Reserve and supported his bold bid to tame inflation. Although there was a recession in 1981 and 1982 after the oil price spike in 1979 and 1980 from the Iranian revolution, the economic downturn was not caused by the price spike. The economic downturn was caused by Volcker's "monetarist experiment" to drive the inflation out of the economy by tightening the money supply. After 1982, with inflation under control, the economy prospered until the early 1990s.[2]

In 1997, Ben Bernanke, before becoming chairman of the Federal Reserve Board, and his cohorts confirmed that the oil shocks were not the cause of the economic maladies of the 1970s. He concluded that the response of the monetary authorities to the oil price spikes had a larger negative impact than the price rises.[3] A study by two economists—Karsten Jeske, one of his colleagues from the Fed, and Rajeev Dhawan of Georgia State University—added that price controls also added to the stagflation because they misallocated goods, such as gasoline, and wasted the time of those who lined up for them.[4]

More recently, some have alleged that high oil prices caused the global economic meltdown. But oil prices had been increasing since the beginning of the first decade of the twenty-first century. A mild recession occurred in 2000 and 2001 after the dot-com and NASDAQ market crashes in 2000. The massive economic meltdown occurred only in late 2007, after years of substantial economic growth despite rapidly increasing oil prices.[5] The earlier, mild recession of 2000–2001 was caused by Fed Chairman Alan Greenspan's monetary expansion from 1995 to 1999, which led to the dot-com bubble in the first place. The huge 2007 meltdown occurred because Greenspan refused to let the 2000–2001 recession take its course—instead re-inflating the money supply even before 9/11 and continuing thereafter. The significant monetary expansion overinflated the already large housing sector of the U.S. economy and created a bubble, which eventually burst.[6] In short, excessive monetary expansion caused both recessions in the new millennium, as it normally does, and oil price increases had nothing to do with either of them.

Ben Bernanke, who took over from Greenspan, then made the same mistake and refused to let the significant economic downturn in late 2007 take its course; he re-inflated the economy, which will probably create a future bubble that will burst. Hopefully, government officials will not be able to blame this future economic calamity on high oil prices, when culpability should rest on their own irresponsible monetary expansion.

19

Myth 8

U.S. Policy Is to Maintain the Flow of Oil at the Lowest Possible Price

AS TECHNOLOGY HAS marched on, the real price of most raw materials, over the long term, has declined.[1] Oil is no exception. But a lower oil price is not always the U.S. government's goal.

When the price of oil is high, the U.S. government does try to put pressure on producing countries—especially OPEC and friendly Persian Gulf oil producers—to produce more and lower it. The government, however, does not want the price to go too low. Again, from 1959 to 1971, the U.S. government imposed controls on imported oil to raise the price of oil for domestic producers—a huge subsidy. Earlier, the Texas Railroad Commission and other state regulatory commissions formed a cartel that restricted and allocated production to try to keep the domestic price of oil higher than market prices.[2] The federal government attempted to aid and abet this cartel. In the early 1970s, when the Nixon administration imposed price controls on the U.S. economy—including the price of oil—the U.S. domestic oil price went from being artificially high to artificially low.[3] In the 1980s, the oil price went so low that, to help the U.S. domestic petroleum industry under the usual guise of national security, then–Vice President George H. W. Bush, deviating from the official Reagan administration free-market rhetoric, went to Saudi Arabia and urged the Saudis to help prop up the price.

The U.S. government regularly imposes import bans on oil from unfriendly producing nations. For example, Libya and Iran have experienced decades of U.S. sanctions on their oil exports. To protest Sudan's human rights record, the United States encouraged international sanctions on its oil exports. These embargoes do marginally increase the price of oil to the U.S. consumer. Slyly, however, the U.S. government knows that it can ban oil imports from any "nefarious evil-doing" country with only a marginal effect on the worldwide market. The market simply reorders, but is a little less efficient—because of slightly increased transportation costs. The overall effect on price is small, however, as long as the sanctioned country sells its oil into the world market somewhere, even if not to the United States.

The only sanctions that really bite are bans on U.S. and foreign investment in such unfriendly oil-producing nations. For example, since 1995, U.S. firms have been banned from investing in Iran; since 1996, the United States has imposed extra-territorial sanctions on foreign firms that invest in Iranian energy projects (Iran-Libya Sanctions Act). The former has deterred U.S. investment in Iran's oil industry and the latter has deterred foreign investment in that business. Thus, because Iran has trouble getting the latest Western oil technology, its production has stagnated—thus raising the world oil price.

In addition, the United States has had chronically bad relations with Russia, Iraq, and Venezuela—all major oil producers.[4] In the most bizarre policy of all, after Saddam Hussein invaded Kuwait, the United States went to war with Iraq to safeguard Persian Gulf oil supplies, according to then-President George H. W. Bush. Yet, before doing so, the first thing Bush did was to lead a comprehensive international ban on trade with Iraq, including that country's principal export—oil. Because enough countries adopted the embargo (unlike the cases mentioned above), Iraq found it difficult to sell its oil anywhere, except through black market channels. As noted in Chapter 10, more oil was removed from the world market by sanctions and the destruction of oil infrastructure during that war than Saddam would have likely taken off the market if he had invaded and occupied Saudi Arabia and the United Arab Emirates in addition to Kuwait. Thus U.S. government policies that were supposed to safeguard oil supplies and keep the price down did just the opposite.

20

Myth 9

*Possession of Oil Means
Economic and Political Power*

POST–WORLD WAR II Japan and Europe (especially Germany)
and the Asian Tigers (Singapore, Hong Kong, Taiwan, and South Korea) grew
into wealthy countries while possessing little or no oil. The U.S. position as a
supplier in the oil market has been in relative decline since the late 1800s, but
during that same period it grew into a world power.

In contrast, the political and economic power of OPEC countries, which
produce a sizeable chunk of the world's oil supply, peak only when the international oil market is tight and prices are high. Even this influence has been
based largely on OPEC's ability to fool policymakers in oil-consuming countries—who often appear surprisingly ignorant of the way the world's energy
markets actually work—into believing that the cartel created the tight market
conditions and can control the long-term price of petroleum significantly above
what the market will bear. Few in the public and in policymaking circles seem
to focus on OPEC's inability to do either. Yet, the same problem has afflicted
prior oil cartels, such as the Seven Sisters and the Texas Railroad Commission,
and cartels for other commodities. Since long-term price support is the very
purpose of a cartel, OPEC has been a flop.

The reason for OPEC's failure is very simple. Oil is a profitable commodity
to sell, and most of OPEC's members are heavily dependent on oil exports to
earn foreign exchange. For example, Saudi Arabia, Iran, and Nigeria rely on
oil for 90 percent of their export revenues, and 75 to 80 percent of Venezuela's
export earnings come from petroleum.[1] Such percentages for these and other
OPEC members dwarf the much smaller percent of U.S. imports accounted
for by oil—about 13 percent. By this standard, OPEC countries are more de-

pendent on the United States to buy their product than the United States is dependent on them to sell it. Thus, the largest petroleum buyer in the world has some market power.

What about oil-driven sovereign wealth funds? Do they pose an economic or security threat to the United States? Sovereign wealth funds are investment funds owned by governments. Sovereign wealth funds from petro-states do invest in the United States, but the real issue is whether such investments bring undue influence in the United States, not whether their funding comes from oil profits. Investment by foreign governments is good for the U.S. economy but does garner some influence in the United States for those governments; however, the net effect is positive. The larger question is not whether the United States should restrict investments by sovereign wealth funds (it should not) but whether the governments operating these funds are taking up productive capital in inefficient and distorting investment mechanisms (they are). They should return such resources to their people, but that is not the United States' problem. Thus, investments in the United States by oil-driven sovereign wealth funds are little threat to U.S. security and benefit the U.S. economy.

21

Myth 10

The United States Must Defend
Autocratic Saudi Arabia Because of Oil

EVER SINCE 1950, the United States has explicitly pledged to defend Saudi Arabia in exchange for oil (an implicit security guarantee preceded this during Franklin Delano Roosevelt's administration). According to Rachel Bronson in *Thicker Than Oil: America's Uneasy Partnership with Saudi Arabia,* since the mid-1970s and the Arab oil embargo, the desert kingdom has maintained the flow of oil at reasonable prices, especially in crisis periods, to stabilize the price.[1] Incredibly, she notes as an example that after 9/11, the Saudis sold more oil to the United States to keep the oil price down.[2] Yet, fifteen of the nineteen hijackers on 9/11 were Saudis; the leader of al Qaeda was a Saudi; the Saudi government and private Saudi money have funded radical mosques, schools, and charities in many Islamic nations and in Saudi Arabia; Saudi private citizens and maybe even the Saudi government have funded militant Islamist terrorists groups; members of the Saudi royal family contributed to charities linked to al Qaeda; the Saudi government was never very enthusiastic about cracking down on the charities or the militants until Saudi Arabia itself became a target of terrorist attacks in 2003; and the Saudis have one of the worst human rights records on the planet (they didn't even abolish slavery until the early 1960s[3]).

Given these facts, increasing the oil flow after 9/11 seems like the least the Saudis could have done. Furthermore, the original reasons Osama bin Laden and al Qaeda began attacking the United States were its maintenance of a military presence in Saudi Arabia long after the first Gulf War had ended and U.S. support for the Saudi monarchy, which is corrupt in bin Laden's (and many other people's) eyes.

All of this may be true, but the conventional wisdom is that the United States must still coddle Saudi Arabia for several reasons: it is the largest net oil exporter on the planet (its share of world production is 13 percent, exporting the vast majority of it); accounts for about 20 percent of the world's proved reserves; produces low-cost, high-quality oil; and is OPEC's swing producer—possessing 85 percent of OPEC's spare capacity—which can ramp up production during a crisis. The conventional wisdom somehow also believes that the United States gets most of its imported oil from Saudi Arabia, when the actual figure is only 18 percent.[4]

As energy journalist Paul Roberts has summarized,

> Whereas the United States might otherwise regard Saudi Arabia, with its anti-Western attitudes and its links to terrorist elements, as a legitimate political enemy, the kingdom's vast oil reserves and especially its enormous surplus capacity have for decades ensured that Washington would overlook such criminal behavior. As one political analyst told me, "the fact that a U.S. president can call up the Saudis and say 'something major is going to happen tomorrow and we desperately need you to pump more oil to reassure the market' has given the Saudis a level of access in Washington that is pretty much unparalleled."[5]

The conventional wisdom ignores several facts. Usually, the something that is happening is an unnecessary U.S. military intervention in the Middle East—for example, both the first and second Gulf wars—in order to "secure" oil supplies. The fact that Saudi Arabia has to be asked to pump more oil indicates that most U.S. military interventions in the regions do quite the opposite.

Another fact, mentioned in more detail earlier, was economist David Henderson's analysis before the first Gulf War that if an aggressive Persian Gulf nation (in his analysis, Saddam Hussein's Iraq) overran the oil producing nations of Saudi Arabia, Kuwait, and the United Arab Emirates, its increased market power would allow production cuts to increase prices that would be equivalent to only less than half of one percent of U.S. GDP. This extreme case demonstrates that oil is a valuable commodity and that whoever owns it has an incentive to sell more into the world market when the price has gone up for economic or political reasons.

It is no different for Saudi Arabia; the country has little else to export to earn foreign hard currency. Oil sales represent roughly 90 percent of Saudi Arabia's export earnings.[6] What is left unsaid is that every crisis (in the Persian Gulf or otherwise) that raises the world oil price gives Saudi Arabia and all other producers an incentive to increase production and exports. Oil is no different from any other product—people can't earn revenues if they don't sell it. The Saudis and the others are not doing this as a favor to the United States or out of altruism; they are doing it out of the self-interest of augmenting their revenues. Furthermore, the Saudis have other incentives to keep the price of oil within reasonable bounds. Having the most petroleum reserves of any nation on the planet makes the Saudis especially vulnerable to long-term price-induced conservation or movement to alternative fuels, which could render their large oil reserves in the ground less valuable.

The biggest threat to the export of Saudi oil has never been takeover by a foreign power, which would likely sell the oil anyway. The most likely threat is an overthrow of the monarchy by ideological radical Islamists, who might rather stick it to the United States and the West than earn the revenues from the oil. But even this threat is overstated. In the case of Iran, after the initial supply disruptions and price increases caused by the Iranian revolution, the fundamentalist Islamic regime there has continued to sell oil into the world market. Such action is all that is needed to avoid major price spikes for U.S. oil imports. Any cutoff of oil to the world by a new Islamist regime in Saudi Arabia would likely be short-lived, because the new regime would undoubtedly be weak and need all the revenue it could get.

At any rate, in addition to the ill effects of a fundamentalist Islamist takeover of the Saudi oil fields being overstated, one of the major causes of such a takeover would probably be the Saudi regime's client status vis-à-vis the United States. The Saudi government realized this threat to its regime when it asked the U.S. to end its military presence their shortly before the U.S. invasion of Iraq in 2003 (replacing Saudi bases with Iraqi bases may have been one of the Bush administration's goals for invading Iraq in the first place). Nevertheless, Al Qaeda keeps attacking the United States because of its continued support of the Saudi monarchy and military presence in other Persian Gulf nations.

Ironically, because Saudi oil normally will be very likely to flow to the world market for economic reasons, U.S. military presence in the kingdom's vicinity merely increases the main threat to Saudi oil exports (if there is any at all)—that is, the U.S. presence fuels Islamist militancy in and around the Persian Gulf. So a U.S. military that is supposed to protect American oil supplies merely protects the despotic Saudi monarchy and likely increases any threat to such Saudi exports.

Finally, with the Cold War long over, the United States need not cultivate the religiously legitimated monarchy, or condone its global export of radical Islamist ideology as a bulwark against communism. That does not mean that the United States should shun Saudi oil or try to undermine or overtly or covertly overthrow the monarchy. But neither does it mean that the United States has to continue to overlook the monarchy's direct or indirect support of Islamist militancy or terrorism simply because the kingdom is the global leader in net oil exports. Once again, markets do work, and Saudi oil will likely be exported no matter what, merely because it is a valuable commodity to sell.

22

Myth 11

*Dependence of Europe on Russian Energy
Is a Threat to U.S. Security*

THE UNITED STATES worries needlessly about Europe's dependence on Russian energy. This one-dimensional view is skewed.

Of particular U.S. concern, Russia provides about a quarter of Europe's natural gas.[1] Russian gas flows through an extensive pipeline system that links Western Europe with natural gas from Russia, Central Asia, Algeria, and the North Sea. Both the Soviet Union and Russia have stopped or reduced energy exports when countries have opposed their political and economic policies— usually to small, relatively poor countries in their traditional sphere of influence that didn't pay market prices anyway. For example, petroleum exports were stopped to Yugoslavia under Tito, Finland in 1958, China in 1959, Latvia in 1990, Lithuania in 1990 and 2006, and Estonia in 2007. Putin's Russia has cut off or curtailed natural gas exports to Ukraine, Belarus, Georgia, Moldova, and Bosnia. In fact, according Andrew E. Kramer in the *New York Times,* a research organization linked to the Swedish Ministry of Defense counted fifty-five politically induced supply disruptions to Eastern European nations since the end of the Cold War.[2]

Political shenanigans, however, can be a two-way street. Russian energy moves to Western Europe through pipelines in Ukraine and Belarus, and they have cut off or threatened to halt the flow in the past or diverted West European customers' energy for their own use. However, the new Nord Stream and South Stream pipelines—traversing from Russia directly to Western Europe, bypassing Eastern Europe using northerly and southerly routes, respectively—may make the political manipulation of supplies more of a one-way (Russian) street. The fear among Eastern European nations is that Russia could then just shut off pipelines to Eastern Europe to attempt to control its "sphere of influence," with little effect on supplies to Western Europe.[3]

What remains unsaid, however, is that supplies to most wealthy Western European countries have never been cut off or reduced.[4] This restraint is perhaps because energy is valuable, pipelines are expensive to build and operate, and Russia is heavily dependent on the hard currency revenues it gets from such big, politically and economically powerful customers (such as Germany) that pay market prices (which former Soviet republics and allies usually don't). Energy is critical for Russia's economy and accounts for 55 to 65 percent of its exports, 40 percent of its government revenues, and 30 percent of its GDP. Historically, changes in Russian GDP are almost completely dependent on changes in Russian oil production.[5] Furthermore, if the Russians cut off gas supplies to Western Europe, the Western Europeans could retaliate by pulling vital investments out of Russia—a threat that former Soviet nations and Eastern European countries cannot wield as effectively as a potential weapon.

Also, any time Russia cuts off or diminishes oil or gas supplies to a country for political reasons, it gets the reputation of being an unreliable supplier—as Arab OPEC did after the 1973 oil embargo and production cutbacks—which could cause its customers to seek alternative suppliers, pipeline routes, or fuels or to permanently reduce consumption by instituting conservation measures. Much to Russia's disappointment, the European Union has diversified its fuel sources, and some countries have cooperated to compete with the attempted Russian pipeline monopoly.

Even if some probability exists that Russia will cut off or reduce gas supplies to Eastern Europe (plausible) or Western Europe (negligible), this threat should not affect core U.S. security interests. As during the Cold War, the United States continues to worry about potential adversaries of regional allies more than the allies do. I guess that's what empires—even informal ones—do.

The United States Has Little Dependence on Russian Energy

The United States itself depends very little on Russian oil and gas. Although Russia has always been one of the largest oil producers, it consumes a significant part of its production, thus lowering its net exports into the world market. Also, a world market for oil exists, and so it matters little who sells to whom as long as the producers sell it into the market—which they are likely to do for substantial revenues. In fact, the Soviet Union and now Russia have never joined OPEC because they want to avoid restrictions on their production and because they have often enjoyed undercutting the OPEC price to earn more revenues. Even during the Cold War, the United States didn't mind becoming dependent on the United States' foremost adversary for oil supplies. One then has to wonder, now that the Cold War is long over, why the United States so fears the amorphous "dependence on foreign oil" or that its allies will be dependent on Russian energy.

With the current state of technology and the physical properties of natural gas, no world market exists. Unlike oil—which is easily transported from one part of the world to another in its existing liquid state via tanker—natural gas must first be frozen, and thus liquefied, before it can be transported by specially built tankers; it is then turned back into gaseous form upon reaching its destination. These processes are expensive (but not totally cost prohibitive) and are only done when long-term contracts for gas can be signed. So the world's natural gas markets remain regional ones that can be reached primarily via pipelines traversing land.

Although Russia has the largest natural gas reserves in the world (27–28 percent of the global total), the United States also has large natural gas reserves and produces 84 percent of the gas it consumes. It adds to this domestic supply with imports, via pipeline, from Canada—another 15 percent of U.S. consumption.[6] So it is unlikely that the United States will ever be as directly dependent on Russia for energy as are the Europeans.

Thus, although little threat to U.S. security exists from European dependence on Russian energy, and the United States has little direct dependence on Russian energy, U.S. hand wringing continues to this day. This angst is evidenced by the uneconomic U.S. governmental jockeying to compete in the Russian sphere of influence over oil and gas pipeline routes to Europe through the Caucuses and Central Asia.[7]

The United States started the competition in the mid-1990s to make political and military inroads into the traditional Russian sphere of influence in Central Asia and the Caucuses around the hydrocarbon-rich Caspian Sea, hoping to pave the way for U.S. energy firms to invest in those regions—a classic case of mercantilism. The United States originally thought that Caspian Sea oil could lessen U.S. dependence on the Persian Gulf, but the Caspian basin has not yet met those high expectations.

In 1997, Sheila Heslin of the National Security Council staff admitted that the United States was trying to build new pipelines from the Caucuses to the Black Sea and Turkey to foil the Russian monopoly on energy transportation in that area. The United States was trying to counter the political influence that the pipelines gave Russia over nations of the Caucuses and Central Asia, which transport their gas to Europe via those Russian routes. As then–U.S. Energy Secretary Bill Richardson stated, "It's . . . about preventing strategic inroads by those who don't share our values."[8] (This also included Iran.) So even before Vladimir Putin took power in Russia, the United States seemed to be pursuing a new Cold War Lite policy toward that nation, never really being serious about integrating it into a post-Cold War Europe.

As oil prices went back up in the new millennium after they were in the doldrums during the 1980s and 1990s and Russia became more assertive under Putin, he pushed back and tried to nix U.S. attempts at alternative pipelines. Russia was also incensed that U.S. military forces remained in Kyrgyzstan and Uzbekistan after the Taliban government was ousted from power in Afghanistan. In response, Russia has augmented its military presence in the Caspian region too.[9] The Russians showed that local military superiority can trump even a superpower. Their attack on Georgia, after a Georgian provocation, threatened the U.S.-sponsored Baku-Tbilisi-Ceyhan (BTC) pipeline and left the faraway United States bereft of options to help out its reckless Georgian ally.

The U.S. government should stop interfering with where oil and gas markets would naturally route pipelines—probably through Russia and Iran. If the Russian government wants to create self-inflicted wounds by meddling, through military presence or intimidation, in its neighborhood's market and by an inefficient maintenance of a state monopoly on pipelines, at least the U.S. government would not be wasting U.S. taxpayer dollars engaged in a competing fiasco halfway around the world.

Self-inflicted inefficiency was also evident in Putin's effective renationalizing of the Russian energy sector after it was initially privatized and taken from the clutches of the Soviet communists. Putin realized that even after the fall of the Soviet Union, Russia had few business prospects other than energy and minerals, and he wanted government control, one way or the other, of those perceived vital sectors. Additionally, after both the 1917 revolution and the 1991 collapse of the Soviet Union, Russia and its energy industries were weak and required assistance from foreign companies to drill in extreme circumstances, but then found excuses to pull the plug on the companies once the nation recovered economically.[10] Putin's economically dubious actions parallel the nationalization of the oil sector in developing nations.

PART III

No Need to Use Military Power to Safeguard Foreign Oil

23

Safeguarding Oil with Military Power Is Mercantilism and Imperialism

CONTRARY TO CONVENTIONAL wisdom, the case has been rendered that oil is no different than any other product and is therefore not "strategic" to the U.S. economy. Also, the argument has been made that there exists a global and relatively free oil market, which will provide petroleum at the cheapest prices possible, making oil independence inefficient, expensive, and even undesirable.

If U.S. politicians, however, abandon their popular pledge to achieve "energy security" and thus independence from foreign oil—which has never come remotely close to being fulfilled since Richard Nixon first enunciated it in the 1970s—and adopt the more feasible, desirable, and honest policy of simply relying on the efficient global oil market to provide petroleum, a new question might arise. People might ask, "If the nation's policy is to rely on the world market to bring us shipments of oil from foreign suppliers, don't we need the U.S. military in the Persian Gulf even more than ever to safeguard those supplies?" After all, almost every other nation tries to safeguard its supply of energy.

Although this question is a good one, it is predicated on assumptions—that oil is strategic to the U.S. economy and that the nation's economic health would be significantly harmed by a supply disruption or high oil prices—that were refuted in earlier chapters. As noted there, the global market for oil ensures that any supply disruption—even if an embargo is directed at particular countries—will be dissipated around the world and merely result in higher prices. Furthermore, industrial economies are able to weather periodic high fuel prices, just as they weather episodic elevated prices for other vital products, such as imported semiconductors.

One other questionable assumption is that oil can be defended through military means. Defending oil is not easy because a lot of parties need to cooperate to get it extracted out of the ground, transported through pipelines, loaded on to tankers, transported to the safety of the open seas, refined, and distributed to customers. At any one point in that chain, some uncooperative party could potentially stop oil's flow. Because of the difficulty of providing the promised defenses of Saudi petroleum during the Cold War, the United States made plans to destroy the oil fields so that they wouldn't fall into the hands of any Soviet invaders. During the Iran-Iraq War of the 1980s, offshore oil platforms, oil-loading facilities, and tankers were all attacked. During the first Gulf War, Saddam Hussein, on his way out of Kuwait with the victorious U.S. military standing idly by, torched the Kuwaiti oil wells. During the recent guerrilla war that followed the U.S. invasion of Iraq, explosions repeatedly shut down Iraqi oil pipelines even though they were being guarded by the most powerful military in the world. In short, war rarely secures oil, and often does quite the opposite.

And as Michael T. Klare points out in *Blood and Oil,*

> Notwithstanding the many American troops now deployed in Centcom's AOR (Area of Responsibility) and the many battles they have fought and won, the area is no more stable today than it was in January 1980, when President Carter issued his proclamation [the Carter Doctrine].[1]

In fact, in the aftermath of the U.S. invasion of Iraq—when Iraqi oil production plunged below prewar levels, stayed there for a long time, and surrounding oil producing nations were destabilized—one could argue that using U.S. military power often is counterproductive to the free flow of oil.

When critics of the oil companies justifiably rail against U.S. government subsidies for "Big Oil," they usually mean favorable regulations and tax loopholes that other industries don't get. Throughout history, these have included sweet leasing terms to explore for and produce oil on public lands; generous oil depletion allowances that reduce taxes on every barrel produced; tax deductions for intangible drilling costs, such as labor, supplies, materials, and repairs; tax write-offs at home for taxes paid by U.S. transnational oil firms to overseas governments (really taxpayer subsidized oil investments in other countries); periodic exemptions from antitrust laws; and special import quotas and production allocations for domestic producers (a government-sponsored cartel).

The critics, however, usually forget about using the U.S. military abroad to safeguard oil flows and allegedly reduce instability and conflict in oil-producing regions of the world. This hidden subsidy distorts the free market for oil and may be at times counterproductive to those goals.

The Persian Gulf

Consumers periodically grouse about the high price of gasoline at the pump, but if this unneeded government subsidy to defend Persian Gulf crude were included therein, it would be higher still—just as it would be if other external costs, such as traffic congestion and environmental degradation, were included. One estimate suggests that the hidden cost of the U.S. military presence in the Persian Gulf, which has grown to massive proportions over the years, would add $5 to the price at the pump for every gallon of imported gasoline.[2]

According to Set America Free, an organization advocating independence from foreign oil, the yearly cost of using the U.S. military to "protect" Persian Gulf oil is $137 billion.[3] By my crude estimate, the United States has been spending more than $334 billion per year (in 2009 dollars) on military forces to be used in the Persian Gulf. Even the former figure is more than four times the approximately $32.6 billion in annual U.S. oil imports from that region, which normally account for only about a quarter of all American imported oil and only about 11 percent of U.S. petroleum consumption. (The top five sellers of oil to the United States are Canada, Mexico, Nigeria, Venezuela, and Saudi Arabia.[4]) My figure is more than ten times the value of U.S. annual oil imports from the Gulf.[5] In short, the societal costs of oil could be reduced if these unnecessary military costs are eliminated.

In the Gulf, the United States has military bases or facilities in Oman, Bahrain, Qatar, Kuwait, the United Arab Emirates, and Iraq. The U.S. had military installations in Saudi Arabia until shortly before the invasion of Iraq. Nearby, U.S. bases or installations are in Egypt, Djibouti, Turkey, Afghanistan, Pakistan, and Diego Garcia in the Indian Ocean.[6] Thus, the United States spends exorbitantly more on safeguarding Persian Gulf than it does on any other expenditure related to energy.[7]

This massive military spending is a subsidy to U.S. oil companies, petroleum-producing nations friendly toward the United States, and oil-consuming nations in Europe and East Asia, which consume much more Persian Gulf oil than the United States (Europe gets 17 percent of its oil from the Gulf and

Japan gets 78 percent from there) and are the United States' primary industrialized economic competitors. But strangely, these allied consuming nations don't see any need to spend money and lives defending their oil imports from the Gulf.

In addition to helping out with the war in Afghanistan, new U.S. bases (since 2001) in Kyrgyzstan and Tajikistan are near the oil-rich Caspian Sea basin, where Kazakhstan and Azerbaijan are the biggest oil producers. The U.S. also had a new military installation in Uzbekistan but has since been kicked out. As American firms won major oil deals with Kazakhstan and Azerbaijan, U.S. arms, aid, advisors, and military training followed to these countries and Georgia (a major pipeline transits Georgian territory).

In the economic realm, to counter the Russian monopoly on energy pipelines running from the Caspian Sea, the United States pushed the construction of an inefficient oil pipeline that went through Azerbaijan, Georgia, and ended in a Turkish port on the Mediterranean. The only purpose was to bypass alternative routes through Russia and Iran, which were more economically reasonable paths for any pipeline but went through potentially adversarial states. In addition to being inefficient, the new pipeline ran close to multiple zones of conflict—Nagorno-Krabakh, Adzharia, Chechnya, Abkhazia, and South Ossetia.[8] This brief Russian war with Georgia threatened the pipeline in that country. So the U.S. government's interference with the market may not have achieved a better outcome.

The reason for all this U.S. government-directed activity: Although most non-OPEC oil production is declining, the most promising areas for oil exploration and production are in Russia, the Caspian Sea (but so far, this area has been disappointing), and West Africa.

West Africa

The United States is building up its military presence in West Africa. The U.S. military's new Africa Command has been set up mainly to safeguard supplies of oil from West Africa. Africa has 10 percent of the world's oil. Between 2000 and 2007, U.S. petroleum imports from Africa increased 65 percent, according to the U.S. Department of Energy. African countries raised their share of U.S. worldwide imports from 14.5 to 20 percent. Nigeria, the leading African oil producer, regularly experiences violence against oil facilities from those who have received few benefits from the profits. Angola, which has had problems with stability in the past, is another major West African producer. Not coincidentally, Nigeria and Angola are the two nations getting the greatest amounts of U.S. security assistance in West Africa.

According to General Charles Ward, then-deputy commander of U.S. forces in Europe, "a key mission for U.S. forces [in Africa] would be to insure that Nigeria's oil fields, which in the future could account for as much as 25 percent of all U.S. oil imports, are secure." The United States wants to establish a presence for the new command somewhere on the African continent, but the exact location hasn't yet been decided. General James Jones, then the U.S. European commander, said that the U.S. Navy's carrier battle groups would shorten their time in the Mediterranean Sea and spend half their time patrolling down the west coast to Africa.

In U.S. defense planning, Africa had long been the only place in the world that was not regarded as strategic to the United States. Obviously, as the U.S. military is being transformed into a protection force to safeguard oil supplies, that idea is changing.

Latin America

The United States is also building up its military presence in Latin America. Venezuela and Mexico are two of the top sellers of oil to the United States. Colombia is also a significant exporter to the United States, but has the potential to sell much more if violence attenuated and more exploration could be done. In addition, the U.S. has expanded its military involvement there past countering drugs and is training and equipping Colombian Army units to guard a key oil pipeline from guerilla attacks. In the spring of 2003, U.S. Special Forces apparently were sent to Colombia to rescue Occidental Oil's pipeline (running from the oil fields to the coast) from attacks by indigenous insurgents.[9] Brazil has recently discovered major oil deposits. Among their other functions, U.S. military bases in Puerto Rico, El Salvador, Curaçao, and Aruba help deter alleged nefarious evildoers (whoever they may be) from creating mischief in the Caribbean/Central American region and thus indirectly protect oil. Such dissuasion could include deterring the virulently anti-U.S. president of Venezuela, Hugo Chávez, who has caused political instability there, and persuading him to keep the oil spigot open to the U.S. (which he would likely do anyway because of his need for cash).

The Caspian Sea and Pacific

The U.S. European Command is training local forces to protect the Baku-Tbilisi-Ceyhan pipeline that runs through unstable Georgia, while the U.S. Pacific Command is using naval patrols to guard tanker routes in the western Pacific, South China Sea, and Indian Ocean from other nations, pirates, and terrorists—especially in the Strait of Malacca.

Conclusion

In other words, before the Cold War ended, and more so after it did, U.S. military deployments have followed the flow of oil. Deployments to safeguard oil have moved beyond the Persian Gulf into these other regions. Michael T. Klare correctly concluded that, "Slowly but surely, the U.S. military is being converted into a global oil-protection service," which protects oil fields and the routes of supply that connect them to the U.S. and its allies. He also noted that oil protection is being conflated with the war on terrorism—aforementioned examples are U.S. involvement in West Africa, Colombia, Georgia, and the Strait of Malacca.[10]

Buying Oil Is Cheaper Than Stealing It

The rationale for this expanded military role in protecting oil, gas, and pipelines is that Kazakhstan, Azerbaijan, Georgia, Nigeria, Angola, Colombia, Venezuela, and even Mexico are no more stable than the Persian Gulf nations. And the Bush administration had encouraged all of these nations, along with Russia, to increase their oil production as an alternative to Persian Gulf oil.

Yet the real reason for the expanded military role may be that the Cold War has been over for some time, and the U.S. military needs something to do to justify and retain the excessively massive budgets that it now enjoys.

Instead, relying on the market to deliver petroleum at the best price would mean that a supply disruption from any supplier would result in increased production by other suppliers and a rerouting of supplies. American consumers might have to pay a higher price until the disruption has passed; but this is still cheaper than funding a massive U.S. military that may actually disrupt supplies by fighting unneeded wars or by its inflammatory overseas bases causing internal upheaval in oil-producing regions.

Using U.S. military power to safeguard oil is a form of mercantilism, which is merely government subsidies and assistance to favored private companies. Like the colonial powers of the eighteenth and nineteenth centuries, which vied for tea, sugar, gold, and slaves overseas, the Western oil imperialists—the industrial powers of the twentieth and twenty-first centuries, including the Americans, the British, the French, and the Imperial Japanese—have competed for oil and even redrawn the map in the Middle East to grab it.[11]

This mercantilism is especially pronounced in the Persian Gulf. Of course, some will argue, however, that because a world market for oil exists, U.S. forces are really safeguarding the largest oil reserves on the planet for all consuming nations; as noted earlier, the U.S. gets only about a tenth of its oil from the Gulf. Yet, about 56 percent of the world's reserves are in the Gulf.[12] After all, the argument goes, as non-OPEC sources (for example, in Alaska, Canada, Mexico, Nigeria, and in the North Sea) peak before OPEC, the world will rely more heavily on OPEC's reserves, especially on Gulf oil.

Nonetheless, even when looked at in this fashion, through military "protection" for oil, U.S. government subsidizes private U.S. companies, friendly oil-producing nations, and European and East Asian consuming nations, because they don't pull their weight in safeguarding such Gulf reserves for the world. Subsidizing oil-consuming economic rivals (European and East Asian allied nations) and even petroleum-importing potential geopolitical rivals (for example, China) makes little sense, because all of these nations (including China) have an interest in keeping the Gulf area stable. These countries can thus channel the resources saved by not helping to safeguard oil into potentially competing economies or militaries.

In the eighteenth and nineteenth centuries, when mercantilism was at its height, free-market economists, such as Adam Smith and Richard Cobden, demonstrated that paying market prices was actually cheaper than substituting such government mercantilist and imperialist policies. Put more straightforwardly, it is cheaper to buy the oil at a higher price on the free market than to use military coercion to subsidize the price.

The reason for this is that the substantial cost of keeping a military force to safeguard Persian Gulf oil—only some which is stationed in the Gulf—is non-contingent. In contrast, the threats to the flow of oil are of low probability (as we will see below) and the costs from any materializing threats are contingent. In addition, any military intervention or war to protect oil usually makes the price go up in the short and medium term.

Furthermore, using military power to ensure adequate oil supplies for the home economy is exactly what Japan did prior to World War II. Franklin Delano Roosevelt did not approve of Japan's empire building in East Asia, and so he effectively cut off U.S. oil exports to the island nation. Because Japan produced little oil, it decided to grab the oil in the Dutch East Indies (now Indonesia). To do so, the supply lines of its military forces would have had to go near the U.S.-occupied Philippines. The Japanese believed that this meant certain war with the United States. So in desperation, they attacked Pearl Harbor, hoping either that a surprise attack would dissuade the much richer United States from fighting or at least that it would give Japan time to build island defenses in the Pacific to resist a U.S. counterattack.

Of course, this is not an attempt to justify the Japanese attack on Pearl Harbor. They did have other options. First, the Japanese could have avoided imitating the Western empires and resisted imperial expansion in East Asia. Second, instead of using military force to seize oil in the Dutch East Indies, they might have purchased it from another supplier or purchased it on the black market. They too should have heeded the classical economists of the eighteenth and nineteenth centuries, who realized that empire was not cost-effective.

Today, the United States seems to be imitating Imperial Japan by using armed force to ensure oil supplies. In fact, the United States may be going beyond the Japanese desire to acquire oil to run their military. Other nations get more oil from the Persian Gulf than does the United States—as noted earlier, the U.S. gets only about a quarter of its imported oil and only about 11 percent of its total consumption from that region. *Yet the Gulf contains more than 50 percent of the world's known oil reserves, and making this area an American lake using U.S. military force allows the American government to have its thumb on the oil supplies and supply lines of many nations—both friend and foe alike.* By having this sword of Damocles hanging over other countries' heads, however, the United States gets only vague "influence" over their actions. Although not a cost-effective policy, such geopolitical influence and imperial glory seem to be the main motives behind the economically irrational use of large U.S. military forces to "defend oil." In the end, the resources used to militarily safeguard oil would be better channeled into the U.S. economy, thus enhancing—instead of dissipating—future U.S. power and the prosperity that primarily underlies it. The U.S. is essentially exchanging vague short-and medium-term "influence" for more rapid long-term decline.

24

Threats to or from Oil

U.S. MILITARY PLANNERS, attempting to justify higher defense budgets and new weapons, often posit unrealistic scenarios of threats to oil supplies. Specific threat scenarios will be analyzed and debunked, but in general, oil is a valuable commodity, and most oil-producing states don't have much else to export. In fact, oil-producing nations get between 65 and 95 percent of their export earnings from oil—much less than the percentage that oil imports account for in developed nations' total imports. Therefore, oil producers have a great incentive to sell it into the world market. Because the oil market is global, they don't even need to be willing to sell it to the United States; the world price, which the United States—along with everybody else—pays, depends only on them bringing the oil to market and selling it to anyone.

Iran is a classic example. Even after its 1979 revolution brought a radical anti-U.S. Islamist ruler—the Ayatollah Ruhollah Khomeini—to power, Iran continued to export oil into the world market. The United States did refuse to buy Iran's oil, but it was only symbolic and fairly costless to do so because Iran merely sold it to someone else, supplies shifted, and sellers displaced by Iran then sold to the United States. Thus, even radical anti-U.S. regimes will sell oil into the market, because they too need export revenues to fund their governments and societies. And that's all the United States needs them to do.

Threats from Oil

Some analysts allege threats come from oil producing nations:

Oil-Producing Nations Sponsor Terrorism—It has been argued that some oil-producing countries—for example, Venezuela, Saddam Hussein's Iraq, Iran, Qadaffi's Libya, and Saudi Arabia—have used oil revenues to sponsor terrorism.

Venezuela has apparently been using its oil revenues to aid the communist guerillas in Colombia, but they do not focus their attacks on the United States. Similarly, contrary to the implication by the George W. Bush administration in its push for war, Saddam's Iraq never sponsored groups that focused their attacks on the United States—instead funding groups aligned against Israel. After the 9/11 attacks, the United States invaded and occupied Iraq, a Muslim country that had no operational relationship to the attacks or to al Qaeda. Homegrown Iraqi terrorists created in response to and fighting against the non-Muslim occupation, then affiliated with al Qaeda.

After the United States quit meddling in Lebanon in the 1980s, attacks by Iran-sponsored Hezbollah of Lebanon on U.S. targets gradually evaporated, and for a long time Iran sponsored no groups that attacked the United States. Evidence exists that after the United States invaded Iraq, the nervous neighboring Iranians aided Iraqi Shi'i militias attacking U.S. occupation forces. After the United States bought off the Sunni resistance in Iraq, which was also attacking Iraqi Shi'a, Iran attenuated its support for the Shi'i militias. And after 9/11, Shi'i Iran actually helped the United States battle al Qaeda, a Sunni terrorist organization. Besides, because the United States has had sanctions on imports of Iranian oil, it hasn't bought any oil from Iran since 1991. Therefore, U.S. dollars for oil are not even helping Iran sponsor groups that attack Israel.

In the late 1970s, Libya sponsored terrorist attacks in Europe until the newly elected President Ronald Reagan began baiting and attacking Libya. The Reagan lore claims to have cowed Libya, but in fact Libya went underground and began a stepped-up terrorist campaign against U.S. targets, sometimes using surrogate groups. Libya's terrorist attacks against such targets attenuated after Reagan left office. In fact, Libya, still an oil-producing state with the same leader—Muammar Qadaffi—agreed to give up its nuclear weapons program and had reconciled with the United States and the West up until recently, when the West saw the chance to be rid of him after an internal rebellion.

At minimum, the Saudi Arabian government, a U.S. ally, has funded schools teaching radical Islam (madrassas) around the Islamic world. But in documents that came to light during 9/11 victims' suit against the Saudi government, charities close to the Saudi royal family were implicated in funding al Qaeda. Unquestionably, private Saudis have supplied money and fighters (most of the 9/11 hijackers were Saudis) to al Qaeda. According to a report from the Council on

Foreign Relations issued in 2002, "For years, individuals and charities based in Saudi Arabia have been the most important source of funds for al-Qaeda. And for years, Saudi officials have turned a blind eye to this problem."[1]

Thus, oil may have funded some terrorism, but most has not been against U.S. targets. Even when anti-U.S. terrorists come from oil producing countries, however, more attention should be paid to the underlying causes of that terrorism rather than reflexively blaming oil. Al Qaeda gets its sustenance from Muslim objections to U.S. military presence or meddling in Islamic countries.

In the cases of Iran, Libya, and al Qaeda mentioned above, U.S. meddling in, attacks on, or occupation of oil-producing countries, respectively, caused the blowback terrorism. Thus, it's not oil revenues, per se, that cause or exacerbate the terrorism, but surprisingly, unneeded U.S. efforts to secure oil with military power.

In fact, most oil-producing governments—for example, Canada, Mexico, the United States, Brazil, Nigeria, Argentina, Angola, Britain, Norway, Russia, Algeria, Qatar, Oman, United Arab Emirates, Kuwait, Bahrain, Azerbaijan, Kazakhstan, India, China, and Indonesia—don't sponsor terrorism. Moreover, some of the most dangerous countries have governments that are U.S. allies and produce little or no oil. For example, unstable Pakistan harbors al Qaeda, Afghanistan has a Taliban insurgency that sometimes uses terrorist tactics, Somalia harbors radical Islamists that the U.S. government helped empower, and Egypt has supplied many al Qaeda members and other Islamist terrorists. Should the U.S. become independent of foreign textiles, rice, and leather goods (some of Pakistan's chief exports); fruits and nuts, handwoven carpets, wool, and cotton (Afghanistan's primary exports other than opium); livestock, Frankincense, and myrrh (some of Somalia's principal exports); or cotton, iron, steel, and rugs (some of Egypt's main exports) to cut revenues for groups in those countries involved in terrorism? Where does it end?

Many terrorists aren't from oil-producing nations and aren't funded by oil revenues—for example, the Tamil Tigers from Sri Lanka (they, not Arab Muslims, invented terrorist suicide bombing), the Irish Republican Army in Northern Ireland, the Basque separatists in Spain, and the Taliban in Afghanistan. Many sources exist for the funding of terrorism, and it is unfair to single out oil. After all, Osama bin Laden and his family made their money in the construction industry, not oil.

Of the four state sponsors of terrorism (not necessarily anti-U.S. terrorism) on the U.S. terrorism list—Cuba, Iran, Sudan, and Syria—only Iran is a major oil producer (Sudan and Syria produce only a small amount of oil).[2] To show how political the terrorism list has become, Cuba and North Korea stopped supporting terrorism long ago, but they were retained on the list because the U.S. government just didn't get along with their governments. Only recently, North Korea was taken off the terrorism list for reasons not related to ending support for terrorism.

In sum, the nexus between oil and terrorism is tenuous. The United States should not become independent of foreign oil merely to try to dry up the funding for terrorism. If the United States were to become completely independent of foreign oil, the increasing demand for petroleum from China, India, and other developing countries would still provide plenty of money to the few oil-exporting nations that sponsor terrorism. Even in the unlikelihood that their oil revenues dried up, terrorists would just find other means of funding their activities—for example, by drug running, kidnapping for ransom, and so on. Many terrorist groups that don't benefit from oil revenues already use these sources of income.

G. I. Wilson, a retired Marine Corps colonel who is an expert on terrorism and asymmetric warfare, has concluded that the conflation of oil and terrorism is a "contrivance" and that "most insurgencies are low-tech in nature. Terrorists don't need oil money. For terrorists, the money flow doesn't come from oil, it comes from drugs, crime, human trafficking, and the weapons trade."[3]

Instead, the faux oil-terrorism nexus should not obscure greater introspection on why al Qaeda, one of the few anti-U.S. terrorist adversaries, is attacking U.S. targets in the first place. It is U.S. meddling and occupation of Muslim lands, primarily to "secure" oil that doesn't need safeguarding.

Unfriendly Petro-States Fund Other Nefarious Activities with Oil Revenues— Richard Lugar, the ranking minority member of the Senate Foreign Relations Committee, alleges that some oil-producing countries are using energy supplies as leverage against their neighbors.[4] Senator Lugar's allegation that certain petro-states, such as Russia, Iran, and Venezuela, use energy supplies to influence their neighbors may be true, but for the most part, this jockeying for advantage shouldn't affect the vital interests of the United States. That these nations want to affect their neighborhood, because what happens there affects their security, should not be foreign to the United States, which does the same thing (and then some). Lugar's nervousness also ignores the reality that those nations' neighbors can have their own means of leverage. For example, some energy travels to Europe from Russia via pipelines that go through Ukraine, allowing that country to threaten to shut off such supplies or divert the gas to its own use, which it has done. In the case of Iran, Israel does not buy oil from the Islamic republic, has a much more potent military than Iran, and probably has about two hundred nuclear weapons.

It is also alleged that oil gives Iran, which has a nuclear program that some fear could be aimed at creating atomic weapons, more revenues to produce such devices. That may be true, but costly U.S. independence from foreign oil may not decrease Iran's oil revenues much, especially if increasing demand from rapidly industrializing nations, such as China and India, increase their imports of foreign oil.

Oil revenues may also embolden the anti-American president of Venezuela, Hugo Chávez. Yet, Venezuela, a small country, poses no military threat to the U.S. superpower. Furthermore, Chávez's anti-Americanism would get a lot less traction in Latin America if the United States stopped its century-old profligate and unnecessary meddling in the affairs of the region.

U.S. Oil Dependence Undermines Democracy Abroad—The claim that U.S. oil dependence—thereby giving more wealth to oil producers—undermines democracy in these countries is just one of the questionable claims by proponents of U.S. independence from foreign oil. Thomas Friedman, a columnist for the *New York Times* and most prominent popular proponent of energy independence, has written that eliminating our need for oil will "protect us from the worst in the Arab-Muslim world. . . . These regimes will never reform as long as they enjoy windfall oil profits."[5] But if oil were not deemed by the U.S. government to be strategic, the nature of such regimes would matter a lot less to U.S. security.

Yet even on a higher plane, David Sandalow, a former assistant secretary of state and senior director on the National Security Council staff, says that a growing batch of scholarship asserts that oil wealth in countries is heavily linked to autocratic governance and corruption. Sandalow notes that recent high oil prices have allowed Hugo Chávez of Venezuela and Vladimir Putin of

Russia to undermine democratic institutions and that oil wealth has facilitated rampant corruption in Nigeria. This essentially converts a "resource curse" argument—economies based on mineral extraction lead to authoritarianism and venality—into and "oil curse" argument.

It is absurd, however, to logically link the wealth derived from sales of a liquid called oil to these social and political outcomes. First of all, even if a correlation between oil wealth and autocracy and corruption exists, cause and effect is suspect. As in the debate on the strategic nature of oil, one should ask why oil—and the wealth derived from it—is unique? Wealth derived from other products or commodities—such as uranium from Niger or diamonds from Sierra Leone— could also provide a financial crutch for authoritarian and corrupt rulers or be used to pay off security forces or even the population. They also provide a periodic financial cushion (when mineral prices are high) for a wayward country to avoid economic reforms. Sandalow does indicate that the oil/authoritarianism and corruption dynamic is not inevitable. Canada, Britain, Norway, and even the United States—all oil producers—will be happy to hear that.

Some proponents of the "oil curse" argument claim that these countries were industrial democracies before the discovery of oil, but even that indicates—as do the fact that many extractive and non-extractive economies have problems with autocracy, corruption, and lagging economic growth—that oil production may not be the defining factor in the generation of countries' severe political and economic problems. Furthermore, the Dutch Disease, a subset of the "oil curse" argument, was first identified in the developed democracy of the Netherlands during its natural gas boom in the 1960s. Dutch gas exports led to higher exchange rates, thus stunting agriculture and manufacturing exports.[6]

In short, there are oil-producing nations that are not autocratic and corrupt, and there are many authoritarian and venal countries that produce little or no oil. Oil probably gets an unnecessarily bad rap here.

Of course, even if it were true that oil wealth leads to authoritarianism and corruption, should the United States discontinue oil purchases from such countries? It could probably list something bad about any country from which it imports items or to which it exports them. Should the United States halt all foreign trade until every country becomes perfect in the eyes of the U.S. government? Moreover, the way to bring new ideas—such as democracy, free markets, and honest business dealings—into autocratic and corrupt nations is not to isolate them, but to increase their trade and interaction with the world. Becoming more integrated into the world marketplace will, if anything, make it necessary for them to adopt better practices.

Besides, even if the United States achieves the false nirvana of independence from foreign oil, dictatorial oil regimes will just sell to someone else, as do oil producers that sponsor terrorism. Even if the "oil curse" is true (which is questionable), artificial U.S. energy independence likely would not diminish rogue nations' oil revenues all that much, because they would just satisfy the burgeoning demand for oil in industrializing countries, such as China and India. Those countries don't much care about the internal politics of the nations that sell them oil.

Even the proposition that swelling oil revenues lead to increasing autocracy has been cogently trashed by Robert Bryce, a fellow at the Institute for Energy Research. He quotes Allan Reynolds, a free-market economist, as saying "cheap oil did nothing to promote economic or political liberty in Algeria, Iran, or anywhere else." Bryce then notes that accumulating oil revenues have not blocked Gulf oil-producing nations, such as Kuwait, Bahrain, and Dubai, from beginning to make their political or economical systems more liberal.[7]

Increasingly Scarce Oil Will Lead to More Conflicts—Lugar also alleges that rising demand for world oil, insufficient supplies, and a rising price will lead to more conflicts over oil.[8] As many historical examples have illustrated, however, gloom-and-doom predictions about running short of oil and experiencing ever-increasing prices have had a long history of being wrong. A higher oil price usually means more exploration and development, new technology being used in those pursuits, and usually an eventual supply glut.

Even if history does not repeat itself, the problem of conflict over oil is largely a self-fulfilling prophecy, as governments erroneously regard oil as a strategic commodity and end up taking counterproductive actions that actually threaten to disrupt the flow of petroleum. As Leonardo Maugeri, a senior executive at the Italian energy company Eni, has concluded,

> The conclusion line is that the wolf is not at the door. And even though dramatization is an unavoidable by-product of everything that concerns oil, there is nothing that dooms us to a vicious struggle for securing our future oil needs in the face of strangling shortages and geopolitical

turmoil. Only the inability of decision makers to grasp this reality and to act accordingly may push us to that brink.[9]

Yet today, China, Russia, and the United States are engaged in such an unnecessary military competition over the Persian Gulf and the Caspian Sea. In the Persian Gulf, the United States is clearly dominant. Although China and Russia sell arms to Iran, the United States provides military assistance to many countries and stations forces on the land and sea in that area. In the Caspian Sea region, in the three-way jousting, Russia has the edge in arming the countries of the Caucuses and Central Asia, because they were in the former Soviet Union. But the United States is making inroads with military assistance to Georgia, Kazakhstan, and Azerbaijan. Russia and the United States both have military forces stationed in Kyrgyzstan, and the Chinese have conducted joint military exercises with that nation.[10]

By examining history, an assessment can be made of Lugar's assertion that future chronic oil shortages and higher prices will mean more wars over such diminishing resources. Since the end of World War II, cross-border aggression has been declining, probably because of the advent of virulent modern nationalism as pushback to any foreign invasion, the proliferation of small arms for those nationalists to use for defense, and the invention of nuclear weapons, which could cause a small war to escalate to a global thermonuclear conflagration. Tight oil markets in the 1970s and for most of the first decade of the twenty-first century did not reverse the overall trend. Aforementioned academic research indicates that if viable markets exist for scarce, nonrenewable resources, conflicts over them are unlikely because it is cheaper to trade for them than to steal them using armed force. So Lugar will have to present more evidence to back his largely unsubstantiated prediction of more wars for scare oil.

Even if more wars over oil occur, the rational response for the United States would be to stay out of them. Historically, if an oil-producing state is involved in a revolution or war, it tries to get production back on line as fast as possible (for example, Iran after its revolution and Iran and Iraq during and after the war between the two of them). There are incentives to do so because war is expensive and has to be paid for, or revolutionary governments are usually weak and need the money to stay in power or carry out their agenda. Any net loss of oil output from a producer because of these causes will likely push up the world price, which will lead other producers to take advantage of the situation and pump more oil to make added money. Such increased production will then put downward pressure on the price.

So in the worldwide market for oil, even if a supplier to the United States is involved in a war or revolution, America most likely can buy oil from another producer. Even if there is a net loss of oil on the world market because of the calamity, it is just cheaper to pay the higher price rather than funding a costly war or maintaining an expensive, forward deployed military to "secure" oil through intimidation ("deterrence" in defense-speak). The annual cost of such forces is a given, but the vague fears are of an oil calamity that probably will never happen. Even if a rare oil crisis happens, as noted previously in this volume, industrial economies are much more resilient to petroleum price shocks than is commonly perceived.

U.S. Dependence on Foreign Oil Leads to the Necessity of Unsavory Alliances—Again, this problem tends to be self-fulfilling. Because U.S. policymakers think that oil is a strategic commodity vital to national security and that military power, rather than the market, must be used to ensure its free flow, they make unsavory alliances with the likes of Islamist Saudi Arabia and the corrupt, militaristic government of Nigeria. Yet, as this book shows, the aforementioned assumptions are false, and such alliances are unneeded.

Specific Scenarios Involving Threats to Oil

Most scenarios that allegedly posit a threat to oil—usually supply disruptions that lead to price increases and economic catastrophe—evaporate under close scrutiny. In general, any supply disruption anywhere in the world, will lead to higher prices. But once again, industrial economies, including the United States, are resilient to oil price increases.

Conquest of More Oil Reserves by an Unfriendly Powerful Nation—During the Cold War, the fear was that the Soviet Union would get control of Iranian or other Persian Gulf oil and use the increased market power to either embargo petroleum to the West or restrict exports and raise the world price. Also, the revenue from that conquered oil could be used to build greater military power that would threaten the West. Of course logic would indicate that these two hypothetical threats are almost mutually exclusive, but this allowed the Pentagon to have a threat to combat no matter what.

Yet even this most severe threat was overstated. The Soviet Union—desperate for foreign currency because it exported little else the world wanted—would have gained more revenue from captured Gulf oil, but to do so, it would have had to sell it into the market, thus restraining world price increases. Furthermore, and just as important, the military and administrative expenses needed to conquer, subdue, and occupy Islamic lands, which would have been very hostile to the atheistic intruder, might well have offset the greater oil revenues. Here the Soviet failure to pacify non–oil producing Afghanistan should have been illustrative. Thus, the net Soviet revenue increase from conquering oil-bearing lands might not have provided many funds to make the USSR stronger.

Besides, if the United States was so concerned about being reliant on Soviet-controlled oil, why did Henry Kissinger attempt a U.S.-grain-for-Soviet-oil swap in the wake of the 1973 oil crisis? He hoped to lessen U.S. reliance on OPEC oil by increasing dependence on America's Cold War archrival.

In reality, in contrast to the theoretical Soviet threat to oil, the biggest actual alleged threat to Persian Gulf oil arising to date has been Saddam Hussein's invasion of Kuwait and the implied threat to Saudi oil. As shown previously, however, economist David Henderson, by estimating the reduction in oil exports and increased price that Saddam could have commanded from increased market power in the worst possible case (his invasion of Kuwait, Saudi Arabia, and the United Arab Emirates), showed that less oil was taken off the market in this supposed horror than via actual universal international sanctions against Iraqi oil exports. Add to this real loss, the petroleum lost from torched oil wells during Saddam's retreat from Kuwait during the Gulf War. In other words, in an attempt to secure oil exports, sanctions and war reduced them.

As for conquered oil giving Saddam additional revenues for his nefarious deeds—at home and abroad—that may have been true, but if Saddam's threat to "strategic" oil had been properly debunked, his other threats were to his people or his neighbors; these threats did not affect U.S. vital interests. He did sponsor terrorist groups, but these focused their attacks on Israel, not the United States. Furthermore, as with any Soviet conquest of oil producing countries in the Persian Gulf, Saddam would have incurred severe military and administrative costs in conquering, occupying, and administering such countries—thus cutting into his net war booty.

Since the early 1990s, the threat of a major power conquering Persian Gulf oil has been very low. Today, the most likely threat is an Iranian conquest of a weak and possibly post-U.S. Iraq. But this threat is improbable because the Iranian regime is weak because of its own internal turmoil. Also, its military was weakened during the Iran-Iraq War and because the United States has refused to sell it parts and new technology for its arsenal of aging U.S.-made weapons. Even if Iran did take over Iraqi oil fields, much of the same analysis would apply to an Iranian conquest as it did to the hypothetical Soviet and Iraqi conquests of oil-producing countries discussed above. Iran would be able, even with its increased market power, to raise the world oil price only so much when it sold oil into the market to get much needed foreign exchange. Iran's greater revenues, also attenuated by the military and administrative costs associated with occupation, might be used to increase support for specific organizations in the Middle East—Hamas and Hezbollah—but those groups do not focus their attacks on the United States.

Reduction in Oil Supplies from War, Internal Upheaval, or Unfriendly Suppliers—Even if a great power doesn't try to grab more oil through aggression, supplies can be disrupted by a war or rebellion in a producing nation or the cessation of exports by an unfriendly nation. The best examples were the Iran-Iraq War and the Iranian revolution, respectively.

Any war in the Persian Gulf—whether it be over oil, such as the First Gulf War, or over other issues, such as the Iran-Iraq War—will increase oil prices. Oil-producing countries not involved in the war, whether in the Gulf or outside it, then have an incentive to pump more oil. This increased production is not done out of altruism, but because these nations want to take advantage of higher prices and to steal market share from the oil-producing combatants, which may have their oil production, transportation, or refining infrastructure damaged or incapacitated by the conflict.

Such increased alternative production will also occur when an oil producing country has a rebellion, such as Iran had in the late 1970s and Nigeria has periodically. Currently, the most severe threat to oil supplies would be a revolution in Saudi Arabia that brought to power a radical Islamist government hostile to the United States. But even Jay Hakes, a former head of the Energy Information Administration and one who thinks that "American dependence on foreign oil. . . . constitutes a grave security and economic risk," acknowledges that "the complete loss of oil from the world's largest exporter, Saudi Arabia, is regarded as unlikely. . . ."[11] Although certainly not a welcome development, even the ill effects to U.S. vital interests of an Islamist takeover of Saudi Arabia have been overblown.

Such a similar revolution already occurred in Iran, with the only difference being that those taking power were virulently anti-U.S. Shi'i Islamic radicals rather than Sunni Muslim militants. So the Iranian case should be illustrative of what might happen with a radical anti-U.S. Islamic regime taking power in Saudi Arabia.

Even after the Iranian revolution in 1978, the fundamentalist Islamic regime in Iran continued to export oil into the world market. Both that revolution and the closely following Iran-Iraq War damaged oil-production facilities and thus reduced exports, but the Iranian regime never refused to sell oil into the global market. The weak, new regime needed all the money it could get to stay in power, fund its security services, win public support by avoiding economic disasters, and finance its activities. (Similarly, Venezuela needs cash to fund its extensive social programs and thus puts aside its many political differences with the United States to be one of America's largest petroleum suppliers; yet it needs only to sell into the world market for the United States to benefit. Venezuela, instead of embargoing oil to the United States, has provided fuel subsidies for some U.S. customers to score political points.)

In contrast to dreamed-up threat scenarios, Iran never intended to use oil as a weapon. Instead, the militant Islamist regime tried to maximize output—exceeding Iran's OPEC quota threefold by the early 1980s—to bring in funds to bolster its fragile revolutionary regime and conduct its war with Iraq, while tweaking Arab OPEC members for supporting Iraq in the conflict.[12]

In fact, even today, after three decades of bad blood between the two countries, Iran would love to sell oil to the United States, but the United States has imposed sanctions on oil imports from that nation. They have had little effect because, as with all unilateral economic sanctions, the market merely reorders. The United States will never be able to isolate Iran, because the world wants its oil, and the Iranians want to sell it. This situation was ideal for the U.S. government, because it could show symbolic displeasure with the new Islamic regime and the taking of U.S. diplomats as hostage without raising the oil price higher than the then record levels caused by the revolution itself.

The problem for the United States came not with the record oil price, but as in the 1973 oil crisis, with the U.S. government's response. Unbelievably, despite the chaos price controls caused in 1973, they were still in effect during the 1979–1980 oil crisis, which once again was U.S. government-induced.

Based on this history, we can safely predict that any new radical Sunni regime in Arabia[13] would need to sell oil into the world market because the commodity is that nation's chief means of acquiring foreign exchange. As in the case of Islamist Iran, the new militant regime would not have to export oil directly to the United States, but only to sell it to someone in the world market. In fact, as it did against the Islamist regime in Tehran, the United States could ban imports of Arabian oil to disapprove of the new regime symbolically, knowing that its sanction would have little effect as long as the new Islamist government in Arabia sold oil into the global marketplace.

However, any damage to the oil infrastructure caused by a rebellion or terrorist attack in Saudi Arabia would cause the world price to go up until other oil-producing nations increased their oil production to take advantage of the higher price or until full Saudi production was resumed. Internal rebels might have even less of an incentive to damage oil infrastructure than would external enemy states, because rebels would realize that they might be desperate to pump valuable oil when they took power. In contrast, an enemy state might want to destroy oil infrastructure to ruin its adversary's economy and ability to finance the war (as in the Iran-Iraq war). Of course, the enemy state might not do this either if it were invading to get the oil.

About this lesser, and somewhat more likely, case, investigative journalist Seymour Hersh reported that "current and former intelligence and military officials portrayed the growing instability of the Saudi regime—and the vulnerability of its oil reserves to terrorist attack—as the most immediate threat to American economic and political interests in the Middle East."[14] The U.S. military presence in Saudi Arabia—now largely withdrawn in response to pressure from the worried Saudi government—and the current American military presence in the Gulf area have contributed to such instability in the kingdom, and the U.S. invasion of Muslim Iraq made it even worse. Continued U.S. meddling in the Gulf region could make the Islamists so powerful that the worst happens and the Saudi monarchy falls. And no matter how severely the Saudi government cracks down on such elements, it will never be entirely secure from their potential attacks as long as it is perceived to be a lackey of the U.S. government, military, and oil companies.

Even in the "catastrophic" instance of a radical Islamist regime taking power in Arabia (a short-term disruption of this magnitude might also occur if Russia ever had a civil war[15]), higher prices could be mitigated in the short-term by the dumping of vast government-held strategic petroleum reserves (globally totaling two billion barrels as of 2008). (By creating these reserves, governments have bought into the fallacy that in a global market for oil, physical control of oil matters.[16])

But in any case, as we have previously seen, even with a higher world price, industrial economies have become much more resilient to oil price spikes. For starters, even though the United States now imports more than 60 percent of its oil, as opposed to 34 percent in 1973, the U.S. economy has become more fuel efficient—reducing the percentage of GDP spend on oil from six percent in the 1970s to only three percent today.[17] Any economic problems that arise are usually caused by pernicious governmental responses rather than as a result of oil price increases. In fact, even during "oil crises," governments underestimate the power of higher prices to ensure that adequate supplies of oil come to market and that those supplies are allocated without disruption—with oil channeled to those who most need it and are willing to pay the elevated cost. Governments regularly underestimate markets because they are under political pressure to restrain the price of a very visible commodity.

Although a Sunni Islamist takeover of Saudi Arabian oil would give the new regime more money to spread its ideology, if the U.S. government realized that oil was not strategic and that the market would best efficiently deliver adequate supplies to meet world demand, such Arabian Islamist efforts could be deemed less of a threat to U.S. interests. Also, if the United States had begun to rely more on the market and had thus withdrawn the bulk of its military forces from the Persian Gulf, any Islamist revolution in Saudi Arabia would likely be much less anti-American. Islamic radicalism in most places is fueled by local issues and affects mainly local governments and citizens. The exception—al Qaeda—is fueled primarily by U.S. occupation of Islamic lands. Eliminating U.S. military presence in the Persian Gulf would probably render any Islamist revolution in Saudi Arabia less likely or merely a local affair, attenuate or even dry up al Qaeda's reservoir of money and recruits, and possibly even make al Qaeda refocus its attention away from attacking U.S. targets.

If the Persian Gulf is unstable, so are other suppliers of oil to the world market—for example, Libya, Nigeria, Venezuela, and states of the Caucasus region and Central Asia near the Caspian Sea. Although the consuming governments and firms will naturally try to diversify supplies, it does not do that much good. Oil taken off the worldwide market in any country because of instability—for example, terrorism, revolution, civil or guerrilla warfare, or workers' strikes—will drive the oil price up. Protecting oil in all of these countries is a Herculean task for even the military of a superpower. If the United States uses land forces to quell the instability and ensure the flow of oil, foreign occupation is likely to make things worse—as it did in the Bush administration's invasion and occupation of Iraq.

So Bush's argument, made when he released his National Energy Policy on May 17, 2001—"If we fail to act [to reduce U.S. dependence on foreign petroleum], our country will become more reliant on foreign crude oil, putting our national energy security into the hands of foreign nations, some of whom do not share our interests"—is a red herring.[18] It is in the common interest of the United States and even unstable, radical anti-U.S. regimes in such countries as Iran, Venezuela, and any future Islamist Arabia to get lucrative oil supplies to market.

Oil Comes from Unstable Areas of the World, Especially the Persian Gulf—
In his State of the Union address in 2006, George W. Bush gave a speech similar to Richard Nixon's in the 1970s (which luckily for Bush, few people remembered). In it, Bush said, "America is addicted to oil, which is often imported from unstable parts of the world." To reduce that addiction, Bush heroically announced the goal of replacing 75 percent of U.S. oil imports from the Middle East region by 2025.[19] Like Nixon's earlier vow of energy independence, one could only wish the president "good luck!"

As production from non-OPEC nations declines, more and more of the world's oil supply will likely come from the Persian Gulf, which has many authoritarian nations, some of which are unstable (as the recent uprisings and protests have shown). The U.S. government's policy has been to keep military forces in the region, usually to support dictators if they have oil (for example, Bahrain, Qatar, United Arab Emirates, and Saudi Arabia), and occasionally to intervene to grab oil under the pretext of spreading democracy (Iraq). Any supply disruptions from war or internal turmoil in unstable areas likely could be mitigated by increased production from other oil-producing nations, which would try to take advantage of the price rise. It is unlikely that instability would hit all oil-producing nations worldwide simultaneously. Even if many Persian Gulf oil states were destabilized simultaneously, as in the case of Saudi Arabia mentioned above, sending American troops to unstable areas to safeguard oil may actually make a supply disruption from internal revolt more likely.

Trying to democratize nations through armed intervention is likely to be ineffective and would also likely disrupt oil production. According to Minxin Pei and Sara Kasper, since 1900, the United States has led seventeen efforts at building democracy in other countries (including the pending cases of Iraq and Afghanistan, which aren't likely to succeed either), but in only four cases did the democracy last ten years or more.[20] Thus, the U.S. success rate is not sterling.

Also, in his address, Bush forgot to mention that many other critical raw materials and products the U.S. imports come from unstable countries—for example, the "strategic" minerals of chromium, cobalt, and platinum-group metals, which are much more rare and valuable than oil. But no one talks of stationing military forces permanently in countries that produce these items.

Another Arab Oil Embargo or Production Cutback—A corollary to the above alleged threat is a future Arab oil embargo or production cutback—or threat of them—to attempt to bend Western or U.S. policy toward the Arab cause. As noted earlier, Western politicians and publics have erroneously perceived the 1973 embargo and production cuts to have been disastrous for the West's economies, when really it was government price controls and excessively expansionist monetary policies that were the real culprit.

In reality, the embargo and production cutback were more disastrous for Arab OPEC. The professionals in the cartel knew that because of the reordering of a market for a fungible product, their embargo was an illusion. In addition, according to energy author Robert Bryce, Ibrahim al-Muhanna, an advisor to Saudi Oil Minister Ali al-Naimi, admitted that the 1973 embargo didn't work because "the oil exporters cheated" by selling oil to middlemen, who then sold it to the United States.

Al-Muhanna also observed that Saudi Arabia and other Gulf oil producers are not interested in cutting the oil flow to the West, because such an action would hurt the Saudis more than the West.[21] The oil producers realized after 1973 that politically motivated production cut backs were disastrous for them, because high prices would spur consuming nations to adopt measures that would reduce the long-term demand for oil—conservation efforts, fuel substitution, and the increased research, development, and production of alternative fuel sources. From 1977 to 1982, as a result of these factors, the United States reversed its increasing dependence on foreign energy by slashing its oil imports by half.[22]

Since the 1973 oil crisis, the cartel's leader, Saudi Arabia—with the most oil reserves and therefore the most to lose from any future permanent declines in demand—has acted to restrain OPEC price rises and to increase its own production to keep prices down. Tellingly, since 1973, although there have been other Arab-Israeli wars, there have been no oil embargoes, politically motivated production curtailment, or threats thereof.

Iran Blocks the Straits of Hormuz—About 40 percent of the world's traded oil and 90 percent of Middle Eastern oil flows through a passage called the Straits of Hormuz, which is a waterway between Iran and Oman where the Persian Gulf flows into the Gulf of Oman. Unlike other maritime choke points in the world, no alternative longer route exists. Only one way out of the Persian Gulf by sea exists. Allegations are that Iran could shut down or interfere with oil tankers going through there to destinations all over the world.

In 1983, Ronald Reagan signed National Security Decision Directive 114, which said that the United States would "undertake whatever measures may be necessary to keep the Straits of Hormuz open to international shipping."[23] Thus, the U.S. government and private analysts have put much effort into analyzing this threat scenario. The scenario, however, is unlikely. Military planners do plan for the worst case but, despite its occasional bluster, Iran has no incentive to close the straits through which it exports the vast majority of its own oil (its one port outside the Gulf is insignificant in oil volume).

Iran did not attempt to close the straits during the fervor of its Islamic revolution in order to poke a stick in the eye of the Great Satan and its Western oil-dependent allies. Even during the ensuing Iran-Iraq War—which saw Iraqi attacks on Iranian oil tankers, Iranian attacks on Iraqi tankers and those of allied nations (for example, those of Kuwait), and a large naval battle between the U.S. and Iran that destroyed half of the Iranian Navy—Iran did not widen the war by stopping all tanker traffic through the straits. This action would have brought international opprobrium and, more importantly, cut off Iran's main source of cash during a knock-down, drag-out war for survival against Iraq. If Iran didn't try to block the straits during this dire situation, it probably won't ever attempt to do so.

One alleged threat scenario would involve Iran trying to sink other tankers while letting its own tankers pass through the straits. But even without U.S. help, the air forces of Iran's Arab adversaries in the Gulf, especially Saudi Arabia's high technology air force, would likely ensure that Iranian tankers were attacked too—thus likely deterring such Iranian attacks in the first place.

The main specific hypothetical threat scenarios seem to be that Iran would launch suicide boats, mine the straits, or fire antiship cruise missiles on any tankers or Western minesweepers that arrive to attempt to clear the mines. Under such fire, it might take up to a month to clear the mines.[24] Eugene Gholz, associate professor at the LBJ School of Public Policy at the University of Texas–Austin, has done a detailed probabilistic study of these three specific threats to oil moving through the straits and finds them all to be overstated. Iran's small, ineffective weapons would likely be ineffective in sinking tankers, which are large and difficult to sink. Gholz believes that Iran's use of small suicide boats is not a likely scenario. It is difficult for a small boat to get near a huge tanker because of the bow wave. Also, it is easier to get suicide bombers to defend the homeland against a foreign invader than it is to attack the vague "world oil market." So recruiting suicide boaters would likely be a problem for Iran.

The Straits of Hormuz are wider than the small main shipping channel that most analysts are familiar with; the straits are twenty miles across, and, to block them, Iran would have to lay many rocket-propelled bottom mines. Iran has 20 mobile antiship cruise missile launchers along the straits. But even if they got multiple hits on one tanker, it would be difficult to sink the ship. In the tanker war between Iraq and Iran in the late 1980s, some tankers survived five hits. So cruise missiles are also likely to be ineffective.[25]

Bryan McGrath, U.S. Navy (ret.), who played in Navy war games involving the Straits of Hormuz, said no participants ever thought the waterway would really be closed for any length of time. In fact, according to McGrath, the most sophisticated group ever to play the role of the Iranians in the games realized that closing the straits was not in its interest.[26]

According to Gholz, even if Iran so desired to commit economic suicide by closing the straits, the effects on the world oil market may not be as severe as assumed. Many routes are available through the passage, thus making the complete interdiction of oil exports unlikely. Also, simply sending more tankers through the waterway would ensure that more oil made it through. In the worst case, if Iran succeeded in blocking the straits, some oil might be transported via the underutilized East-West Pipeline that runs from the Gulf through Saudi Arabia to its port city of Yanbu on the Red Sea.[27]

As for sub-state groups or pirates (hostage takers) terrorizing ships to deter tankers from going through the straits, the problem for them is mounting enough attacks and sustaining them at a high enough level, using limited resources, to cause such deterrence. Getting people aboard huge tankers from small boats is not that easy and also would probably reduce the number of successful attacks.

China's Newfound Interest in the Persian Gulf Is a Threat to the United States—China's huge population and rapid economic growth have made it the world's second largest consumer of energy. In the future, it will be in first place. For the first time in China's long history, it has become a net importer of oil. During the coming decades, China is projected to increase its demand for oil by about 4 percent per year, but its oil production is expected to stagnate. Yet compared to U.S. imports of almost 70 percent of its oil consumption, the Chinese import only 34 percent.

Thus, the rapidly growing country has naturally formed commercial relationships with oil-producing nations all over the world, such as Nigeria, Venezuela, and Russia.[28] Some U.S. anti-China hawks have alleged that China is attempting to ally with oil-producing nations that don't get on well with the United States. There is apparently some truth to this accusation, but not for the nefarious Chinese intent implied. According to an employee of a Chinese oil company that has dealings in Iran, "Basically we will choose those countries not enjoying a good relationship with the United States because there is almost no hope for Chinese companies to go into those pro-U.S. countries."[29] Perhaps China would not become an adversary if the United States government did not create a self-fulfilling prophecy.

China is also importing greater amounts of petroleum from the Persian Gulf. The Saudis are anxious to sell to what will soon be the largest market for oil in the world. But according to Evan Medeiros, a political scientist at RAND and fellow at the Council on Foreign Relations, the Chinese are so preoccupied with their periphery in East Asia that the Gulf is still not a vital interest for them. Medeiros has said allegations that the Chinese are developing a "string of pearls"—a line of bases and allied nations—on a route from China to the Gulf do not square with reality. The Chinese do, however, have an interest in maintaining stability in the Gulf but are leery of the costs of getting involved there—something the U.S. government should emulate.

Moreover, Medeiros has concluded that the Chinese government cares less about where its oil comes from than it does about price shocks, which may harm the regime's fragile legitimacy through inflation, thus creating social upheaval.[30] However, someone needs to tell the Chinese that a rising price for oil, by itself, will not cause general price inflation, because people will have less money to spend on other goods, thus driving their prices down and offsetting the oil price increase.

Upon closer examination, the Chinese military threat to Persian Gulf oil evaporates into thin air. First, the power projection capabilities of the Chinese military are only rudimentary. The Chinese military can barely project power into its periphery in East Asia, let alone half way around the world to the Persian Gulf.

Because a Chinese military threat to the Gulf is so ridiculous, anti-China hawks have focused on Chinese economic "penetration" of oil-producing countries. This alleged threat involves China's attempt to lock in long-term oil purchase contracts with petroleum-producing nations or Chinese state-owned oil companies aggressively exploring and attempting to produce oil in such countries.

As Eugene Gholz and Daryl Press conclude, neither is a threat to the United States. Even if the Chinese lock in long-term contracts to purchase oil, those agreements do not mean China will consume any more oil than it would have otherwise. Oil-producing countries not contracting with China will sell oil to the United States and other countries. Thus, such long-term contracts will not significantly change the world price for oil.

Also, in a worldwide oil market, aggressive oil exploration and development by China's state-owned oil-producing companies is at least neutral, and could even be helpful, to the United States. The Chinese have been so zealous in trying to get oil for their rapidly expanding economy that they will drill where Western private companies won't because of political or geological risk. Their companies are state-owned, have the risks underwritten by the Chinese government, and don't have to answer to private stockholders. If Chinese companies fail to find oil in risky places, it is costly only to them. If they get lucky and strike oil, they add to the world's supply, thus putting downward pressure on the price. However, overall, the U.S. Department of Energy concluded that the Chinese oil strategy is "economically neutral" to the United States.

Gholz and Press correctly conclude that the only real oil-related dangers to the United States from China are increased Chinese demand for oil, which puts upward pressure on price, and a possible self-fulfilling prophecy of deteriorating U.S.-China relations because of erroneous U.S. perceptions of a Chinese threat to oil supplies. First, many analysts think that rising oil prices throughout most of the first decade of the twenty-first century were substantially due to increasing Chinese demand.[31] Yet the resilient U.S. economy continued to grow for most of these years, despite substantial oil price increases, until loose U.S. monetary policy caused a housing bubble, which ultimately burst and plunged the world into a deep recession. And because the world benefits tremendously from increased commercial ties with a rapidly growing China, any higher oil prices caused by that growth are probably worth paying. In the past, however, higher prices have caused the market to discover and produce more oil, thus ultimately reining in such price increases.

Second, there is no need for rising tensions or military confrontation with China because of the largely empty threat that that nation poses to U.S. oil supplies. China would have little incentive to try to threaten the flow of petroleum to the United States. A healthy U.S. market is pivotal for Chinese economic growth, which is tied to China's exports—many of which go to the United States. Also, the Chinese have invested much money in the U.S. economy. Disincentives for war are one of the many advantages of economic globalization. During the first year of the Bush administration, a U.S. spy plane was shot down near China and the crew captured; but the crisis was solved peaceably between the two countries, which some analysts attributed to the high degree of economic interdependence between the two nations (something the United States and the Soviet Union never had).

In fact, the Chinese should be more worried about a U.S. threat to their oil, rather than vice versa. Because the United States has many military facilities and forces deployed or permanently based around the Persian Gulf, China fears a U.S. cutoff of its petroleum imports in any U.S.-Chinese foreign policy crisis—say over Taiwan. So the Chinese government, like the U.S. government, is attempting to diversify sources of, and transportation routes for, its imported oil. For example, the Chinese have committed to building a pipeline from Kazakhstan to the east coast of China to deliver natural gas over land, so they can cut down their tanker traffic from the U.S.-controlled Persian Gulf, which has much cheaper gas. In addition, the Chinese state-owned oil companies regularly overpay in an attempt outbid Western companies to get petroleum resources in oil-producing nations. So perhaps the U.S. threat to Chinese oil supplies is causing China to take economic measures to ensure those supplies, which are, in turn, being perceived by U.S. anti-China hawks as somehow threatening.

Like the Americans and Europeans, the Chinese are beginning to provide oil-producing nations with arms exports (for example, $1.6 billion to the Middle East from 1995 to 2002) to curry favor with them—although not on the vast scale of that of the United States (during the same period, to the same region, the U.S. shipped almost $47 billion in weapons) or European nations.[32]

These are the types of foolish uneconomical "strategic" games that governments—including the U.S. government—play instead of relying on the efficient world market to bring them oil at the cheapest possible price. But the Chinese seem smarter than the United States in trying to acquire their oil by mostly commercial means, instead of using force and getting bogged down in Middle Eastern quagmires. Such tar pits suck up national resources, make the home country poorer, and, in the long term, drain its power. Instead of regarding as a threat even Chinese commercial activities to obtain oil, the United States should withdraw militarily from the Persian Gulf and adopt China's commercially oriented model (except for using state-owned companies to procure the oil).

U.S. Military Protection of Oil Is Counterproductive to U.S. Security

Not only is U.S. military intervention to safeguard oil costly (in lives and money) and unneeded (oil is not strategic and the above alleged threats to it have been debunked), but such meddling erodes, not enhances, U.S. security.

As noted earlier, the classical economists of the eighteenth and nineteenth centuries realized that simply paying for resources on the free market was cheaper than expensive military expenditures required to imperially steal them and accompanying administrative spending needed to occupy countries. Historically, many empires have become overextended—with military and administrative expenditures exceeding the empire's ability to pay for them—and have fallen. Fighting two small wars in Iraq and Afghanistan have helped push up U.S. budget deficits and national debt to record and dangerous levels. When combined with an economic meltdown, the United States is in danger of decline, especially in the face of dramatic economic growth by China and India. If the United States does not retract its global military presence (a main purpose of which is to dominate oil), reduce its defense and federal budgets significantly, and plow the money back into private economic growth, it may even be eclipsed as a great power (much as France and Britain were after their exhausting victories in World Wars I and II).

Furthermore, the U.S. Constitution says that the government should "provide for the common defense," not create a worldwide military empire. The first responsibility of any government is to provide for the security of its people and territory. On September 11, 2001, the U.S. government failed in this primary mission. Not many Americans focus on the fact that this heinous attack was blowback from U.S. intervention in the Islamic world. Al Qaeda attacks the United States primarily because of its military presence in Islamic countries (especially Persian Gulf nations) and its support for corrupt dictators in those nations.

Although U.S. support for Israel is a factor in motivating the blowback terrorism, even Kenneth Pollack, a hawkish Middle East analyst who advocated invading Iraq, admitted that U.S. backing of corrupt and autocratic dictators in the Middle East breeds terrorism and rebellion. Michael Klare of Hampshire College added that increasing our military presence in this region will only breed more violence, which will require even more U.S. troops and longer deployments—thus creating a spiraling cycle of mayhem.[33]

Dr. Steven Kull, who regularly polls people globally on their attitudes, said his research in the Islamic world

> does show that anti-American feelings do make it easier for al Qaeda to operate and to grow in the Muslim world. In this context, it is not surprising that three out of four respondents favor the goal of getting the U.S. to withdraw its military forces troops [sic] from all Islamic countries. . . . Though al Qaeda and America are both seen as largely illegitimate, America is seen as the greater threat. It is as if Muslims are living in a neighborhood where there are two warlords operating. They do not like either one, but one is much more powerful.[34]

Thus, given no need to have the extensive U.S. military presence around the world—and especially in the Islamic Persian Gulf—to safeguard oil supplies, withdrawing those forces would actually lower costs, reduce such blowback terrorism to the American homeland, and improve U.S. security.

In sum, retracting the U.S. oil-based empire would preserve and enhance long-term American power and security. Buying oil on the market, and ending the connection between U.S. government foreign and security policies and such transactions, would make U.S. citizens safer and conserve U.S. power longer—especially if some resources were shifted from the military to the private economy, the true bedrock underlying all other indicators of national power.

PART IV

Policy Prescriptions

LEONARDO MAUGERI, an executive for the Italian energy company Eni, best summed up the sorry state of oil policy:

> There is reason to believe that the Western obsession with Persian Gulf oil security is largely overstated. By the same token, its main corollaries, the perceived need for a soft or hard form of control of the Persian Gulf and the parallel quest for "oil independence" from it, are the result of a dangerous and even naïve miscalculation, both in political and economic terms.[1]

Current U.S. policy in the Persian Gulf brings the worst of all worlds for U.S. national security. The harsh reality is that, whether intended or not, the policy is an expensive mercantilist and imperial one. The policy of using military force to secure oil is a subsidy to oil companies, U.S. oil-producing allies in the region, and rich petroleum consuming nations that get more oil from the Gulf than does the United States. Using taxpayer dollars to subsidize U.S. transnational corporations is a modern form of mercantilism (read: welfare).

The free market can provide petroleum more cheaply than investing in large military forces to "protect" oil that would flow anyway because it is profitable to export. The cost-effectiveness of the free market—compared to an imperial policy similar to that of Imperial Japan prior to and during World War II— was demonstrated by the classical economists in the eighteenth and nineteenth centuries. If anyone really needs to defend oil (questionable) and has the biggest intrinsic incentive to do so, it is the producing countries that net 65 to 95 percent of their export revenues from it—not the faraway United States. Thus, if the United States withdrew its forward presence from the Gulf, the Gulf Cooperation Council (GCC) states would then have an incentive to do more for their own defense. In other oil-producing areas around the world—for example, the Caspian Sea, West Africa, and so on—the same holds true; market forces and regional security organizations should be more heavily relied on to get petroleum to consumers.

Thus, one would have to suspect that this expensive U.S. imperial policy is undertaken deliberately—not to guard oil supplies for the United States, which will probably flow anyway, but to have the U.S. finger on the oil supplies of both allied (Europe, Japan, South Korea, India, and so on) and potentially rival (Russia and China) nations. The policy could be undertaken out of simple ignorance about the oil market, but presidents have advisors who are qualified to know how that market works, and some presidents have even been oilmen—for example both George H. W. Bush and George W. Bush. So a deliberate imperial policy is more likely.

Non-Muslim U.S. military forces are stationed in Muslim nations to carry out this imperial policy—thus motivating blowback terrorism against American targets, both abroad (for example, attacks on U.S. embassies, military bases, and businesses) and at home (for example, the 9/11 attacks).

Maugeri once again best summarizes the problem:

> Stationing Western troops in an Islamic Arab country is anathema to any Muslim, an act of impiety and an offence against the sacredness of the Holy Land of the believers. It is something that will lead to further alienating the indigenous populations. By embarking on a long-term military and political presence in the Middle East to secure its oil supply,

the West would provide a boost to the radical Islamists most effective weapon. . . ."[2]

Such imperial policies, although done in the name of promoting U.S. security, do just the opposite.

Therefore, the U.S. government should make the following policy changes:

1. Let the market provide the U.S. economy with all the oil it needs at the lowest price free commerce will allow. Understand that during a severe oil crisis, the price of petroleum will rise. But even oil producers in the crisis area will then have a powerful added incentive to get whatever oil they can to market. Also, producers not involved in the crisis area can increase production dramatically to take advantage of the higher prices.

2. If the market could provide oil even during a crisis, the United States could withdraw all ground and air force units, pre-positioned supplies on land and at sea, and even warships from the Persian Gulf area; it could also abandon bases in Oman, Qatar, Kuwait, Iraq, Bahrain, Saudi Arabia, and the United Arab Emirates that house, store, maintain, and repair them. To get real cost savings from this prescription, all of these military units would have to be disbanded. If military forces are just brought back from overseas to U.S. bases, rather than decommissioned, it actually may cost more to operate and support them than it did before. Foreign countries sometimes provide host nation support to help defray some of the costs to the taxpayer of basing U.S. forces abroad. If roughly half the U.S. armed forces—five divisions of the army, five active air wings of the air force, five Marine Expeditionary Brigades, and 144 ships (including six aircraft carriers)—could be eliminated from the force because the Persian Gulf no longer had to be defended, the U.S could save roughly $334 billion per year (in 2009 dollars).[3] This is no small amount when an economic meltdown and massive federal budget deficits make an unnecessary and counterproductive imperial oil policy no longer tenable cost-wise.

3. A retraction of U.S. military presence from the Persian Gulf would not only save taxpayer dollars in a time of severe economic crisis, but would

actually make America and its homeland more secure. Although not often highlighted by the U.S. government, foreign policy establishment, or media, fundamentalist Islamist militants, such as al Qaeda, attack U.S. targets at home and abroad primarily because the non-Muslim U.S. stations troops in or occupies Muslim nations. If U.S. forces withdraw from their unneeded postings in the Persian Gulf, including Iraq, this would reduce the amount of "beating on the hornet's nest" that U.S. foreign policy usually carries out.

4. To complete the sea change in U.S. policy, the United States might want to withdraw from other Islamic nations too. The U.S. should completely quit Somalia, because such meddling largely created an Islamist militant threat where little existed before. In Afghanistan, which has sometimes been erroneously deemed to be strategic because of its proximity to Iran and Persian Gulf, the United States should quit attempting the hopeless task of rebuilding the central government in an anarchic, decentralized land and of undertaking the equally fruitless effort of freeing the country from poppy cultivation. The United States should withdraw, while threatening to conduct heavy future strikes against any Afghani government that threatens to harbor anti-U.S. terrorists. Meanwhile, the United States should focus its efforts on creating effective carrots and sticks to get the Pakistani government to apprehend or kill the remaining leadership of al Qaeda, who are thought to be holed up in that country. (This task would be easier if the United States stopped fighting a Pakistani ally—the Afghan Taliban.) If this can't be done satisfactorily, and military action has to be taken to try to kill that leadership, the United States should focus on using "low footprint" cruise missiles, unmanned CIA drones, or Special Forces to carry out the attacks. This type of attack was successfully used to kill Osama bin Laden. The United States has been using drones in Pakistan but should drop all of the unneeded meddling in Afghanistan, which just unnecessarily stirs up the Islamic militants' ire against the United States.

5. As a fallback, if U.S. policymakers cannot be introspective enough to realize that they need to fully abandon a foreign policy in the Persian

Gulf that is overextended (especially in times of economic meltdown), imperialistic, and counterproductive to U.S. security, maybe they can at least go halfway.

President Barack Obama at least seems to be cognizant that U.S. actions have some effect on Arab and Islamic public opinion, which in turn affects the motivation to commit terrorist acts by the most radical fringe of Islamist militants. In responding to former Vice President Dick Cheney's comments that Obama's more relaxed policies on interrogation and torture would make the U.S. vulnerable to future terrorist attacks, Obama correctly noted that the Bush administration's harsher policies merely inflamed Arab and Islamic opinion against the United States.

Obama is on the right track but needs to look even deeper at the root causes of anti-U.S. terrorism. Because the non-Muslim military presence on Muslim soil is such a key motivator, if Obama does not want to abandon the U.S. policy of using U.S. military power to safeguard Persian Gulf oil, he should at least move that presence offshore as much as possible.

All U.S. land bases for ground troops, aircraft, and their pre-positioned equipment should be removed from the region. This is ever more crucial in the wake of increased instability in the region caused by street opposition in some of these countries in 2011. The U.S. Fifth Fleet, headquartered in Bahrain, should be dismantled and the base abandoned. Any U.S. carrier groups in or near the Persian Gulf should be sent from the United States and should make as few port calls in the Gulf as possible. As suggested by Daryl Press at a workshop on energy security at the Massachusetts Institute of Technology, this "over-the-horizon" strategy could also include heavy U.S. bombers based at Diego Garcia, an island in the Indian Ocean, to provide long range coverage over the Persian Gulf to deter any adversary (say Iran) from attacking oil fields and to provide heavy bombing in the event that deterrence failed. The over-the-horizon strategy relies on air and sea presence rather than the more inflammatory presence of ground forces to provide security in the Gulf. Over-the-horizon strike capabilities have improved since they were used effectively to deter a greater Soviet enemy from the Gulf in the 1980s (before the extensive U.S. presence on land was established after the U.S. victory in the first Persian Gulf War).[4]

Following Lisa Margonelli's solution of giving up the U.S. role of sole protector of Gulf oil would further dilute the U.S. military presence. U.S. allies that are large consumers of imported oil from the Gulf—for example, European and East Asian nations—could provide vessels for multilateral naval patrols. These allies are often nervous about providing ground troops for U.S.-led military operations in the Gulf—it can lead to combat deaths that are unpopular at home—but they are less skittish about providing ships for naval patrols, which usually result in many fewer casualties. The United States could also rely more on Middle Eastern, Asian, and African security forces to be the first line of security for oil flowing from those regions. If the U.S. government is too nervous to rely entirely on the market to provide oil, at least other countries could take over some of the burden of "defending" the flow.

If the United States relies more on offshore military power or on its allies to help safeguard the flow of oil, such military forces should still intimidate OPEC to keep prices slightly below what they would have been without any U.S. or allied presence in the Gulf. Of course, if the United States entirely withdrew its forces from "protecting" Gulf oil, its allies would probably at least increase their naval presence there—thus allowing the U.S. to free ride—for once—on allied efforts to ensure lower-than-market oil prices. Of course, as the classical economists in the eighteenth and nineteenth centuries taught, it is cheaper for whichever nations are providing Gulf security to simply pay higher prices for the oil, rather than to spend vast sums to defend it from fairly low probability threats.

Furthermore, although the U.S. Strategic Petroleum Reserve and other governments' oil stockpiles are also unnecessary interventions in the world petroleum marketplace, they do provide an added security blanket against short-term supply disruptions for nervous world leaders who don't really believe the market, by itself, can deliver oil most reliably and cheaply. Although imperfect, they are better than using military force, or threat thereof, to guard against high oil prices or supply disruptions.

The retraction of the American empire would reduce the chances of terrorist attacks on U.S. ships—like the bombing of the U.S.S. *Cole* in

2000—and generally reduce the footprint of the U.S. military presence in or near the Gulf, thus reducing anti-American terrorism emanating from Arab and Islamic nations. As a hedge against any very rare severe crisis, the United States, however, could sign agreements for access to bases in the region in case of emergency.

Conclusion

In 1990 and 1991, during the first Gulf War, the United States safeguarded oil with forces brought from over-the-horizon—many from those stationed in the United States and Europe. Subsequent to that war, the principal threats to the oil flow (if even these were really threats to the world market for a monetarily valuable commodity)—Saddam Hussein's military or the Soviet Union—had either been severely crippled or had dissolved, respectively. Only after these threats had evaporated did the United States then decide to set up its first-ever bases for land-based forces and pre-positioned weapon storage sites in the Gulf. Because the Cold War had ended, United States could and did shift forces from Europe and East Asia to the Persian Gulf.[5]

So we must assume that because the worst threats to oil had diminished after 1991, the new bases and land-based forces in the Gulf were needed for the more imperial ends of keeping a U.S. thumb on the oil supply lines around the world, rather than for safeguarding the flow of oil from imaginary enemies.

Of course, empire has a steep price in blood and treasure that the United States, which is instead supposed to be a republic, can no longer afford. Not only does this unneeded securing of oil using force smack of the costly, unnecessary, and immoral Japanese policy prior and during World War II, but it also inflames Islamist terrorists and motivates them to attack U.S. targets. Osama bin Laden returned home after fighting to successfully displace the non-Muslim Soviet Union from Islamic Afghanistan, only to find more non-Islamic forces in his homeland of Saudi Arabia, which houses Islamic holiest shrines. This non-Muslim military presence on Muslim lands was the chief motivator for bin Laden declaring war on the United States and launching a series of heinous terrorist attacks, including that of 9/11.

Reducing or eliminating the U.S. military presence in the Islamic Persian Gulf would save much money at a time when the fragile U.S. economy can no longer afford such an overseas empire, would save U.S. lives by avoiding unneeded wars for oil, and would evaporate the primary fuel that fires the ability of al Qaeda to garner money and terrorists from radical Muslim populations. In short, going to war for oil is unnecessary, expensive in blood and treasure, and dangerous for U.S. security.

Notes

Chapter 1

1. Using quantitative research, Miroslav Nincic, a professor at the University of California at Davis, demonstrates that it is easier for U.S. presidents to increase their popularity by going to war to avoid a loss to an acquired geopolitical position (a "protective" intervention) than it is to enhance their approval ratings by starting a conflict to secure a net foreign policy gain (a "promotive" intervention). See Miroslav Nincic, "Loss Aversion and the Domestic Context of Military Intervention," *Political Research Quarterly* 50, no. 1 (March 1997): 97. Some evidence for Nincic's research seems to be provided by George W. Bush's approval ratings during the invasion and occupation of Iraq. When the "protective" justifications for the war—feared Iraqi weapons of mass destruction and alleged operational links between Saddam Hussein and al Qaeda and the 9/11 attacks—fell through, Bush's and the war's popularity declined as a "promotive" justification—bringing democracy to Iraq and the Middle East—was then emphasized. Of course, the guerrilla war quagmire that ensued also torpedoed public support for the president and the war. Although never a stated goal of the war, perhaps securing U.S. oil supplies, a "protective" objective, should have been used because it likely would have been more popular than the "promotive" goal. It was for Bush's father during the first Persian Gulf War in 1991. Thus, wars for oil that are economically irrational can unfortunately still be politically advantageous to politicians.

2. Lisa Margonelli, *Oil on the Brain: Petroleum's Long, Strange Trip to Your Tank* (New York: Broadway Books, 2008), 26.

3. Daniel Yergin, "It's Still the One," *Foreign Policy.* http://www.foreign policy.com/articles/2009/08/17/Its _still_the_one, 3 (accessed August 24, 2009).

4. Donald Losman, *Economic Security: A National Security Folly* (Washington, DC: Cato Institute Policy Analysis No. 409, August 1, 2001), 9.

5. Margonelli, *Oil on the Brain,* 104–6

6. Paul Roberts, *The End of Oil: On the Edge of a Perilous New World* (Boston: Houghton Mifflin Company, 2005), 94–95.

7. Thomas E. Woods Jr. *Meltdown: A Free-Market Look at Why the*

Stock Market Collapsed, the Economy Tanked, and Government Bailouts Will Make Things Worse (Washington, DC: Regnery Publishing, Inc., 2009), 125–26.

8. Losman, *Economic Security*, 3.

9. Marshall Goldman, *Petrostate: Putin, Power, and the New Russia* (New York: Oxford University Press, 2008), 139, 179.

10. Goldman, *Petrostate*, 3–4, 7–10.

Part 1, Chapter 2

1. Antonia Juhasz, *The Tyranny of Oil: The World's Most Powerful Industry —and What We Must Do to Stop It* (New York: HarperCollins, 2008), 22.

2. Leonardo Maugeri, *The Age of Oil: What They Don't Want You to Know About the World's Most Controversial Resource* (Guilford, Connecticut: The Lyons Press, 2006), 9; and Juhasz, *Tyranny of Oil*, 43–44.

3. Daniel Yergin, *The Prize: The Epic Quest for Oil, Money and Power* (New York: Free Press, 1992), 86–87, 95, 112.

4. Yergin, *The Prize,* 226.

5. Yergin, *The Prize,* 178.

Chapter 3

1. Yergin, *The Prize,* 11–12, 173.

2. Roberts, *End of Oil*, 38.

3. Yergin, *The Prize,* 158–163; and Juhasz, *Tyranny of Oil*, 77–78.

4. Yergin, *The Prize,* 13, 78–80, 170–71, 176.

5. Michael T. Klare, *Blood and Oil: The Dangers and Consequences of America's Growing Dependency on Imported Petroleum* (New York: Metropolitan Books/Henry Holt and Company, 2004), 149.

6. Maugeri, *Age of Oil*, 25.

7. Yergin, *The Prize,* 194–95, 211–18, 222.

8. Yergin, *The Prize,* 246–47, 252–58.

9. Juhasz, *Tyranny of Oil*, 4–5.

10. Yergin, *The Prize,* 372, 378.

11. Yergin, *The Prize,* 273–79.

12. Klare, *Blood and Oil*, 10.

13. Margonelli, *Oil on the Brain*, 209.

14. Yergin, *The Prize,* 395.

15. Yergin, *The Prize,* 401.

16. Juhasz, *Tyranny of Oil*, 82.

17. Quoted in Klare, *Blood and Oil*, 36–37.

18. Quoted in Robert Bryce, *Gusher of Lies: The Dangerous Delusions of "Energy Independence."* (New York: PublicAffairs, 2008), 51.

19. Klare, *Blood and Oil*, 36, 38.

20. Margonelli, *Oil on the Brain*, 209–10.

21. Margonelli, *Oil on the Brain*, 92–93.

Chapter 4

1. Yergin, *The Prize,* 333–38, 344, 346–48, 376–77, 379, 382, 450.

2. Yergin, *The Prize,* 316–19.

3. Yergin, *The Prize,* 319–20, 322.

4. Herbert Feis, *The Road to Pearl Harbor: The Coming War Between the United States and Japan* (Princeton, N.J.: Princeton University Press, 1950), 19, which was noted in Yergin, *The Prize*, 310, 314–16.

5. Yergin, *The Prize,* 277–307.

6. Yergin, *The Prize,* 319.

7. Yergin, *The Prize,* 356–58.

Chapter 5

1. Klare, *Blood and Oil*, 29–30.

2. Maugeri, *Age of Oil*, 55–56.

3. Klare, *Blood and Oil*, 39–40, 149.

4. Maugeri, *Age of Oil*, 74–75.

5. Maugeri, *Age of Oil*, 59–61.

6. Quoted in Richard H. Curtiss, "Truman Advisor Recalls May 14, 1948 Decision to Recognize Israel," Information Clearing House, www.informationclearinghouse.info/article4077.htm.

7. Maugeri, *Age of Oil,* 77.

8. Rachel Bronson, *Thicker than Oil: America's Uneasy Partnership with Saudi Arabia* (New York: Oxford University Press, 2006), 20.

9. Quoted in Yergin, *The Prize,* 537–38.

10. Yergin, *The Prize,* 402–3, 406–7, 409–10, 412, 427–29, 499–500.

11. Bronson, *Thicker than Oil,* 45.

12. Klare, *Blood and Oil,* 12.

13. Yergin, *The Prize,* 433–36, 448–49.

14. Yergin, *The Prize,* 452, 453, 455, 468, 470–74, 476, 477.

15. Bronson, *Thicker than Oil,* 71.

16. Yergin, *The Prize,* 537.

17. Jay Hakes, *A Declaration of Oil Independence: How Freedom from Foreign Oil, Can Improve National Security, Our Economy, and the Environment* (Hoboken, New Jersey: John Wiley & Sons, Inc., 2008), 90.

18. Ben Zycher, "OPEC," in David Henderson, ed., *The Concise Encyclopedia of Economics,* http://www.econlib.org/cgi-bin/printcee.pl.

19. Yergin, *The Prize,* 555–58.

Chapter 6

1. Juhasz, *Tyranny of Oil,* 92–94.

2. Yergin, *The Prize,* 521–24, 531–32.

3. Quoted in Yergin, *The Prize,* 704.

4. Maugeri, *Age of Oil,* 72, 80–83.

5. Juhasz, *Tyranny of Oil,* 100–101.

6. Juhasz, *Tyranny of Oil,* 5, 116, 122, 126.

7. Maugeri, *Age of Oil,* 83.

8. Hakes, *A Declaration,* 14–16.

9. Yergin, *The Prize,* 567, 571–72.

10. Maugeri, *Age of Oil,* 121, 228–29.

Chapter 7

1. Quoted in Bryce, *Gusher of Lies,* 68.

2. Bronson, *Thicker than Oil,* 116.

3. David Sandalow, *Freedom from Oil: How the Next President Can End the United States' Oil Addiction* (New York: McGraw-Hill, 2008), 1.

4. Maugeri, *Age of Oil,* 103, 112–13.

5. Bronson, *Thicker than Oil,* 119–22.

6. Quoted in Editorial, "Realism in Oil Prices," *Business Week,* September 28, 1974, 116.

7. Henry Kissinger and James Schlesinger quoted in David Henderson, *Do We Need to Go to War for Oil? Independent Policy Report* (Oakland, CA: The Independent Institute, 2007), 2.

8. Yergin, *The Prize,* 631, 634.

9. Paul W. MacAvoy, *Energy Policy: An Economic Analysis* (New York: W.W. Norton & Company, 1983), 20.

10. Juhasz, *Tyranny of Oil,* 96.

11. Vaclav Smil, *Oil* (Oxford, England: OneWorld, 2009), 162–63.

12. Bryce, *Gusher of Lies,* 206.

13. Roberts, *End of Oil,* 215.

14. Sandalow, *Freedom from Oil,* 39, 42.

15. Roberts, *End of Oil,* 103.

16. Yergin, *The Prize,* 639, 642–43,

17. Volcker cited in Hakes, *Declaration,* 20–21.

18. Bohi cited in Losman, *Economic Security,* 4–5.

19. Bronson, *Thicker than Oil,* 126–28.

20. Quoted in Yergin, *The Prize,* 617–18.

21. Yergin, *The Prize,* 685–86.

22. Juhasz, *The Tyranny of Oil,* 103.

23. MacAvoy, *Energy Policy,* 20.

24. Hakes, *Declaration,* 44, 60.

25. CIA estimate quoted in Morris A. Adelman, *The Genie Out of the Bottle: World Oil since 1970* (Cambridge, Massachusetts: MIT Press, 1995), 178.

26. Yergin, *The Prize,* 687–88, 718–726.

27. Yergin, *The Prize,* 646, 648–52, 664–65, 782, 783.

Chapter 8

1. Allan H. Meltzer, "Inflation Nation," New York Times, May 4, 2009, A19.

2. Bronson, *Thicker than Oil,* photo captions after p. 162.

3. Hakes, *Declaration,* 89, 93.

4. Maugeri, *Age of Oil,* 128.

5. Bronson, *Thicker than Oil,* 162.

6. Klare, *Blood and Oil,* 45–46.

Chapter 9

1. Goldman, *Petrostate,* 137–38.

2. Goldman, *Petrostate,* 35–37, 43, 49, 50–52, 82.

3. Michael Lynch, "'Peak Oil' Is a Waste of Energy," *New York Times,* August 25, 2009, A15.

4. Yergin, *The Prize,* 717–18.

5. Hakes, *Declaration,* 75.

6. Maugeri, *Age of Oil,* 136–37.

7. Hakes, *Declaration,* 78.

8. Margonelli, *Oil on the Brain,* 200–203.

9. Hakes, *Declaration,* 76–77.

10. Yergin, *The Prize,* 769–70.

Chapter 10

1. Maugeri, *Age of Oil,* 153.

2. Bronson, *Thicker than Oil,* 192.

3. Hakes, *Declaration,* 79.

4. Maugeri, *Age of Oil,* 147.

5. David Model, *Lying for Empire: How to Commit War Crimes with a Straight Face* (Monroe, ME: Common Courage Press, 2005), 211–12.

6. Roberts, *End of Oil,* 105.

7. Quoted in Yergin, *The Prize,* 773.

8. Quoted in Sandalow, *Freedom from Oil,* 21.

9. Both James Baker and National Security Directive 54 quoted in Juhasz, *Tyranny of Oil,* 328.

10. Klare, *Blood and Oil,* 50.

11. Klare, *Blood and Oil,* 51.

12. Henderson, *Do We Need to Go to War for Oil?,* 10.

13. Henderson, *Do We Need to Go to War for Oil?,* 10.

14. Eugene Gholz and Daryl G. Press, *Energy Alarmism: The Myths That Make Americans Worry about Oil* (Washington, DC: Cato Policy Analysis No. 589, April 5, 2007), 12–13.

15. Henderson, *Do We Need to Go to War for Oil?,* 11, 13.

16. Hakes, *Declaration,* 80–81.

17. Yergin, *The Prize,* 774–75, 781–83.

18. Bronson, *Thicker than Oil,* 204, 218–19.

19. Maugeri, *Age of Oil,* 169–71, 174.

20. Klare, *Blood and Oil,* 53.

21. Klare, *Blood and Oil,* 53–54.

22. Bryce, *Gusher of Lies,* 28–30.

23. Alex Spillius, "Wikileaks: Saudis 'Chief Funders of al-Qaeda,'" *The Telegraph,* www.telegraph.co.uk/news/worldnews/wikileaks/8182847/wikileaks-saudis-chief-funders-of-al-Qaeda.html

24. Bronson, *Thicker than Oil,* 241–42, 244–45.

25. Juhasz, *Tyranny of Oil,* 321.

26. Roberts, *End of Oil,* 91–93.

27. Klare, *Blood and Oil,* xvi.

28. Roberts, *End of Oil,* 304.

29. Hakes, *Declaration,* 94–95.

30. Quoted in Bryce, *Gusher of Lies,* 26, 67.

31. Roberts, *End of Oil,* 110–112.

32. Klare, *Blood and Oil,* 5, *100–101;* and Bryce, *Gusher of Lies,* 24.

33. Klare, *Blood and Oil,* 90–91.

34. Energy Intelligence Research, *Iraqi Oil and Gas: A Bonanza-in-Waiting*

(Spring 2003), cited in Juhasz, *Tyranny of Oil*, 325–26, 353–54.

35. As cited in Klare, *Blood for Oil*, 104.

36. Juhasz, *Tyranny of Oil*, 325.

37. Quoted in Juhasz, *Tyranny of Oil*, 323.

38. Both men were quoted in Juhasz, *Tyranny of Oil*, 319.

39. Juhasz, *Tyranny of Oil*, 321.

40. Ron Suskind, *The Price of Loyalty: George W. Bush, the White House, and the Education of Paul O'Neill* (New York: Simon and Schuster, 2004), 129.

41. Hakes, *Declaration*, 97–98.

42. Roberts, *The End of Oil*, 10.

43. Juhasz, *Tyranny of Oil*, *341–42*, 348. Hakes also implies this reason as an underlying motivation for the U.S. invasion of Iraq; *see* Hakes, *Declaration*, 95.

44. Hakes, *Declaration*, 86.

45. Henderson, *Do We Need to Go to War for Oil?*, 13.

46. Roberts, *End of Oil*, 337.

47. Goldman, *Petrostate*, 79.

48. Maugeri, *Age of Oil*, 186–87.

49. Hakes, *Declaration*, 83

50. Maugeri, *Age of Oil*, 187–88, 193.

51. Yergin, "It's Still the One," 2.

Chapter 11

1. Yergin, "It's Still the One," 2.

2. Maugeri, *Age of Oil*, 180.

3. Hakes, *Declaration*, 126.

4. Morris H. Adelman, "The Real Oil Problem: Behind the Myths of an Oil Crisis and an Oil Weapon is a Very Real Danger Posed by a Clumsy and Shortsighted Cartel." *Regulation*, March 22, 2004, Vol. 27:1, CATO Institute, 16–21. http://media-serveramazon.com/exec/drm/amzproxy.cgi/MzYwIPvT8...EF8T

Vzcu2qLVdTQHaiaYDaYdaea_X2 BQX5QegQ==$GALOG0116407317 .html and CNBC. "The Hunt for Black Gold" Broadcast Segment (September 24, 2008).

5. Blaise Allaz and Jean-Luc Vila, "Cournot Competition, Forward Markets, and Efficiency," *Journal of Economic Theory*, Vol. 59:1, February 1993: 1–16.

6. Juhasz, *Tyranny of Oil*, 132.

7. Juhasz, *Tyranny of Oil*, 131–33.

8. Juhasz, *Tyranny of Oil*, 5–7, 13.

9. Yergin, "Its Still the One," 3.

10. Juhasz, *Tyranny of Oil*, 26–27.

11. Hakes, *Declaration*, 87–88.

12. Roberts, *End of Oil*, 97–98, 107.

13. Quoted in Juhasz, *Tyranny of Oil*, 126, 128.

Part II, Chapter 12

1. Goldman, *Petrostate*, 179.

2. Hakes, *Declaration*, 84–85.

3. Margonelli, *Oil on the Brain*, 290.

4. Maugeri, *Age of Oil*, 261.

5. Sandalow, *Freedom from Oil*, 42.

6. Goldman, *Petrostate*, 85.

7. Gholz and Press, *Energy Alarmism*, 11–14.

Chapter 13

1. Federal Trade Commission Report on Spring/Summer 2006 Nationwide Gasoline Price Increases, August 2007, http://www.ftc.gov/reports /gasprices06/P040101Gas06increase .pdf and Margonelli, *Oil on the Brain*, 26.

2. Hakes, *Declaration*, 136; and Adelman, "The Real Oil Problem."

3. Richard L. Gordon, *An Economic Analysis of World Energy Problems*, (Cambridge, Mass.: MIT Press, 1981), 121–122.

4. Maugeri, *Age of Oil*, xi.
5. Maugeri, *Age of Oil*, 259–60.

Chapter 14

1. Bryce, *Gusher of Lies*, 279.
2. Newt Gingrich, *Drill Here, Drill Now, Pay Less: A Handbook for Slashing Gas Prices and Solving Our Energy Crisis* (Washington, DC: Regnery Publishing, Inc., 2008), 148–50.
3. Bryce, *Gusher of Lies*, i.
4. CNBC. "The Hunt for Black Gold."
5. Smil, *Oil*, 165.
6. Maugeri, *Age of Oil*, xv–xvi, 202, 204–5
7. Also, in a 1972 book, Morris Adelman refuted the 1970s installment of the peak oil thesis that the world's oil resources would soon be exhausted. See Morris Adelman, *The World Petroleum Market*, (Baltimore, Md.: John Hopkins University Press, 1972.) Yergin, "It's Still the One," 3.
8. Lynch, "'Peak Oil,'" A15.
9. Yergin, "It's Still the One," 4.
10. Lynch, "'Peak Oil,'" A15.
11. Maugeri, *Age of Oil*, xiv.
12. Roberts, *The End of Oil*, 54–56.
13. Gholz and Press, *Energy Alarmism*, 1, 5–7.
14. Maugeri, *Age of Oil*, 219.
15. Roberts, *The End of Oil*, 48, 52, 56.
16. Quoted in Juhasz, *The Tyranny of Oil*, 284.
17. Juhasz, *The Tyranny of Oil*, 290–92, 297.
18. Bryce, *Gusher of Lies*, 39.
19. Maugeri, *Age of Oil*, 219–20.
20. Losman, *Economic Security*, 6.
21. Bryce, *Gusher of Lies*, 256–258.
22. Roberts, *End of Oil*, 271.
23. Maugeri, *Age of Oil*, 3–4.
24. Ronnie Lipschultz and John Holdren, "Crossing Borders: Resource Flows, the Global Environment and International Stability," *Bulletin of Peace Proposals 21* (1990): 121–33.
25. Jon Barnett, "Security and Climate Change," *Global Environmental Change 13* (2003): 11. Also, for an analysis of pernicious internal effects of high oil prices on the stability of oil producing countries, see Gordon, *An Economic Analysis*, 232–233.

Chapter 15

1. Losman, *Economic Security*, 7.
2. Losman, *Economic Security*, 8.
3. Losman, *Economic Security*, 7.
4. Henderson, *Do We Need to Go to War for Oil?*, 5.
5. Comments of MIT economist Olivier Blanchard in Massachusetts Institute of Technology Security Policy Studies, *Energy, National Security, and the Persian Gulf* (Boston: MIT SSP, February 22, 2008), 12–13.
6. Sandalow, *Freedom from Oil*, 24–25, 42, 132.
7. Goldman, *Petrostate*, 169, 204.
8. Bryce, *Gusher of Lies*, 11–12, 16, 18, 206.

Chapter 16

1. Losman, *Economic Security*, 9.
2. Margonelli, *Oil on the Brain*, 104–6.
3. Sandalow, *Freedom from Oil*, 162–66.
4. Margonelli, *Oil on the Brain*, 107, 114.
5. Hakes, *Declaration*, 145–49.
6. Margonelli, *Oil on the Brain*, 116–17.
7. Margonelli, *Oil on the Brain*, 108, 116–18.
8. Margonelli, *Oil on the Brain*, 106–8.
9. Margonelli, *Oil on the Brain*, 114.
10. Margonelli, *Oil on the Brain*, 101, 105.

Chapter 17

1. Certain authors, such as Richard L. Gordon and Morris Adelman, seem to be pro-oil industry rather than pro-oil market. Gordon implies agreement with Adelman's advocacy of protecting the domestic oil industry to guard against potential supply disruptions stockpiling oil in the Strategic Petroleum Reserve, subsidizing the U.S. oil industry to increase domestic oil production, government involvement to reduce the price of oil and a heavy ad valorem tax on oil imports. See Gordon, *An Economic Analysis*, 235, 241, 243.
2. Roberts, *End of Oil*, 94–95.
3. Sandalow, *Freedom from Oil, 3, 15–16;* Roberts, *End of Oil*, 295; and Energy Information Administration, "Annual Energy Review 2009," http://www.eia.gov/electricity/
4. Calculated from Energy Information Administration, "International Energy Outlook 2010," http://eia.gov/oiaf/ieo/world.html.
5. Roberts, *End of Oil*, 5.
6. Gingrich, *Drill Here*, xiii, 6.
7. Klare, *Blood and Oil*, 8.
8. Bronson, *Thicker than Oil, 251;* and Klare, *Blood and Oil*, 7–8.
9. Hakes, *Declaration*, 173.
10. Margonelli, *Oil on the Brain*, 30–31.
11. Sandalow, *Freedom from Oil*, 18.
12. Roberts, *End of Oil*, 191.
13. Hakes, *Declartion*, 129–130.
14. Bryce, *Gusher of Lies*, 9.
15. Roberts, *End of Oil*, 13
16. Gingrich, *Drill Here*, xiii.
17. Gingrich, *Drill Here*, xiii.
18. Roberts, *End of Oil*, 168–69.
19. Bryce, *Gusher of Lies*, 284–85.
20. Roberts, *End of Oil*, 181–82, 184–85.
21. Sandalow, *Freedom from Oil*, 66–67, 75.
22. Bryce, *Gusher of Lies*, 206.
23. Roberts, *End of Oil*, 175, 193.
24. Hakes, *Declaration*, 6.
25. Sandalow, *Freedom from Oil*, 141–48.
26. Roberts, *End of Oil*, 87, 88, 90.
27. Hakes, *Declaration*, 174, 214.
28. Roberts, *End of Oil*, 191.
29. Roberts, *End of Oil*, 202–4, 206.
30. Hakes, *Declaration*, 182, 215–16.
31. Roberts, *The End of Oil*, 77.
32. Sandalow, *Freedom from Oil*, 131–34.
33. Hakes, *Declaration*, 216.
34. Marc Labonte and Gail Makinen, *Energy Independence: Would It Free the United States from Oil Price Shocks?* (Congressional Research Service, January 11, 2002).
35. Gingrich, *Drill Here*, 148.
36. Kathleen Parker, "A Crude Reality about Energy Independence," *Washington Post*, (August 2, 2009). www.washingtonpost.com/wp-dyn/content/article/2009/07/31/AR2009073102609.html.
37. Sandalow, *Freedom from Oil*, 3.
38. Sandalow, *Freedom from Oil*, 54.
39. Juhasz, *Tyranny of Oil*, 85–86.
40. Roberts, *End of Oil*, 299.
41. Goldman, *Petrostate*, 180, 207.
42. Council on Foreign Relations, *National Security Consequences of Oil Dependency,* Task Force Report No. 58, October 2006, p. 4.

Chapter 18

1. Woods, *Meltdown*, 125–26.
2. John H. Wood, *A History of Macroeconomic Policy in the United States* (London: Routledge, 2009), 170–72.
3. Ben Bernanke, et al., "Systematic Monetary Policy and the Effects of Oil Price Shocks" (*Brookings Papers on Economic Activity*, 1997).

4. Rajeev Dhawan and Karsten Jeske, "How Resilient is the Modern Economy to Energy Price Shocks?" Federal Reserve Back of Atlanta, Economic Review, (third quarter 2006), 21–32.

5. Henderson, *Do We Need to Go to War for Oil?*, 5.

6. Woods, *Meltdown*, 80–82.

Chapter 19

1. Maugeri, *Age of Oil*, 176.

2. Richard Gordon mentions that not only the U.S. government has an interest in keeping oil prices high, but domestic oil, coal, and nuclear power produces and even envrornmentalists share an interest in doing the same. See Gordon, *An Economic Analysis*, 233–234.

3. Losman, *Economic Security*, 3.

4. Bronson, *Thicker than Oil*, 21–22.

Chapter 20

1. Sandalow, *Freedom from Oil*, 171.

Chapter 21

1. Morris Adelman has debunked this myth. Adelman is cited in Gordon, *An Economic Analysis*, 233.

2. Bronson, *Thicker than Oil*, 3.

3. Bronson, *Thicker than Oil*, 86.

4. Klare, *Blood and Oil*, 26.

5. Roberts, *The End of Oil*, 286

6. Energy Information Administration, *Saudi Arabia: Background*, http://www.eia.doe.gov/cabs/Saudi _Arabia/Background.html.

Chapter 22

1. Goldman, *Petrostate*, 166.

2. Andrew E. Kramer, "Eastern Europe Fears New Era of Russian Sway: Concerns On Pipeline: Nations See a Continent Further Split Over Natural Gas," *New York Times,* October 13, 2009, A1.

3. Kramer, "Eastern Europe Fears," A1.

4. Goldman, *Petrostate*, 49, 82, 156–157.

5. Goldman, *Petrostate*, 13, 80, 82; and Klare, *Blood and Oil*, 154.

6. Goldman, *Petrostate*, 139, 179.

7. Goldman, *Petrostate*, 3–4, 7–10.

8. Quoted in Klare, *Blood and Oil*, 154–157

9. Klare, *Blood and Oil*, 154–157.

10. Goldman, *Petrostate*, 172–174.

Part III, Chapter 23

1. Klare, *Blood and Oil*, 6.

2. Margonelli, *Oil on the Brain*, 203.

3. Bryce, *Gusher of Lies*, 47–48.

4. See www.eia.doe.gov/pub/oil_gas/ petroleum/data_publications/ company_level_imports/current/ import.html

5. The total number of barrels of crude oil the U.S. imported from the Persian Gulf per day in 2009 was 1,656,000 (U.S. Imports of Crude Oil, www.eia.doe.gov/dnav/pet/hist/ LeafHandler.ashx?n=PET&s+MCRI MUSPG28f=A. This figure was taken times 365 days and times the $54 average price per barrel of oil in 2009 (*Historical Crude Oil Prices*, Table at www.inflationdata.com/inflation/ inflation_rate/historical_oil_prices_ table.asp) to give a total value of U.S. oil imports from the Persian Gulf for 2009 of $32.6 billion. For a crude calculation on what the U.S. annually spends defending the Persian Gulf, I took the basic budget for national defense (account 050) and added the cost of the two wars, which totaled $668.3 billion in estimated outlays for 2009. I then divided by two because

the wars in Afghanistan and Iraq were getting about equal funding per year, getting $334 billion annually. The data for this calculation comes from U.S. Office of Management and Budget, "Data Sets: Federal Budget 2009—Budget Authority and Outlays by Function, Category, and Program" (Table 27–1), http://maneyes.alphaworks.ibm. com/maneyes/datasets/federal-budget-2009-budget-authority/versions/1. During the post–Cold War era, the Pentagon's strategy had spoken of fighting two major regional wars nearly simultaneously. For political reasons, these conflicts were never named, but the Department of Defense was believed to be conducting planning for wars in Iraq and North Korea. Because the Persian Gulf has been the location of the two biggest U.S. military actions in the last two decades and few other threats requiring large forces exist, it is not stretching it to allocate roughly half the U.S. defense budget to defending the Gulf. Even if lesser costs are assigned to safeguarding Persian Gulf oil, the costs are still many times greater than the value of the oil the U.S. imports from the Persian Gulf.

6. Juhasz, *Tyranny of Oil,* 321.
7. Hakes, *Declaration,* 101.
8. Klare, *Blood and Oil,* 132–33.
9. Juhasz, *Tyranny of Oil,* 321–23.
10. Klare, *Blood and Oil,* 6–7, 72.
11. Roberts, *End of Oil,* 38.
12. "Worldwide Look at Reserves and Production," *Oil & Gas Journal* 106, no. 48 (December 22, 2008): 23–24.

Chapter 24

1. Quoted in Bryce, Gusher of Lies, 56.
2. Bryce, *Gusher of Lies,* 57–58, 60.
3. Quoted in Bryce, *Gusher of Lies,* 57.
4. Richard Lugar, Forward to Sandalow, *Freedom from Oil,* xii.
5. Thomas Friedman, "The Energy Wall," *New York Times,* December 1, 2006, 31.
6. Terry Lynn Karl, "The Peril of the Petro-State: Reflections on the Paradox of Plenty," *Journal of International Affairs 53, no. 1* (Fall 1999): 43.
7. Bryce, *Gusher of Lies,* 72–74.
8. Lugar, Forward to Sandalow, *Freedom from Oil,* xi–xii.
9. Maugeri, *Age of Oil,* xvi.
10. Klare, *Blood and Oil,* 147.
11. Hakes, *Declaration,* 2–3.
12. Maugeri, *Age of Oil,* 136–37.
13. The Saud family rules Saudi Arabia. If the clan were overthrown, the "Saudi" would undoubtedly be dropped from the country's name.
14. Seymour Hersh, "King's Ransom," *New Yorker,* October 22, 2001, http:// www.newyorker.com.
15. Gholz and Press, *Energy Alarmism,* 15, 21.
16. MIT SSP, *Energy, National Security, and the Persian Gulf,* 8, 10.
17. Sandalow, *Freedom from Oil,* 39, 42.
18. George W. Bush, National Energy Policy Speech in St. Paul, Minnesota, May 17, 2001, transcript available: http://articles.cnn.com/2001-05 -17/politics/bush.transcript_1_ district_energy_model_of_energy _efficiency_darker_future?_s=PM :ALLPOLITICS
19. George W. Bush, State of the Union Address, January 31, 2006. Transcript available: http://www. washingtonpost.com/wp-dyn/content/article/2006/01/31AR200601310 1468.htm
20. Minxin Pei and Sara Kasper, "Lessons from the Past: The American Record on Nation Building"

(Carnegie Endowment for Peace Policy Brief, May 2003).

21. Quoted in Bryce, *Gusher of Lies*, 241.

22. Hakes. *Declaration*, 8.

23. Quoted in Bryce, *Gusher of Lies*, 98.

24. MIT SSP, *Energy, National Security, and the Persian Gulf*, 17–18.

25. Eugene Gholz, *Assessing Iran's Threat to Oil Flows through the Strait of Hormuz* (Washington, DC: Briefing at the Cato Institute, July 7, 2009).

26. Comment by Bryan McGrath, U.S. Navy (ret.) at the briefing *Assessing Iran's Threat to Oil Flows through the Strait of Hormuz*. (Washington, DC: Briefing at the Cato Institute, July 7, 2009, conducted by Eugene Gholz).

27. Eugene Gholz cited in MIT SSP, *Energy, National Security, and the Persian Gulf*, 15.

28. Roberts, *End of Oil*, 145.

29. Roberts, *End of Oil*, 257.

30. Evan Medeiros cited in MIT SSP, *Energy, National Security, and the Persian Gulf*, 23–24, 26, 28.

31. Gholz and Press, *Energy Alarmism*, 1, 8–10.

32. Klare, *Blood and Oil*, 168–177.

33. Pollack cited in Klare, *Blood and Oil*, 182–83.

34. Steven Kull. "Negative Attitudes Toward the United States in the Muslim World: Do They Matter?" (Testimony before the Committee on Foreign Affairs, Subcommittee on International Organizations, Human Rights, and Oversight, U.S. House of Representatives, May 17, 2007).

Part IV

1. Maugeri, *Age of Oil*, 267.

2. Maugeri, *Age of Oil*, 267.

3. This is an extremely rough calculation, cutting half the forces and half the U.S. budget for national defense, based on the traditional defense posture of being able to fight two major regional contingencies nearly simultaneously—one believed to be in the Persian Gulf. (The United States has had two major wars in the Persian Gulf in the last two decades.) The calculation was based on service data for their force structures listed in House Report 111–230-Department of Defense, Appropriations Bill, 2010. For the Navy, see: http://ecip.loc.gov/cgi-bin/cpquery/?&sid=cp111HUNm&refer=&r_n=hr230.111&db_id=111&item=&sel=TOC_81084&. For the Army, see: http://ecip.loc.gov/cgi-bin/cpquery/?&sid=cp111 HUNm&refer=&r_n=hr230.111&db_id=111&item=&sel=TOC_75084&. For the Air Force, see: http://ecip.loc.gov/cgi-bin/cpquery/?&sid=cp111HUNm&refer=&r_n=hr230.111&db_id=111&item=&sel=TOC_87168&. For the Marine Corps, see: http://en.wikipedia.org/wiki/List_of_United_States_Marine_Corps_brigades. To see the derivation of the defense budget savings figure, examine Chapter 23, Note 5.

4. MIT SSP, *Energy, National Security, and the Persian Gulf*, 8–9.

5. MIT SSP, *Energy, National Security, and the Persian Gulf*, 6.

Index

About the Author

IVAN ELAND is Senior Fellow and Director of the Center on Peace & Liberty at The Independent Institute. Dr. Eland is a graduate of Iowa State University and received an M.B.A. in applied economics and a Ph.D. in Public Policy from George Washington University. He has been Director of Defense Policy Studies at the Cato Institute, and he spent 15 years working for Congress on national security issues, including stints as an investigator for the House Foreign Affairs Committee and Principal Defense Analyst at the Congressional Budget Office. He also has served as Evaluator-in-Charge (national security and intelligence) for the U.S. General Accounting Office (now the Government Accountability Office), and has testified on the military and financial aspects of NATO expansion before the Senate Foreign Relations Committee, on CIA oversight before the House Government Reform Committee, and on the creation of the Department of Homeland Security before the Senate Judiciary Committee. Dr. Eland is the author of *Partitioning for Peace: An Exit Strategy for Iraq*, *Recarving Rushmore: Ranking the Presidents on Peace, Prosperity, and Liberty*, *The Empire Has No Clothes: U.S. Foreign Policy Exposed* and *Putting "Defense" Back into U.S. Defense Policy*, as well as *The Efficacy of Economic Sanctions as a Foreign Policy Tool*. He is a contributor to numerous volumes and the author of 45 in-depth studies on national security issues.

His articles have appeared in *American Prospect, Arms Control Today, Bulletin of the Atomic Scientists, Emory Law Journal, The Independent Review, Issues in Science and Technology (National Academy of Sciences), Mediterranean Quarterly, Middle East and International Review, Middle East Policy, Nexus, Chronicle of Higher Education, American Conservative, International Journal of World Peace, The Freeman*, and *Northwestern Journal of International Affairs*. Dr. Eland's popular writings have appeared in such publications as the *Los Angeles Times, San Francisco Chronicle, USA Today, Houston Chronicle, Dallas Morning News, New York Times, Chicago Sun-Times, San Diego Union-Tribune, Miami Herald, St. Louis Post-Dispatch, Newsday, Sacramento Bee, Orange County Register, Washington Times, Providence Journal, The Hill*, and *Defense News*. He has appeared on ABC's World News Tonight, NPR's Talk of the Nation, PBS, Fox News Channel, CNBC, Bloomberg TV, CNN, CNN-fn, C-SPAN, MSNBC, Canadian Broadcasting Corp. (CBC), Canadian TV (CTV), Radio Free Europe, Voice of America, BBC, and other local, national, and international TV and radio programs.

INDEPENDENT STUDIES IN POLITICAL ECONOMY